Also by Richard Stengel

Mandela's Way

You're Too Kind

January Sun

RICHARD STENGEL

INFORMATION WARS

HOW WE LOST THE GLOBAL BATTLE
AGAINST DISINFORMATION
— & —
WHAT WE CAN DO ABOUT IT

Atlantic Monthly Press
New York

FIRST EDITION

Published simultaneously in Canada
Printed in the United States of America

First Grove Atlantic hardcover edition: October 2019

This book is set in 11.75-pt. Janson Text LT Pro by Alpha Design & Composition of Pittsfield, NH.

Library of Congress Cataloging-in-Publication data available for this title.

ISBN 978-0-8021-4798-1
eISBN 978-0-8021-4799-8

Atlantic Monthly Press
an imprint of Grove Atlantic
154 West 14th Street
New York, NY 10011

Distributed by Publishers Group West

groveatlantic.com

19 20 21 22   10 9 8 7 6 5 4 3 2 1

For Mary, Gabriel, and Anton

CONTENTS

GLOSSARY OF ACRONYMS

BBG—Broadcasting Board of Governors
CDA—The Communications Decency Act
CN—Congressional Notification
CSCC—The Center for Strategic Counterterrorism Communications
CVE—Countering violent extremism
DC—Deputies Committee
DRL—Democracy, Human Rights, and Labor
EAP—East Asian and Pacific Affairs
ECA—Educational and Cultural Affairs
EUR—European and Eurasian Affairs
FLEX—Future Leaders Exchange
GEC—Global Engagement Center
H—Office of Congressional Affairs
IVLP—International Visitors Leadership Program
J—Civilian Security, Democracy, and Human Rights
L—Legal Department
NCTC—National Counterterrorism Center
NEA—Near Eastern Affairs
NSC—National Security Council
PA—Public Affairs
PC—Principals Committee
PDP—President's Daily Brief
P—Under Secretary for Political Affairs
R—Under Secretary for Public Diplomacy and Public Affairs
SCA—South and Central Asian Affairs
S—Secretary of State

INTRODUCTION

The first thing you notice when you walk into the White House Situation Room is how cramped and stuffy it is. There's so little space that if people are already sitting at the table, you have to slowly snake your way in between them like you're taking a seat in the middle of a row in a crowded movie theater. *Excuse me . . . Pardon me . . . Sorry.* And try not to bump the National Security Advisor. For some reason, the air-conditioning doesn't work all that well, so it can get pretty fragrant. And unless you're the President of the United States, every guy keeps his suit jacket on and his tie tightened.

It was early in 2014, and it was my first time in the room with President Obama. I was the new Under Secretary of State for Public Diplomacy. He was in shirtsleeves and came in without greeting anyone—focused, intense, all business. I had known President Obama when I was a journalist and had that chummy, jokey rapport with him that journalists and politicians cultivate. But this was a side of him that I had never seen before.

The meeting was about the role of international broadcasting, which was part of my brief at the State Department. International broadcasting meant the legacy organizations that were better known during the Cold War: Voice of America, Radio Free Europe, Radio

Liberty. You may not pay attention to them anymore, but they still have a $750 million budget—a nontrivial number even to the federal government. Ben Rhodes, the President's deputy national security advisor, sketched out the topic and then called on me. I started to lay out all the traditional stuff that these entities were doing, and I could see the President was impatient. "I caught the pass, Rick," he said without a smile. Hmm. In a nanosecond, I pulled back to 30,000 feet and said, well, the real problem was that we were in the middle of a global information war that was going on every minute of the day all around the world and we were losing it.

Then, a different response from the head of the table. "Okay," the President said, "what do we do about it?"

That is the question. There is indeed an information war going on all around the world and it's taking place at the speed of light. Governments and non-state actors and individuals are creating and spreading narratives that have nothing to do with reality. Those false and misleading narratives undermine democracy and the ability of free people to make intelligent choices. The audience is anyone with access to a computer or a smartphone—about four billion people. The players in this conflict are assisted by the big social media platforms, which benefit just as much from the sharing of content that is false as content that is true. Popularity is the measure they care about, not accuracy or truthfulness. Studies show that a majority of Americans can recall seeing at least one false story leading up to the 2016 election.[1] This rise in disinformation—often accompanied in authoritarian states by crackdowns on free speech—is a threat to democracy at home and abroad. More than any other system, democracies depend on the free flow of information and open debate. That's how we make our choices. As Thomas Jefferson said, information is the foundation of democracy.[2] He meant factual information.

Disinformation is as old as humanity. When the serpent told Eve that nothing would happen if she ate the apple, that was disinformation. But today, spreading lies has never been easier. On social media, there are no barriers to entry and there are no gatekeepers. There is no fact-checking, no editors, no publishers; you are your own publisher. Anyone can sign up for Facebook or Twitter and create any number of personas, which is what troll armies do. These trolls use the same behavioral and information tools supplied by Facebook and Google and Twitter to put poison on those platforms and reach a targeted, receptive audience. And it's just as easy to share something false as something that's factual.

One reason for the rise in global disinformation is that waging an information war is a lot cheaper than buying tanks and Tridents, and the return on investment is higher. Today, the selfie is mightier than the sword. It is asymmetric warfare requiring only computers and smartphones and an army of trolls and bots. You don't even have to *win*; you succeed if you simply muddy the waters. It's far easier to create confusion than clarity. There is no information dominance in an information war. There is no unipolar information superpower. These days, offensive technologies are cheaper and more effective than defensive ones. Information war works for small powers against large ones, and large powers against small ones; it works for states and for non-state actors—it's the great leveler. Not everyone can afford an F-35, but anyone can launch a tweet.

Why does disinformation work? Well, disinformation almost always hits its target because the target—you, me, everyone—rises up to meet it. We ask for it. Social scientists call this confirmation bias. We seek out information that confirms our beliefs. Disinformation sticks because it fits into our mental map of how the world works. The internet is the greatest delivery system for confirmation bias in history.

The analytical and behavioral tools of the web are built to give us information we agree with. If Google and Facebook see that you like the Golden State Warriors, they will give you more Steph Curry. If you buy an antiwrinkle face cream, they will give you a lot more information about moisturizers. If you like Rachel Maddow or Tucker Carlson, the algorithm will give you content that reflects your political persuasion. What it won't do is give you content that questions your beliefs.[3]

So, what do we do about it?

First, let's face it, democracies are not very good at combating disinformation. I found this out firsthand at the State Department, where the only public-facing entities in government that countered ISIS messaging and Russian disinformation reported to me. While autocracies demand a single point of view, democracies thrive on the marketplace of ideas. We like to argue. We like a diversity of opinion. We're open to different convictions and theories, and that includes bad and false ones. In fact, we protect them. Justice Oliver Wendell Holmes famously argued that the First Amendment protects "the thought that we hate."[4] And frankly, that's a handicap when it comes to responding to disinformation. It's just not in our DNA as Americans to censor what we disagree with. "The spirit of liberty," said Learned Hand, "is the spirit which is not too sure that it is right."[5]

Disinformation is especially hard for us to fight because our adversaries use our strengths—our openness, our free press, our commitment to free speech—against us. Our foes use free media just like political candidates do. They understand that our press's reflex toward balance and "fairness" allows them to get their own destructive ideas into our information ecosystem. Vladimir Putin knows that if he says the sun revolves around the earth, CNN will report his claim and find an expert who will disagree with it—and maybe one who supports it just to round out the panel. This quest for balance is a journalistic trap that Putin and ISIS and the disinformationists exploit. In a fundamental way, they win when an accepted fact is thrown open for debate. Treating both sides of an argument as equal when one side is demonstrably false is not fair or balanced—it's just wrong. As I used to tell the foreign service officers who were working to counter disinformation, "There aren't two sides to a *lie*."

What is perhaps most disturbing is that disinformation erodes our trust in public discourse and the democratic process. Whether it's Mr. Putin or ISIS or China or Donald Trump, they want you to question not only the information that you are getting but also the means through which you get it. They love the stories in Western media about information overload and how social media is poisoning the minds of young people. Why? Because they see us questioning the reliability of the information we get, and that undermines democracy. They want people to see empirical facts as an elitist conspiracy. Social media was a godsend to their disinformation efforts. On Facebook and Twitter and Instagram, information is delivered to you by third parties—friends, family, celebrities—and those companies don't make any guarantee about the veracity of what you're getting. They can't; it's their economic model. And your friends are not exactly the best judge of what's fact and what's not. Under the law, these companies are not considered publishers, so they are not responsible for the truth or falsity of the content they are delivering to you. That is a mistake. They are the biggest publishers in history.

Not that long ago, the internet and social media were seen as democratizing and emancipating. The idea was that universal access to information would undermine authoritarian leaders and states. In many cases, it does. But autocrats and authoritarian governments have adapted. They have gone from fearing the flow of information to exploiting it. They understand that the same tools that spread democracy can engineer its undoing. Autocrats can spread disinformation and curtail the flow of accurate information at the same time. That's a dangerous combination for the future of democracy.

This challenge is different from those we've faced before. It is not a conventional military threat to our survival as a nation, but it is an unconventional threat to our system of beliefs and how we define ourselves. How do we fight back without changing who we are?

As you will see, I don't believe government is the answer. In a democracy, government is singularly bad at combating disinformation. That's in part because most of those we are trying to persuade already distrust it.[6] But it's also not good at creating content that people care about. That's not really government's job. Early on at the State Department, I said to an old media friend, "People just don't like government content." He laughed and said, "No, people just don't like bad content."

This is not a policy book, though there is policy in it. It's not a traditional memoir, though the book is in the first person. It's not journalism, though I've tried to use all the skills I learned over a career as a journalist. Is it history? Well, it's somewhere between the whirlwind of current reporting and what we once called history. But with today's accelerated news cycle, where memoirs come out a few months after the actions they describe, it's more like history as the Greeks saw it, a narrative about the recent past that provides perspective on the present. It's the story of the rise of a global information war that is a threat to democracy and to America—a story that I tell through my own eyes and experiences at the State Department.

I spent a little under three years at State during President Obama's second term, from early 2014 to the end of 2016. I came to it after seven years as the editor of *Time* and a lifetime as a journalist. As head of *Time*, I used to say my job was to explain America to the world, and the world to America. That's not a bad definition of my job at State. I brought other experience with me as well. I spent three years working with Nelson Mandela on his autobiography. I was the head of the National Constitution Center in Philadelphia. The official description of my job at the State Department was to support U.S. foreign policy goals by informing and influencing international audiences.[7] Some people called it being "propagandist in chief," but I liked to say that I was the chief marketing officer of brand America.

The story is not a view from the top. Despite that opening anecdote, I was not in the Oval Office conferring with President Obama on key decisions. But it's not a view from the bottom either; I was the number-five-ranked person at the State Department. In the grand scheme of things, the Under Secretary for Public Diplomacy isn't a big deal, but the job is not a bad vantage point from which to tell this particular story. No, I couldn't see everything that the President or the Secretary of State saw. But in government, it's harder to see below you than above you. While I missed a lot of what those below me saw, I saw a lot of what those above me missed.

There's a lot in the book about how government and the State Department work. I found government too big, too slow, too bureaucratic. It constantly gets in its own way. And sometimes that's not a bad thing. Like, now. I used to joke with my conservative friends that they should be in favor of big government because big government gets nothing done. But at the same time, I came to realize that the only people who could really fix government are those who understand it best. The dream of an outsider coming in to reform government is just that—a dream. This also bears repeating: I found that the overwhelming number of people in government are there for the right reasons—to try to make things better. To work for the American people. To protect and defend the Constitution. They are true public servants. Even when I grew frustrated, I never doubted that.

The rap on me in government was that I saw every problem as a communications problem. I wouldn't say this was quite true, but I saw that communication was a critical part of every problem. And that not thinking about and planning for how to communicate something generally made the problem worse. And you know who else saw it that way? ISIS and Vladimir Putin and Donald Trump. For all three of them, communications—what we in government called messaging—was not a tactic but a core strategy. They all understood that the media cycle moves a lot faster than the policy cycle, and policy would forever play catch-up. They knew that it was almost always better to be first and false than second and true. One problem with the U.S. government is that we didn't really get that; we saw messaging as an afterthought.

Even though my position had enormous range—covering educational and cultural exchanges as well as public affairs—I ended up focusing on two things: countering ISIS's messaging and countering Russian disinformation. Before I went into government, smart people told me to find a few things to concentrate on and not to worry about the rest. As it turned out, I felt like these two issues found me. History happened, I jumped in, and I worked on them to the exclusion of almost everything else. Both involved a global trend: the weaponization of information and grievance. ISIS perfected a form of information warfare that weaponized the grievances of millions of Sunni Muslims who felt spurned by the West and by their own leaders. Russia spent decades developing its own system of information warfare, which helped Putin weaponize the grievances of Russians who felt a sense of loss at the fall of the Soviet Union.[8] In fact, our word "disinformation" is taken from the Russian *dezinformatsiya*, which was reportedly coined by Stalin.[9] Both ISIS and Russia saw and depicted America as a place riven by hypocrisy, racism, and prejudice, and the primary source of global injustice. This book's narrative is chronological, and the story rotates back and forth between Russia and ISIS, a structure that reflects the reality of my job. I tell the story in real time with the knowledge I had at the time.

And then, two-thirds of the way through my time fighting these battles, Donald Trump entered the American presidential race, and it felt like everything suddenly connected. The information battles we were fighting far away had come home. Trump employed the same techniques of disinformation as the Russians and much the same scare tactics as ISIS. Russian propagandists had been calling Western media "fake news" long before Donald Trump. The Russian disinformation techniques we saw around the annexation of Crimea and the invasion of Ukraine were transposed to the American election space. Only this time, they were done in English—pretty poor English mostly—not Russian. For ISIS, Trump's candidacy confirmed all that they had been saying about the Islamophobia of the United States and the West. Trump's "Muslim ban" was propaganda gold for ISIS. All three of them—ISIS, Putin, and Trump—weaponized the grievances of people who felt left out by modernity and globalization. In fact, they used the same playbook: ISIS sought to Make Islam Great Again; Putin yearned to Make Russia Great Again; and we know about Mr. Trump. The weaponization of grievance is the unified field theory behind the rise of nationalism and right-wing strongmen.

I found that there was a malign chain of cause and effect among the three. In fighting Assad and seizing territory in Syria, ISIS helped create an exodus of Syrian refugees, millions of whom made their way to Europe. Putin's indiscriminate bombing in Syria accelerated that mass relocation. Then Russia, through disinformation, helped weaponize the idea of immigration by stoking fears of refugees and terrorism. And along came Donald Trump, who made the fear of immigration a central part of his campaign.

I see that very clearly now, but did I see it then? Not really. Did anyone in the U.S. government see it? I'm not sure. If people did see it, they didn't talk about it, and not much was done about it. I'm not sure how much we could have done anyway.

Every scene in the book is designed to show how both Russia and ISIS weaponized information and grievance; how Russian disinformation entered the American election; how Donald Trump weaponized griev-ance and used many of the same techniques and strategies as Russia and ISIS did; how government isn't much good at responding to a threat like this. In many ways, the fight against ISIS's messaging looks like a success story. We actually did a fair amount, and ISIS went from seeming omnipresent on social media to being confined to the dark web. But the truth is, I don't know that what we did made any difference. Crushing ISIS militarily had a heck of a bigger effect than dueling with tweets. As I used to tell my military colleagues, losing a city to ISIS sends a terrible message, but taking a city is the best message of all. Ultimately, it's not a military fight; it's a battle of ideas between Islamic extremists and the much larger audience of mainstream Muslims. ISIS was always more of an idea than a state, and that idea is far from dead.

The fight against Russian disinformation was murkier. It was dif-ficult to get started, didn't gain much traction, and then mostly faded away. Combating Russian disinformation was harder than counter-ing ISIS in part because everyone agreed that ISIS was an irredeem-able enemy, while lots of people at State and the White House were ambivalent about hitting back at Russia. Some of that hesitance came from people who didn't think it was the government's job to counter any kind of disinformation, which is a fair point. Some of it came from people who thought that countering Russia's message only made things worse. And some came from people who felt that it was more effective to treat Russia as a fellow superpower (even though it was not) than a fading regional player.

But the scale of Russian disinformation was beyond what we were capable of responding to. The Russians had the big battalions; we had a reluctant, ragtag guerrilla force. They also had the element of surprise. Maybe a few old Cold Warriors might have seen it coming, but mostly we did not. It hadn't been all that long since the 2012 election when people had mocked Mitt Romney for saying that a revanchist Russia was our number one geopolitical foe. Frankly, it's not that they were so sophisticated, it's that we were so credulous. The Global Engagement Center, created during my final year and designed to be a centralized hub for countering all kinds of disinformation, is potentially a powerful weapon in this fight.

Finally, when it came to countering Donald Trump's disinformation, we were pretty much paralyzed. No one wanted to do that. Let me correct that: plenty of people wanted to do it, but almost no one thought it was practical or right or legal to do so. Moreover, everyone at the White House and at the State Department thought, Well, Hillary is going to win, and the White House really didn't want it to look like we were putting our finger on the scale. After all, the Russians and Trump were preparing to question the integrity of the election when Trump lost. No one wanted to give them any evidence they could use to say the election was rigged, which is precisely what they would have done.

For the first six weeks after Donald Trump entered the race in June 2015, Russia did almost nothing to support him. The Russians seemed as bewildered as the rest of us at what he was doing. They were always and resolutely anti-Hillary, but it took them a while to become pro-Trump. They were reading the polls too. When they did come around to supporting him, it was pretty clear they didn't think he would win. What they wanted was a loss close enough that they could question the legitimacy of Mrs. Clinton's victory. They were as surprised by Trump's victory as, well, Trump was.

I saw Russian disinformation enter the American presidential campaign and was alarmed by it, but to this day, I'm not sure what impact it had. Russian messaging had a lot of reach but hardly any depth. Sure, Russian ads and stories on Facebook reached 126 million people, but those 126 million people saw exponentially more content than a few Russian ads.[10] Moreover, as data today suggests, the ads themselves were not very successful. People didn't recall them or act on them. What had a more significant effect was the false and deceptive content that the Russians seeded onto all platforms, not just the buying of ads on Facebook. But in the end, disinformation tends to confirm already held beliefs; it's not really meant to change people's minds. Disinformation doesn't create divisions; it amplifies them.

So, did Russian disinformation tip the election to Donald Trump? I don't know. By televising hundreds of hours of Trump's campaign speeches, CNN did a whole lot more to elect him than Russia Today did. Televising his rallies sent a message to voters: this is important, pay attention—after all, we are. And millions of voters' deeply held antipathy to Hillary Clinton did a lot more to defeat her than a few hundred Russian trolls in St. Petersburg. The Russians sought to sow doubt about the election, hurt Hillary, and help Trump, without any expectation that it would tip the balance.

My experience in government changed my view of the information and media industry in a fundamental way. As a journalist, I had always seen information as the lifeblood of democracy. That's how the Framers saw it too.[11] Like so many, I saw the rise of the internet as a fantastic boon to global freedom and democracy—the more knowledge people had, the better able they would be to choose how to govern themselves and live their own lives. I still do. But these new tools and platforms are neutral. As Aristotle said of rhetoric, it can be used for good or ill. I came to see that dictators and autocrats and con men quickly figured out how to use these new tools to fool and intimidate people. They used the tools of democracy and freedom to repress democracy and freedom. We need to use those same tools to protect those values.

I had always believed in the notion that the best ideas triumph in what Justice William O. Douglas called "the market place of ideas."[12] This notion is found in John Milton and John Stuart Mill and is a bedrock principle in our democracy. But everyone presumed that the marketplace would be a level playing field. That a rational audience would ultimately see the truth. I think we all now know that this is a pipe dream. Unfortunately, facts don't come highlighted in yellow. A false sentence reads the same as a true one. It's not enough to battle falsehood with truth; the truth does not always win.

In foreign policy, there's the classic divide between realism and idealism. When it came to information, I'd always been an idealist. I believed that sunlight was the best disinfectant. I left office as an information realist. Disinformation, as I said earlier, isn't a new problem, but the ease with which it can be spread on social media is. Today we are all actors in a global information war that is ubiquitous, difficult to comprehend, and unfair. It is a war without end, a war without limits or boundaries. A war that we still don't quite know how to fight.

To say the truth is under attack is a beautiful phrase. But the problem is that people have their own truths, and these truths are often at war with one another. We no longer seem able to agree on what is a fact or how to determine one. The truth is, it's impossible to stop people from creating falsehoods and other people from believing them.

So, looking back, there was a lot that we saw that we did something about. There was a lot that we saw that we didn't or couldn't do anything about. And there was a lot that we just didn't see. I saw part of the picture but not all of it. I wish I had been able to connect the dots faster. I wish I had been able to do more. And there was always the sense that it couldn't happen here.

PART I

Welcome to State

The Turnstile

When you walk into the 21st Street entrance of the State Department, you have to show your ID to the uniformed guards standing outside the building. They peer down at your card to check the tiny expiration date in the upper left-hand corner before waving you through, exactly the way they have been doing it since the Korean War.

Once you're past the guards, you have to pass through two tall, automated metal doors. To get them to open, you step onto a four-by-six-inch magnetic carpet in front of them. Some mornings you just had to touch the carpet and the doors would spring open. Sometimes you had to jump up and down. And sometimes you had to open the doors yourself. On many mornings, you would see diplomats in sensible suits hopping up and down before putting their shoulders to what must have been a two-hundred-fifty-pound door.

Once you were through the double doors and into the lobby, you needed to pass through one of five clunky-looking metal turnstiles that probably didn't look modern when they were installed 25 years ago. You inserted your card in a horizontal slot in the main part of the turnstile and then entered your PIN on the keypad. The problem was the keypad. It was loose and soggy, and the smudged protective plastic cover made typing hard. About a third of the time when you typed in your number, it didn't register. When that happened, you moved over to the next turnstile and started all over again.

So, each morning, as you entered what everyone always called "the Building" to do your day's work for American diplomacy, there were a series of small fraught negotiations that failed about as often as they succeeded.

The Lobby

That eastern entrance to the State Department was the main entrance when the Building opened in 1941. It was designed in the late 1930s to be the home of the War Department. But a few years after construction started, the War Department realized that it had already outgrown the building's capacity and commenced work on what would become the Pentagon. It was decided that the new building would house the State Department.[1] The site, in a part of the District known as Foggy Bottom, was not a very glamorous location, then or now. For the employees of the State Department, who had been in the ornate Old Executive Office Building on Pennsylvania Avenue, it was like moving to a much less desirable zip code.

Established in 1789 under President George Washington, the State Department was the first cabinet-level agency to be created under the new executive branch. It was responsible—then and now—for managing the foreign affairs of the U.S. government. The first Secretary of State, Thomas Jefferson, had a staff of one chief clerk, three subordinate clerks, a translator, and a messenger. There were just two diplomatic posts, London and Paris. Today, the department has more than 40,000 employees, over 200 diplomatic posts, and a budget of $50 billion. In addition to the high-level diplomacy conducted by ambassadors and envoys, the State Department does more prosaic tasks, like issuing passports for American citizens and visas for foreigners traveling to the United States.

The architecture of the State Department is not what most people think of when they imagine Washington, D.C. With its unadorned limestone art moderne exterior and its portico of rectangular columns that look like a giant sideways sans serif letter *E*, State's new headquarters owes more to Mussolini than to Pierre L'Enfant. When you enter the two-story terrazzo lobby, with its floor-to-ceiling pink Tennessee marble, you are greeted by an enormous 50-foot-wide mural called *Defense of*

Human Freedoms, which was designed for the War Department. At the center of the painting, four panels depict small-town American life and Roosevelt's four freedoms: freedom of speech, freedom of worship, freedom from fear, and freedom from want. These freedoms are defended by American GIs on the left side of the panel in gas masks and on the right side by American infantrymen in helmets firing M16s. Across the top of the mural stretches the wingspan of a B52 bomber. In 1954, the diplomats of the State Department found it to be too warlike for an agency dedicated to peace, and the mural was covered up by plywood and draperies, which were only removed two decades later.[2]

The Marshall Office

My office was on the fifth floor of the original building. I shouldn't say "my office"—it was the office of the Under Secretary of State for Public Diplomacy and Public Affairs, and it was a plum. In fact, it had been the office of Secretary of State George Marshall when the building first opened. The ceiling is 25 feet high (when my youngest son first saw it, he said, "Dad, you could have two basketball hoops on top of each other") and featured three enormous, round lights that looked exactly like the flying saucers in the 1951 movie *The Day the Earth Stood Still*.

The office was a strategic asset in a city of beautiful offices. After all, people did make a correlation (inaccurate though it might be) between the size of one's office and how much power one had. For that reason, I liked to have meetings with foreign ambassadors and ministers in my office, where I would serve tea and coffee and let them take it all in. (The office came with its own State Department china.)

There was another anomaly about the office, one that was not necessarily an advantage: it wasn't on the seventh floor. The seventh floor was where the Secretary sat, as well as his two deputies and all the

Under Secretaries except one: me. Yes, the seventh floor was a physical space, but it was also the mythic locus of power in the Building. The phrase "the seventh floor" was uttered hundreds of times a day at the State Department: "The seventh floor isn't happy." "The seventh floor wants to do the deal." "The seventh floor is going up against the NSC." Just as the phrase "the White House" is shorthand for the President, "the seventh floor" represented the Secretary of State.

My office was on the fifth floor and not the seventh thanks to the astute real estate sense of one of my predecessors, Judith McHale, who was Under Secretary for Hillary Clinton. In 2008, after she was sworn in, she was shown the dark, rather grotty office on the seventh floor where the Under Secretary for Public Diplomacy normally sat. At the same time, someone mentioned that the Marshall office on the fifth floor in the old State building had just finished its renovations and was available. Judith chose beauty over proximity to power, and almost every morning when I walked into that lovely space, I silently thanked her.

But because I was not physically on the seventh floor, I was constantly walking or trotting—and sometimes sprinting—to it for meetings. And it was a hike. The State Department was the most nonintuitive, mazelike structure I've ever worked in. One reason is that when the building was expanded in 1961, the new parts were grafted on to the old building in a completely inorganic way. To remedy that, the hallways were numbered and marked with a rainbow of colors. The legend was that Henry Kissinger had the halls painted different colors so that he could find his way around—though the idea that Secretary Kissinger was wandering the halls of the Harry S. Truman Building strikes me as implausible. I would leave early for meetings to factor in the time I would be lost. What helped one navigate is that there were enormous posters from different countries at the end of each hall. So I always remembered that my office was at the juncture of the picture from Thailand (a boy walking across a rope bridge over a river) and one of a Hindu temple in India, and that when I was going up to the seventh floor, I turned left at the picture of a snowy St. Basil's Cathedral in Moscow.

Even after a decade in the building, foreign service officers would still get lost. But at least after a few months I stopped having to send text messages to my staff to come and rescue me. Like so many people there, I figured out a few different ways to get to where I had to go and then stuck to those paths religiously. It was a little like diplomacy.

The 8:30

Washington is an early-morning culture. When I was editor of *Time*, one of the first things I did was change the regular all-hands editorial meeting from 10 a.m. to 9:30 a.m. People were aghast. At State, meetings usually began at 8:30, but many started at 8, or even 7:30. But there was one meeting at the State Department that was the most exclusive in the building, and it was known only as "the 8:30." It was the Secretary's meeting.

When I first started talking to people about joining the State Department, some State veterans said to me, "You have to make sure that you're at the 8:30." Condoleezza Rice had an 8:30. Madeleine Albright had an 8:30. Secretary Clinton had an 8:30. For all I know, Thomas Jefferson had an 8:30. Secretary Kerry continued the tradition. This was an invitation-only meeting from the Secretary for about a dozen senior staff, and it set the tone—and much of the action—for the day. It was a chance to see and hear the Secretary first thing. In the building, the 8:30 was something of a mystery. Not everyone knew about it. It was a little like a secret society. And like any good secret society, it had its rules and protocols.

My day did not actually begin with the 8:30, but it was because of the 8:30 that I scheduled an 8. After I had gone to a few of the

Secretary's meetings, I realized that I needed to be briefed about what was happening. So I started a small meeting in my office at 8 to go over what might come up and what public diplomacy equities would be useful to talk about. On my staff at State, I had four "special assistants." These were bright young foreign service officers who were like my eyes and ears on what was going on in the world and, more important, in the Building. They each "covered" geographical areas as well as policy functions. So, one might handle Asia, refugees, and legal affairs. Another handled South America, educational exchanges, and consular services. Each morning, one of the "specials" would meet me at 8 to go over material before the 8:30. Usually, they stood in front of my desk (young foreign service officers will always stand unless you tell them to sit) and gave me an overview of what the Secretary was doing that day, what had happened in the news that might affect some of our issues, and what to look out for.

It was also useful because it gave me something to do while I attempted to log on to State's outdated computer system, which was impossibly slow and required two automated fobs plus several passwords. And that was not even for the classified computer system, the so-called high side, which took even longer. On a good day, this process took 7 to 8 minutes; but on many mornings, it could take half an hour, especially if you had to call IT, which was not infrequent. I hadn't seen a computer system like that since the 1990s. I sometimes used to try to calculate how many millions of dollars a year the American taxpayer was paying for State employees to wait for their computers to boot.

Like so many in government, I had gotten used to communicating with the staff and department on Gmail, which was faster, easier to use and search, and didn't take an eternity to get on. This started during the nomination and confirmation process—when you didn't yet have a government account—and continued pretty much until the end. While the State system was not so clunky that I'd resort to a private server, I completely understood why so many people used alternative means for unclassified communication. Although you weren't supposed to use Gmail for official business because of the Presidential Records Act, which mandated the preservation of all federal emails, few of the politicals followed that rule. What most people did was then send the Gmail chain to their federal email address. I know I did.

At 8:20, I would dash out of my office for the trek to the seventh floor. After walking up the staircase (it was much faster than the elevators, which were often shut down for dignitaries), I went through a side door that took you to what was known as "Mahogany Row." Mahogany Row is the rather claustrophobic suite of offices where the Secretary and the two deputies sit. It got its name from the dark wood paneling, but to my inexpert eye, it looked, well, fake. In fact, almost everything on Mahogany Row *was* fake. When the suite of offices was first opened in the new State Department building in 1961, it looked more like a 1950s motel with sliding glass doors, wall-to-wall carpeting, and acoustical-tile ceilings. When the wife of then Secretary of State Christian Herter arrived for a diplomatic reception for Queen Frederika of Greece and saw it for the first time, she burst into tears.

Over the next 25 years, money was privately raised to turn the reception rooms and the executive suite into a space that looked like it was from the early Federal period. In came the Hepplewhite chairs, the Duncan Phyfe tables, and somber oil portraits of all the former Secretaries. Mahogany Row was finally finished in the mid-1980s. When I first visited there to meet with Secretary Kerry, it gave me a kind of historical vertigo. After entering the building through the modern 1960s deco entrance lobby on the south side, you took the elevator to the seventh floor, where you stepped back into the 19th century.

When visitors go to Mahogany Row, they have to check in at an imposingly high desk, where security guards verify your name and take your cell phone. They take your phone because Mahogany Row is a

SCIF—a sensitive compartmented information facility, always pronounced "skiff," like the boat. A SCIF is a secure area protected from electronic surveillance where you could review classified information. In the early security briefings I had at the department, I was told by State security that you were liable to be spied on by a hostile foreign power in any part of the Building that was not a SCIF.

Outside the side door to Mahogany Row were a couple of Victorian-looking cubbyholes for State employees to store their phones. You put your phone in a small compartment and got a tiny key. One of the unintended benefits of being in meetings on Mahogany Row is that people weren't surreptitiously checking their phones. A few times in those early weeks, I was sitting in a meeting on the seventh floor and felt my BlackBerry buzz in my pocket. I would instantly leap up, excuse myself, and dash outside to lock it up, praying all the while that I had not allowed the Russians or the Chinese to penetrate the seventh floor.

The 8:30 took place in the Secretary's conference room, which was cattycorner to the entrance to his office suite. It was a narrow rectangular room with terrible acoustics. The Secretary was always the last to arrive—usually a few minutes late. He'd scoot into the room in shirtsleeves, sit down, and start talking. He moved fast and didn't like to waste time. It was always a bit of a stream of consciousness—what was on his mind at that moment. By 8:30 he'd had his PDP—President's Daily Brief—and perhaps even had a phone call with Bibi Netanyahu or Sergei Lavrov. His engine was already revved. In fact, John Kerry had as much energy as any human being I've ever known. When I walked beside him down the long corridors of the State Department, I always had to skip a little to keep up. He's permanently leaning forward. That was his attitude about the world as well. To plunge in, to move forward, to engage. There's no knot he doesn't think he can untie, no breach that he can't heal. For him, the cost of doing nothing was always higher than that of trying something. As he often said, "If we don't do it, it won't happen."

The Secretary sat at the head of a long, rectangular table. To his right was the Deputy Secretary of State for policy, and to his left was the Deputy Secretary of State for Management. Next to the Deputy for policy sat the Secretary's chief of staff, and next to the Deputy for Management sat the Under Secretary for Political Affairs. The other regulars in the meeting were the Under Secretary for Management, the Secretary's two deputy chiefs of staff, the assistant secretary for public affairs, legislative affairs, and the spokesperson. The assistant secretary for public affairs was the only assistant secretary there. Only three of the six Under Secretaries were invited. Even though there were no place cards at the table, there was a strict seating chart. Before I went to my first meeting, my chief of staff drew a makeshift diagram for me and said my chair was between those of the head of policy planning and the deputy chief of staff on the south side of the table. I sat in the wrong place my first couple of times, until someone kindly pointed out the correct seat.

The first words out of the Secretary's mouth were almost always some version of, "A lot going on," "Lots of balls in the air," "A lot of crap happening." (One morning he said with a smile, "When have I not said that? I've got to stop saying that!") Some mornings the Secretary launched into a tour of the international waterfront. He would touch on half a dozen issues, from helping the Syrian "moderates" to the civil war in the Congo to an upcoming trip to Kazakhstan. He would often talk about what was bothering him, like the uselessness of Congress ("They have a complete inability to do their job"); the habitual leaks from meetings he attended at the White House ("With our usual discretion, there it is on the front page of the *New York Times*"); the fecklessness of certain world leaders ("He doesn't understand the first thing about economics"); Americans' lack of interest in international relations ("There are no exit polls on foreign policy"); and the vagaries of Washington ("This is a city of snow wimps!"). He understood that just hearing what was on his mind had value for us.

In general, people would speak rapidly and tell the Secretary something he ought to know (Sir, an American in our embassy in Lima was arrested for assault); or what they were doing (Sir, I'm meeting with the deputy foreign minister of Malaysia to discuss counterterrorism efforts); or just something he might find amusing or interesting (I once surprised him by saying that CCTV, the Chinese state broadcaster, had the biggest news bureau in Washington, with more than 350 people).

On mornings when something was bothering him or we were in the midst of one crisis or another, or he just seemed a little down, he would sidle into his chair and mumble something. That was a universally understood signal. Because when we went around the table, people would then say, "Nothing this morning, Sir." There were days when almost the whole table of 15 people did that. Sometimes it's diplomatic to say nothing. But even on those days, when the meeting ended, he would bound out of his chair and offer some exhortation, like "Go get 'em," or "Let's get it done."

Comms and the 9:15

At State, and pretty much everywhere in Washington, "comms" is the standard shorthand for "communications," which basically means any and all of the outward-facing stuff, from a local newspaper interview to a speech at the United Nations. After the 8:30, I jumped into the comms meeting, which was held just across the hall in the chief of staff's office. The comms meeting was even smaller than the 8:30 and consisted of the chief of staff, the deputy chief of staff, the spokesperson, the assistant secretary for public affairs, and the chief speechwriter.

We sat at a round wooden table in a room that had a lovely view looking south toward the Lincoln Memorial. This was the most informal and candid meeting of the day. It ranged much further afield than simply comms. Yes, we might complain about a negative story that was in that morning's *Washington Post*, but we would also look ahead to the Secretary's speeches, trips, and interviews and try to plan not just for the current crisis but for the one around the corner. There was always a lot of discussion of what the White House did or didn't want us to do. And there was always a fair amount of wry laughter.

This was dangerous, because the chief of staff's office had a discreet side door that led directly to the Secretary's private office, and often the Secretary would pop in to say something or call out for the chief of staff. I remember once spending much of the meeting discussing the fact that the Secretary wanted to take his windsurfing board on a trip to the Middle East because he would have a day at Sharm al-Sheikh, in Egypt, which had a beach. We were all laughing about this when he poked his head in, and then became pretty silent. He didn't take the board on the trip.

The centerpiece of the comms meeting was that day's press briefing. For reasons that were unclear, the State Department was the only government agency besides the White House that did a daily press briefing. I personally thought this didn't make much sense and caused way more problems than it solved, but I was in a distinct minority on that one. Our spokesperson was then Jen Psaki, who had come from the White House communications shop. Jen was very good at what she did: she was smart, good-humored, hard to rattle. She was also routinely pilloried, caricatured, and memed by Russian state media, which coined the word "Psaking," defining it as talking about something you didn't understand. She took this in stride. Every morning, she would list the issues that were likely to come up that day in the briefing and go over her answers on the trickier ones. We would tweak and make suggestions. It was a good way of getting a waterfront view of policy.

The actual press briefing was held in the public affairs briefing room, a cramped, subterranean space with a podium at the front, behind which was perhaps the worst step-and-repeat banner I'd ever seen, bearing the words, "U.S. State Department." It made viewers think they were seeing double. The foreign press, as they were called, had little cubbyholes and desks off the briefing room. They were a some-what motley crew that ranged from crackerjack correspondents for big foreign news organizations like the BBC, *Die Welt*, and the *Guardian* to reporters from obscure Asian newspapers who barely spoke English. Add to that the handful of correspondents from state-supported Rus-sian outlets who delighted in asking adversarial questions with dozens of often inane follow-ups. The whole crew was presided over by Matt Lee, the senior diplomatic correspondent for AP, a crotchety, contrarian, immensely knowledgeable reporter who for some reason was always given the first question at the briefing.

On Mondays and Wednesdays, I would dash out of the comms meeting to make the large formal meeting that was called the "Senior Staff Meeting" on the calendar but was always referred to as the "9:15." This was the more general meeting for the top 100 or so people at the department—all six Under Secretaries and their chiefs of staff, the 25 or so assistant secretaries and their deputies, the heads of bureaus, and any ambassadors who might be in town. On Mondays, the 9:15 was held in the Holbrooke Room, a large, low-ceilinged, secure space. This meeting always showed one curious characteristic of foreign service officers. There were days when I arrived at, say, 9:10 and the entire room was empty and I thought, Maybe the meeting has been canceled? Do I have the wrong day? At State, people were not late for meetings, but they were never early either. What was uncanny was that no matter how large or small the meeting, people would arrive a minute or two, sometimes just thirty seconds, before it was scheduled to begin. So, the Holbrooke Room could be empty at 9:10 and then have 100 people sitting down at 9:14. And when the Secretary arrived at, say, 9:18, it looked for all the world as if everyone had been sitting there chatting happily for half an hour.

The centerpiece of the Holbrooke Room was an enormous, polished wooden table around which the senior staff sat. There were place settings on large pieces of white cardboard. To an outsider, the name cards would mean nothing: they contained a single capital letter. D or P or J or R. The tradition was that each Under Secretary and each Deputy Secretary was referred to by a single initial. Thus, the Under Secretary for Political Affairs was always known as P. The Deputy Secretary for political affairs was known as D. The Under Secretary for Management was M. The Under Secretary for Economic Growth, Energy, and the Environment was E. That all made sense. But my title, Under Secretary for Public Diplomacy and Public Affairs, was known as R. Why R? No one had a good answer, except that P, D, and A were already taken.

I generally sat between J (Civilian Security, Democracy, and Human Rights) and T (Arms Control and International Security). Some of the assistant secretaries sat at the end of the table, but most stood against the wall opposite where the Secretary sat. The 9:15 was the most communal of the department's meetings. In the minutes before S arrived (yes, that's the initial used for the Secretary), you could hear the hum of chatter and gossip. (Gossip was the lingua franca of the foreign service.) When he strode in, everyone got quiet. He usually began with a folksy hello. Because this was a more public meeting, the Secretary's demeanor was both more upbeat and more formal than it was at the 8:30. He usually mentioned the same concerns he'd had at the 8:30, but typically in a shorter, sanitized version, along with a handful of announcements. He also regularly delivered what the department referred to as "attaboys" to individuals or departments that had done something positive.

This meeting was less for the Secretary than for the workhorses of the department: the regional assistant secretaries. The State Department was divided between functional bureaus—like mine, arms control, and international security—and regional bureaus, like Europe and Eurasian Affairs, African Affairs, and Near Eastern Affairs. Geography was power at the State Department, and the regional bureaus were the powerhouses in the Building. Dean Acheson compared them to the barons at a feudal court.[3] The analogy was still apt. At State, it was important to own territory. And people protected it fiercely. If you tried to launch a program in one of the assistant secretary's regions and she objected, it went nowhere. State was a Jeffersonian culture in the sense that the institution seemed to believe that the regions knew better than the center.

The Secretary would go around the room and call on the assistant secretaries. Yes, they were the workhorses, but there was definitely a show-horse aspect to this meeting, as the assistant secretaries gave a kind of bravura tour of their own areas with names and details designed to impress everyone with the depth and the reach of their knowledge. The assistant secretary for Africa might say, "Mr. Secretary, there was a coup in the Congo, and I've been in touch with our embassy. No danger to any U.S. personnel. You're going to meet with the president of Nigeria next week and the trip is coming along well. I spoke to him yesterday, and I sent up a read-ahead memo on the trip this morning."

At these meetings, you realize pretty quickly that there is no such thing as "the foreign policy of the United States." We talk about it all the time, and the media writes about it, but it's an invented idea. If you walked into the State Department and said, "I'd like a copy of the foreign policy of the United States," no one would know what you were talking about. There is no such document. The foreign policy of the United States is mostly what the President and the National Security Council signal is our policy, and then folks at the State Department interpret it according to their own lights. People react to what is urgent and important, and figure out a way forward. Oftentimes, foreign policy seemed to be made by whoever made a convincing case—because often no one else had a case to make.

In government in general and at State in particular, meetings are not preparation for work, they *are* the work. People prepared for meetings, they participated in them, and then they summarized what had happened for another meeting. In government, meetings are the product. People judged how they had done that day by how the meetings had gone. My specials would sometimes say, "We crushed that meeting, Sir." When a meeting didn't go so well, people plotted about how to make the follow-up go better. I almost never heard anyone at a meeting at State say something was going badly. At worst, people would say it was "moving along" or "progressing." Delivering bad news was avoided, and in fact, people often prefaced their remarks by saying, "And some good news from . . ." Two sentences I never heard uttered at a State Department meeting: "Let's make it bigger." "Let's do it faster."

The Foreign Service

State is an observational culture. In 1775, when the forerunner of the department was created as a committee of Congress, it was set up to watch and report the goings-on of the world. That original mission is still in the DNA of the Building. At State, people were good at *monitoring* things. Almost everything was retrospective. Every meeting recounted something that had already happened, and then every subsequent meeting recounted that recounting. And then there were the "summary of conclusions" memos, even if there were no conclusions. At *Time*, we used to have meetings about what we were doing that day, but we also had weekly and monthly planning meetings to plot out the quarter or the year. Early on, I asked my acting chief of staff when all the planning meetings were. She didn't know what I meant. There weren't any.

At State and elsewhere in Washington, there was a lot of *admiring the problem*. We'd look at an issue—say, the concern that the Mosul Dam in Iraq was about to collapse—and examine it from every possible angle. Then memos were written covering each theory of the case. New memos were then signed off on and circulated. Then task forces were formed that spurred another round of memos. Then meetings of higher-ups were convened to examine the task forces' findings. The problem wasn't solved, but the bureaucracy was satisfied.

State was also a passive, risk-averse culture. There was safety in inaction. It was always easier and safer to say no than yes. A no never got you in trouble the way a yes could. It was the opposite of entrepreneurial. Consensus was prized above initiative. People did things the way they had been done before. At an early meeting, I asked my staff if they could name one public diplomacy program that had been discontinued. As hard as it was to start something new at State, it was almost impossible to end something old. When I arrived, the two countries that received the most public diplomacy money were Japan and Germany—a continuing legacy of World War II. As one longtime foreign service officer once told me, diplomacy is an 18th-century profession, managed by a 19th-century bureaucracy, using 20th-century technology.

The dominance of the assistant secretaries at the 9:15 reflected something else: the permanence of the foreign service and the temporariness of political appointees like me. Under Secretaries are almost all political appointees, while about half the assistant secretaries were foreign service officers. The perception of the foreign service was that political appointees come and go, while the foreign service abideth forever.

While there have been ambassadors and consuls from the earliest days of the republic, the foreign service was created only in 1924. Today, to become a foreign service officer, you have to pass the foreign service officer test, a 3-hour exam, and then go through a rigorous interview and vetting process.[4] Only a few hundred people are selected a year out of more than 15,000 applicants.[5] The foreign service likes to boast that it has a lower acceptance rate than Harvard. The old joke was that the foreign service was "pale, male, and Yale." But the lone example of that species I saw at the department was John Kerry. To a person, foreign service officers were decent and diligent; they were devout internationalists, who generally much preferred to be in the field than in Washington, D.C. They cared deeply about their work and America's role in the world.

In a deep and unshakable way, the culture of the foreign service *was* the culture of the State Department. It was a culture of gatherers, not hunters. They didn't like to make mistakes, or ever appear not to know something. I remember when I was going on a trip to Peru; every single foreign service officer I spoke to said the same thing to me: "Great ceviche."

Like officers in the military, everyone in the foreign service changes jobs every two or three years. Because most jobs were two or three years in length, foreign service officers were not particularly beholden to their current boss. A year into a two-year rotation in Washington and they were already foraging for their next assignment. Sometimes they would spend two years at the Foreign Service Institute learning a language and then only two years at the post where they would need to speak that language. And then they might come back and study a different language! I remember thinking, If I spent two years training a correspondent to speak Mandarin, I'd want that darn reporter to spend more than three years in Shanghai.

Foreign service officers were not political. That is true in the sense that they are not appointed, but it is also true in the sense that I never knew who might be a Republican or a Democrat. It just wasn't evident in any way and didn't matter. For them, politics really did stop at the water's edge. Part of the reason is that they were all members of one party: the foreign service party. They were loyal to two main things: the idea that international affairs mattered and the foreign service itself. The foreign service did many things well, but what it did best was inculcate loyalty and belief in the foreign service.

Coming from the media world in New York, I found the culture of the State Department to be unfamiliar. I thought that I had experienced bureaucracy at Time Inc. when I ran *Time* magazine, but that operation was astonishingly lean compared with the State Department. People often said to me, Oh, you come from a big international business, so this must seem like small potatoes to you. In fact, my editorial budget at *Time* was under $100 million a year when I became editor in 2006. My annual budget at State was $1.1 billion. Yes, that's *b* for "billion." I found that people in government often had no real concept of the vast amounts of money they had and how it dwarfed the sums available in the private sector. Foreign service officers always complained about how little money they had in their budgets and were often demoralized when it was cut by 2 or 3 percent. "How can I do what I did last year if my budget is cut by 3 percent?" Very rarely did anyone think, Maybe I shouldn't be doing exactly what I did last year.

I wouldn't call *Time* a glamorous place, but it felt glamorous compared with the State Department. In fact, the State Department of 2014 felt more like the *Time* magazine of the 1980s. Among foreign service officers, there were lots of boxy, out-of-fashion suits and bad haircuts.

But the thing that always made me laugh was how many mustaches there were. You could be at a meeting with 10 men sitting at the table and 5 of them had mustaches. And the varieties! Handlebars, lampshades, chevrons, and even the occasional Fu Manchu. These looked like mustaches they had grown in the '80s and never shaved off.

The department was very hierarchical in terms of structure, but in some ways, that was deceiving. What I found confounding was that when a senior leader made a decision, the counterforces of those who disagreed with it were mobilized. In the Building, the phrase for this was "anti-bodies," as in, "There are a lot of anti-bodies to that policy in the Building." I found that when people disagreed with a decision, they began their response with, "I think that's exactly right, but . . ." Nobody would openly oppose something, but then people would work behind the scenes to undermine it. Sometimes you discovered that actions you had signed off on were still not done months or years later.

Meetings Are Action

When the 9:15 was over, people filed out, chattering, and headed back to their offices. When I first started, my then chief of staff had a daily meeting at 4:30 p.m., known as "vespers," to go over everything that happened that day. Lots of offices at State had vespers. What I found was that by 4:30, I'd pretty much forgotten what had happened at the 8:30 and the comms meeting and the 9:15 as I went pell-mell through my day. After a month or so, I decided we should move vespers to 10 a.m., when I had everything fresh in my mind from the morning meetings.

So after the 9:15 ended, I would head back downstairs exactly the way I had come. And there, waiting in my office, in a U shape at the north end of my office, was my front office staff. I mentioned having four special assistants, but I also had two traditional assistants—one did my schedule and one did logistics and travel. I had a chief of staff. And the chief of staff had a deputy, who was the head of R's policy planning staff. I had a speechwriter, a social media person, an advisor for countering violent extremism, a military aide, a congressional liaison—and I'm sure I'm forgetting a few others. This, by the way, isn't counting the bureau heads who reported to me, the assistant secretary for educational and cultural affairs, the assistant secretary for public affairs, or the coordinator of International Information Programs. So, when we had a meeting in my office for just R front office staff, there could be 16 or 17 people. At *Time*, I had one assistant.

Each smaller meeting at State was a microcosm of a bigger meeting. So my little morning meeting recapitulated the Secretary's 8:30. My chief of staff would lay out the day, and then we would go around the room, starting with the special assistants, who would review what was happening in their realm. Everyone in there felt that they were looking out both for me personally and for R equities, and I appreciated it. State was "turfy," and people were adept at protecting their territory.

I discovered that my chief of staff, a foreign service officer, would schedule me with one meeting after another throughout the day so that I had no time to think or even react to what had happened in the last meeting. When she would say to me, "You're back-to-back today," she wasn't kidding. This came from a variety of things, including the simple one of trying to cram as much work into a day as possible. But the other aspect of this in Washington was what I thought of as the "infantilization of principals." This was the idea that principals—basically political folks—should be kept so busy, with absolutely everything done for them, that they never really made any decisions or choices other than the ones baked in for them by staff. Basically, every principal in Washington had so much staff, all of whom were so eager to write or contribute something, that you could go your entire day, every day, just reading off a piece of paper or a cue card of what you were supposed to say or do at a meeting. And many principals did just that. At meetings in the White House Situation Room I was often amazed that principals of agencies and cabinet officers would just numbly read from the notes that had been prepared by staff. I sometimes wondered why we didn't hire actors. They certainly would have read the scripts better.

Pretty much everyone at State filed out promptly at 5 p.m. I had never seen that before. If you send an email to foreign service officers or civil servants at 5:05 p.m., don't expect to hear back until the following morning. And if you send it at that same time on Friday, don't expect to hear back until Monday morning. They either didn't look at it or didn't think it was appropriate to answer during non–office hours. At first, when I didn't get answers to my emails, I thought that perhaps the server was down or that there was some other technical problem. I remember having IT guys come to look at my dusty old Dell desktop. Some of this had to do with the State Department work ethos, which was that something asked for today could actually be done tomorrow—or even next week. But part of this was the idea that to so many at State, even the simplest email was looked at as a kind of barbed weapon, a digital Trojan horse that might be a trap of some kind. An email could get you in trouble. It was a federal record. Folks were terrified of making a mistake. Hence, the answers were almost always bland and noncommittal.

So at 4:30 we summarized the day, and then we were all back in at 8 the next morning to do it all over again. As one longtime foreign service officer said to me, "Holding back the hands of time is a 24/7 job."

PART II

Getting There

Luck = Opportunity + Readiness

It was 2013, and I was in my seventh year as editor of *Time*, and I was having lunch with Melody Barnes, the former Obama domestic policy advisor at the White House, with whom I'd become friends over the years. I wanted to know about her post-government life. At the end of the lunch, she turned to me and asked, out of the blue, Would you ever be interested in working at the State Department?

Why do you ask? I said.

She said her good friend was recruiting people to work for Secretary Kerry.

Would there be a particular job that you might want?

The only one I could think of—and knew a little bit about, in part because it had been held by former journalists—was the Under Secretary for Public Diplomacy. She smiled when I said that, and then we said goodbye.

Ten days later I was sitting in Secretary Kerry's elegant outer office on the seventh floor of the State Department. Unbeknownst to me at the time I had lunch with Melody, the person in the job had just told the Secretary that she would be leaving that summer.

Melody had mentioned our lunch to her friend, a longtime aide to Secretary Kerry, who was then recruiting people from outside the department. She liked the idea; she mentioned it to Kerry, who also liked the idea. I had known Senator Kerry a bit over the years. I had never actually covered him, but I'd been the national editor for *Time* when he had run for president in 2004. I'd always admired him and hoped that he didn't remember the story I'd edited about how he'd never win Iowa and never go on to become the Democratic nominee.

I'd always known I'd do some form of public service. In my first summer as editor, I wrote a cover story called "The Case for National Service," and we published an annual national service issue thereafter. I truly believed in the Framers' idea of citizen service as a foundation of democracy.

A few days after the lunch with Melody, I got an email from David Wade, Secretary Kerry's chief of staff, asking me if I was serious. I said I was.

I did a little research about the job. It was created only in 1999, under Bill Clinton, when a bill sponsored by Jesse Helms and Joe Biden abolished the U.S. Information Agency (USIA) and transferred its public diplomacy programs to the State Department to be managed by the newly created Under Secretary at State.[1] It hadn't been an easy change: the USIA people felt that their mission had been devastated, and the State people didn't love the idea of an information agency at the department. In the 17 years since the job's creation, it had been empty for as long as it had been filled. The longest-serving Under Secretary had been Karen Hughes, at two years.

After being ushered into Secretary Kerry's outer office, I sat on the light-blue-and-white-striped chaise on the right, with two chairs in front of it. Kerry bounded into the room with a big smile and a "Great to see you, Rick." He took one of the chairs in front of the chaise and launched into how important public diplomacy was in the 21st century and how he'd like to reinvent it and I would be the ideal person for the job: I really want your help figuring out what the narrative is for this new century. He's a terrific salesman. When he finally paused after the tornado of words, I smiled and said, "You had me at 'hello.'"

I expected him to smile, but he didn't (perhaps he didn't know the movie?) and then launched into a second, just-as-enthusiastic round of selling me on the job. In the middle of this second effort, I said,

Whoa, Mr. Secretary, I'm going to do it—I'd love to do it. Count me in. Then he leaned back, sighed, and gave me a clap on the shoulder. I saw firsthand what a tenacious negotiator he was. He wouldn't even take yes for an answer.

Vetting Is Painful

For anyone who has been vetted for a Senate-confirmed job, what I'm about to write will be painfully familiar. The process is byzantine, detailed beyond imagining, uncomfortable, and invasive. It's not hard to see why it keeps some good people from going into government. (It can also keep bad people out.) Let's start with the SF86 Form, from the Office of Personnel Management, which is the standard questionnaire for national security clearances. Filled out, the form can run to hundreds of pages, as mine did. A State Department nominee also has to fill out the Senate Foreign Relations Committee questionnaire. Mine was again over a hundred pages. I won't go into all the details—and the details are endless—but here's one: For the SF86 and the Senate Foreign Relations questionnaire, you have to list every foreign trip you've taken over the past 14 years, every significant relationship you had with any foreign national on each trip, and, to the best of your ability, an estimate of how much you drank on these trips. Oh, and whether you used any illegal drugs.

Those questions are a legacy of the Cold War, when Congress and the intelligence community worried about State employees being blackmailed by Russian spies. One assumption seems pretty intuitive: if you drank too much on a foreign trip, you were more likely to be a target of a Russian *kompromat* operation.

As a nominee, you also needed to be investigated by law enforcement, and for that you were assigned a "special investigator," who, well, investigated you. The investigator would question your neighbors, your work colleagues, your elementary-school teachers, and ask them if you drink too much, if you use drugs, if you are abusive, if you are trustworthy, and, oh, if you are loyal to the country.

My investigator—let's call him Mike—was a burly, no-nonsense former cop who seemed to want to get the job done with a minimum of hassle. My introduction to Mike came when he sent me an email telling me that he would be working on my investigation. His first email to me was about a late payment on a J.Crew credit card, and why my balance was past due.

Mike also asked for names of friends and colleagues whom he might contact. But then the investigator can also call people on his own. A few weeks later I got a worried late-night telephone call from a neighbor I hadn't seen in months.

"Rick, did you do anything wrong?"

"No," I said. "Why?"

"Because I got a call from law enforcement asking me whether I think you might be a spy or a foreign agent or whether you might be working for a terrorist organization."

The Confirmation Process

At the time of my nomination, there were already dozens of nominees who had not been scheduled for a vote and dozens more who had gotten through various committees and were waiting for a vote from the Senate. Almost all nominations were voted on by what the Senate called "UC"—unanimous consent. The Senate had to confirm hundreds of political nominees every year, and if it took up each one individually for debate and a vote, it probably wouldn't have time to get to any other business. "UC" simply meant that if no one objected to or put a hold on your nomination, it would go through via voice vote.

From the moment I was officially nominated, I was assigned a ground-floor office at the State Department. Just beyond the main elevators there are a couple of corridors with nondescript offices reserved for nominees. The idea is that the Senate wouldn't look kindly on a nominee using her official office before she was confirmed, so you're meant to make do with a temporary one. Mine was a small, dingy office with a tiny window that overlooked an alley. I wasn't allowed to see my official office, and I had to be escorted anywhere I needed to go in the Building.

Pretty quickly, I began to suss out the idiosyncrasies of the State Department. I was besieged with emails, memorandums, and reports, and basically every one—*every one*—was way too long. I don't mean an extra paragraph or page; I mean 3 to 5 to 10 times too long. There seemed to be some reward mechanism for writing long memos. It was as if people at State were paid by the word. There was also a process for everything, no matter how big or small, that always had to be followed. There was a process for nominees to meet the department, and there was a process for how I had to be escorted to my office. Oftentimes this process wasn't written down anywhere but was part of a tradition known only by the foreign service.

The main way the department got you ready for confirmation hearings was by holding what were known as "murder boards." Murder boards are practice runs for the hearing. You are put in a room like the hearing room, seated at a table up front, while a range of State Department officers pretend they are Senators and pepper you with possible questions and then critique your answers. In preparation for my murder board, I was given about a dozen comically large notebooks (we're talking over 700 pages each) that covered everything from the origins of the Public Affairs Department to the Foreign Assistance Act of 1962.

It was like learning a new language. I've already mentioned that every bureau has an initial, but then every regional bureau also has an acronym: there's EUR (European and Eurasian Affairs), NEA (Near Eastern Affairs), EAP (East Asian and Pacific Affairs), and SCA (South and Central Asian Affairs). On top of that, every functional bureau had an abbreviation: ECA (Educational and Cultural Affairs), INL (International Narcotics and Law Enforcement Affairs), DRL (Democracy, Human Rights, and Labor), and on and on. And then individual programs had acronyms: IVLP (International Visitors Leadership Program), YALI (Young African Leadership Initiative), EUSIR (Fulbright European Union Scholar-in-Residence). People have entire conversations in acronyms, except for the occasional verb to connect the initials.

I struggled with what you might call governmentspeak, or Washingtonese. I had spent most of my life speaking like a journalist. It didn't occur to me that I would have trouble transitioning to speak like someone in government. (Later I would joke that when I was a journalist, I didn't know a whole lot and tried to make as much controversy as possible, but now that I'm in government, I know a lot more and try to make as little controversy as possible.) In fact, Washingtonese is a kind of anti-controversy speech. It's full of euphemisms and indirection and the passive voice. My fallback was always, "Senator, I welcome that question, but I will have to get back to you on that."

My guidance from H was useful: The hearing is pass/fail; you're not graded on every question. The key is to give a "perception of readiness." When you're on safe ground—benefits to the taxpayer, jobs, prosperity, the flag—don't hold back. And don't be afraid to be dull—this is not the time to wheel out your bold proposal on income redistribution. You can use notes—but not too many! And remember the 80-20 rule—let the Senators speak for 80 percent of the time. And absolutely no joking.

I had to learn the structure and history of public diplomacy and the intricacies of the public diplomacy budget; the difference between 0.7 funding and ECE funds (don't ask). There were 3,540 public diplomacy (PD) and public affairs (PA) positions. There were 189 public affairs offices abroad. Some 50,000 people participated in education-exchange programs in more than 160 countries. About 800,000 international students contributed almost $23 billion to the U.S. economy. And I had to always refer to *foreign* audiences, because the U.S. Information and Educational Exchange Act of 1948 (known as Smith-Mundt) still governed how public diplomacy operated, and it prohibited the distribution of State Department–produced material in the physical United States. The law was not only pre-internet; it was pre–color TV.

Each nominee had the option of reading an opening statement, and everyone does so. I worked on mine for a few weeks. I talked about why I cared about public service; mentioned my father, who would have been very proud; and talked a little about my work with Nelson Mandela. When I was happy with my draft, I was instructed to share it with State and H, which would then offer comments and suggestions. This was my first experience of the State "clearance process" and the group culture of the foreign service. H and L (the legal department) had a few factual suggestions. But what I was taken aback by was that foreign service officers I did not know blithely deleted whole paragraphs and added new ones—in my own voice—without even informing me.

By the time the hearing came around, I felt ready. I won't bore you with my entire written statement, except to note that the theme that I talked about at the top was the theme that would be the overwhelming focus of what I did during my three years at State. And that was the rise of disinformation, how that was facilitated by social media, and what we needed to do about it:

Every day all over the world, there is a great global debate
going on. It is about the nature of freedom and fairness,
democracy and justice. It is happening in all the traditional
ways, in coffee shops and on street corners, but it is also
taking place on the new platforms of social media. The
reach, the scale, the speed of that debate are like nothing
before in history. I have been in that debate all of my life.
America has to be in that debate. We need to lead it. And we
cannot rest on our laurels. Every minute, there are attacks
and misstatements about America and American foreign
policy that cannot be left to stand. Social media is a tool
that can be used for good or ill. It is a powerful medium for
truth, but it is an equally powerful medium for falsehood.
My Senator from long ago, the great Pat Moynihan, used
to say, "You're entitled to your own opinions, not your own
facts." Well, today, more and more, people feel entitled to
their own facts. They choose the facts that conform with
their point of view. Even though it is easier than any time
in human history to find information to rebut lies, less of
that seems to be happening than ever. We cannot resign
ourselves to this; we need to fight it.[2]

The actual hearing was an anticlimax. It was a busy day in the
Senate, and this was far from the most important thing going on. I
don't think there were ever more than five Senators in the room at
one time, and often there was only one. My principal questioner was
Marco Rubio. He began by saying that some people around the world
look at all the debate in our society as evidence of how fractured and
polarized we are, but he sees it as a source of strength. I agreed with
him wholeheartedly and said that my whole career as a journalist was

to highlight this debate and that it made our democracy richer and stronger. Thank you, Senator Rubio. And then it was over.

H was hoping for a pre-Thanksgiving unanimous-consent vote in the Senate. We'd been told that November 22 was the day. But something a little more momentous happened in the Senate that day. Harry Reid, the Senate Majority Leader, frustrated with Republican intransigence on nominees, invoked the so-called nuclear option, the most fundamental change in the Senate's rules in more than a generation. By a simple majority vote, the Democratic Party changed the longtime rules of the Senate that required 60 votes for confirmations. Now all nominations, except those to the Supreme Court, would need only a simple majority to be confirmed.

In theory, this should have made things easier. But the Republicans responded by blocking unanimous-consent votes on nominees and forcing every nomination to the floor. That meant that every nominee would now take between 8 and 30 hours of debate to get confirmed. There were 87 nominations pending—and I was one of them.

In fact, the Senate adjourned on December 21 without voting on any of the 28 State nominees. It had already been five months, and now the wait got longer.

It was not until February that they held another vote. In the end, I was confirmed 92–8. All the nays were Republicans. It was good to be in, and good to have some opposition, but not too much. (A vote of 100–0 means you never made any enemies.) It had been a year since Secretary Kerry had clapped me on the shoulder in his office.

PART III

The Job

Wrong Foot

My first day began in an inauspicious way. The calendar said my first official meeting as Under Secretary of State for Public Diplomacy and Public Affairs of the United States of America was with the Russian Special Envoy for Cultural Cooperation, Mikhail Shvidkoy, the country's highest public diplomacy official.

Umm, how did this come about? I asked my acting chief of staff.

Well, the envoy "happened to be in the Building," she said, and both the European bureau and public affairs thought it made sense for me to see him while he was here. After all, she said, the two of you are the co-chairs of the Bilateral Presidential Commission Working Group on Education, Culture, Sports, and Media.

I felt awkward about this. Our relations with Russia were at a sore point. The much-heralded "reset" had proved a bust. I asked my chief of staff, Was this meeting going to send a message one way or another? Should I punt? Everyone told me that I was overthinking it, and canceling it would be worse.

I was given a BCL on the meeting. BCL is short for "briefing checklist," This is the top of the BCL:

> **Under Secretary Stengel's Meeting with Russian Federation's Special Envoy for Cultural Cooperation Mikhail Shvidkoy**
>
> Your first meeting with Shvidkoy (Shh-vit-koy) is an opportunity to begin a strategic relationship with <u>Russia's most senior public diplomacy official</u>. **Your overarching objective is to establish a relationship that enables us to advance a more positive U.S.-Russia agenda through people-to-people relations with Russia.**

The memo went on to talk about "key objectives" and then came the part of traditional State memos that I always liked best: "Watch Out For." Here the memo said the Russians wanted to repatriate the remains of the Russian pianist Sergey Rachmaninoff and would float a proposal about Fort Ross in California.

I also got a bio of Shvidkoy. He sounded like he might be entertaining. He had written three books on the theater, and was the host of two television shows.

We met in a nondescript conference room off my office because he would be bringing a number of staff and therefore I would have to as well. At State, we always mirrored the number of aides that the foreign official had. He had three, and so did I.

Shvidkoy looked a lot like Nikita Khrushchev—short, stocky, bald. He was bumptious and impatient. After the perfunctory handshakes, our two teams took their seats on opposite sides of the long, rectangular table.

We got off on the wrong foot, not because of personality but because of policy. Just before the meeting, we had received word that our annual bilateral cultural meeting with the Russians—the U.S.-Russia Bilateral Presidential Commission Working Group for Education, Culture, Sports, and Media, which the Russians apparently loved—had been canceled by the White House because of Russia's behavior in Ukraine. I thought it best not to sugarcoat this, and I announced it right at the top. Russian diplomats never show surprise. I could have announced that President Obama was inviting President Putin to be his partner on *Dancing with the Stars*, and they would have just nodded, expressionless. Shvidkoy barely acknowledged what I had said and did not bring it up again. Russians are from the "never apologize, never explain" school of diplomacy.

The primary issue they wanted to talk about was Fort Ross, which had been the one and only Russian colony in the contiguous United

States. In 1812, a Russian American shipping company chartered by the czar built a settlement about 90 miles north of San Francisco. The settlers planted crops, bred livestock, and constructed a simple Russian Orthodox chapel. But by 1841, their plans changed, and they sold the fort. Decades later, California turned Fort Ross into a park. In 2009, California was considering closing the park, and the Russian Ambassador Sergey Kislyak met with then California Governor Arnold Schwarzenegger and implored him to keep it open.[1] Now Shvidkoy was advocating that it become part of the National Park Service, which would protect it. This was a pretty remote possibility, as either the President would have to issue a proclamation under the 1906 Antiquities Act, or Congress would have to pass a bill establishing it as a national monument. Right then, no one was looking to do the Russians any favors.

When I explained that this was very unlikely, Shvidkoy launched into a speech. He said Russia had "sovereignty" over Fort Ross because of "history" and certain "rights." Mr. Shvidkoy was clearly unhappy with my answer and seemed to imply that Russia should just annex it. That didn't seem like a good plan. I looked around the room, and all my State colleagues were stone-faced. Is that what diplomacy is? Listening to crazy stuff and not acknowledging it?

After his speech, Shvidkoy seemed to lose his energy and switched abruptly to the Rachmaninoff case. Rachmaninoff was a great Russian artist, he said, and his remains should be sent back to the homeland. When he finished, I said that the State Department didn't have any jurisdiction over the remains of the pianist and that he would need to take it up with the Rachmaninoff estate. That seemed to be enough for Mr. Shvidkoy. He looked at his watch, glanced at his colleagues, stood up, shook my hand, and then they all filed out. If he was playing the part of the gruff, humorless unbending Russian apparatchik, it was a flawless performance.

Rethinking Rethinking

I must have gotten a dozen memos in the first few weeks about convening meetings to "reimagine PD" or "rethink PD" or create "PD for the 21st century." I didn't get any memos about diplomacy in general or policy or media or China or Russia or anything else. The way it works at the State Department is that foreign service officers each had a "cone," kind of like a major in college—politics, economics, consular affairs, management, public diplomacy. They were an economics officer or a political officer or a public diplomacy officer. They received special training in these fields, and they mostly stayed in their cones for their entire career. In many ways, public diplomacy was the cone that, as the comedian Rodney Dangerfield used to say, "don't get no respect." PD officers had a bit of an inferiority complex. They were underrepresented in the ambassadorial ranks, the great goal of all foreign service officers. Politics and economic officers didn't have to justify what they did. But public diplomacy was kind of nebulous.

I was thinking less about reimagining PD than defining it in the first place. I disliked the mushy language around public diplomacy and I absolutely hated the phrase, so often used to describe PD, "winning hearts and minds." Everything we've learned in the last 50 years from social science and psychology suggests that changing someone's mind is a nearly impossible task. The more you try to change an embedded view, the more likely people are to double down in their beliefs (i.e., the "backfire effect"). In the department, public diplomacy was described as people-to-people diplomacy, in contrast to state-to-state. Everyone also talked about "telling America's story," which was the earnest phrase used during the Cold War. In all my reading, I hadn't seen a very good definition of PD. The one I liked best was also the briefest: Joe Nye's phrase "soft power."[2] I generally felt that the more time we spent talking about PD rather than policy, the more we marginalized ourselves.

The other thing that irked me was all the discussion of the "golden age" of public diplomacy during the Cold War. Very often a Representative would say, We used to know how to counter the Russians. In fact, PD was seen as a success only *after* the fall of the Berlin Wall. Before then, PD practitioners were blamed for not getting our message across. The fabled United States Information Agency (USIA) never really had a seat at the table, and the sainted Edward Murrow famously complained about it ("If you don't include us in the takeoff, we can't help you on the crash landing"). Members of Congress had this naive idea that without USIA, the Berlin Wall would never have fallen and the Soviet Union would still exist. If anything, it was more Edward G. Robinson and Mr. Ed than Ed Murrow that led to the fall of communism. American popular culture was the secret weapon, not schmaltzy USIA documentaries about African American athletes and musicians.

On my first morning as Under Secretary, I sent out a message to all public diplomacy officers abroad that commended them for what they did, but said that we had to use the power of social media and mobile technology. For PD officers in the field, these missives from newly confirmed political appointees must be somewhere between forgettable and comical. For them, each new person has his or her priorities that tend to last for only as long as that person stays in the job, which in the case of the Under Secretary for Public Diplomacy had not been very long.

There was a lot of resistance and just plain lack of knowledge about digital and mobile. State officials were equipped with clunky old BlackBerrys, and plenty of officers didn't even have that. People were resistant to social media. At that time, there were only a few dozen State Twitter accounts, and even the Secretary did not have one. Later, at a town hall meeting I had for our ambassadors, an ambassador to a small European country raised his hand and said that his problem with social media was that it's too easy to make a mistake.

Getting more folks on digital platforms was a challenge. I had a tour of International Information Programs, a bureau under public diplomacy that had once been part of USIA and helped create content in support of policy. Staff escorted me to a large conference room to proudly show me . . . *magazines.* Spread across an enormous rectangular table were all the print magazines they produced and distributed around the world. I guess they thought that I, as a former magazine editor, would be pleased to see all the wonderful magazines they produced. In fact, I was horrified. I had just sent out a message about focusing on social media, and here they were showing me glossy legacy products from the 1970s. Heck, didn't they know the magazine business was dying? I eventually killed about half the titles.

Silos, Silos, Everywhere

A couple of weeks after my confirmation, I got my State Department email address—with the domain state.gov—but there was very little in my inbox every morning. I was still getting more State Department email at my Gmail address than at my government one. I noticed that while my inbox sat empty, my staff received all kinds of internally produced news summaries and lists of clips and press releases. It was strange that there was no process to get you set up digitally—no set of lists or schedules. In fact, it took months to get on the lists I needed to be on to get news articles about the State Department, to get op-eds and editorials about foreign policy, to get the rundown of weekly meetings—and even then, I'm sure I wasn't on nearly all the lists I needed to be on. Occasionally, a longtime State Department hand would say, Hey, what's that list? I didn't even know about that one.

The truth was, few people at State knew what was going on in a 360-degree way. I was stunned, for example, to find that people at the

State Department didn't seem to know when the Secretary of State was giving a speech. Or what it was about. Or where it was taking place. In those first few months, when I'd mention to other Under Secretaries that the Secretary was giving a speech on, say, arms control or countering violent extremism, they would say, Really! How did you know about that?

This siloification extended far beyond the Secretary's speeches. When the European bureau made a statement about some action of Putin's or the Africa bureau condemned an action by a terrorist group in Mali, almost no one knew about it. There was no cross-promotion. Statements were issued from their silos and then not amplified. Public Affairs was often quite reticent about chiming in on such statements. They didn't see their role as amplifying other statements—after all, they had their own statements to make! They thought it was the Secretary's job to make speeches and the press's job to report on them, and that's how our policies got out to the public. Very 20th century. We literally didn't have a single person assigned to tweet or be on social media while the Secretary was speaking.

One of the first ideas I had was to form a digital hub in PD that would not originate content but rather share, amplify, and coordinate it. Nobody seemed to be doing this. It would take only a handful of people—three or four—who could retweet and repost what the department had done that day. It would essentially be an aggregator of content for the department. But it could also refute false information about U.S. foreign policy. It would be a hub, and that's what I called it. I thought it was a no-brainer. But the no-brainer was me, it turned out. Everyone objected. Public Affairs didn't like the idea and said it was their function. International Information Programs thought this was their function. The seventh floor was skeptical and didn't really understand the purpose.

I talked about it all the time. I wrote an action memo to the Secretary. And nothing happened. S did not sign the action memo. I didn't get the go-ahead from management to hire people. I was frustrated and didn't understand what was happening. It was my first experience with how ideas get blocked within the department. Ideas died at State because people saw them as violating their turf, not because they weren't good. They died not because anyone overtly objected—they died from a kind of aggressive passivity. It took me a while to understand Colin Powell's dictum that in government no idea on its own is good enough to rise; every idea needs a coalition to succeed.

The Birth of Counter-Messaging

When I first looked at the structure of R and the bureaus underneath it, one piece didn't seem to fit: CSCC, the Center for Strategic Counterterrorism Communications. All the other parts—Public Affairs, Educational and Cultural Affairs, International Information Programs—had been cobbled together from the 1999 legislation that created the office of public diplomacy, but CSCC was new. It had been created in 2010 by Secretary Hillary Clinton in collaboration with CIA chief Leon Panetta to combat the communications of a radical terrorist group that was using revolutionary new techniques to get out its message: al-Qaeda. Remember, this was 2010. Al-Qaeda had shot videos of Ayman al-Zawahiri sitting on a hillside in Pakistan giving a jihadist lecture directly to the camera for 54 minutes. They then uploaded that video to YouTube, where it got a few thousand views. That was cutting-edge back then.

The genesis of CSCC occurred at a Situation Room meeting in 2010. The U.S.'s drone war against terrorists was having success on the ground but wounding the image of America abroad. At that meeting, State's coordinator for counterterrorism pitched the idea of an information war room to combat terrorist messaging and help America's image in the process. According to observers, Obama replied, "Why haven't we been doing that already?"

That was enough to launch the idea, and Secretary Clinton came up with a plan for a small, nimble entity that could coordinate across the government to counter al-Qaeda's media in real time. It would live at the State Department but essentially be an interagency group staffed from across the government. Executive Order 13584, issued on September 15, 2011—about a year after that first Situation Room discussion—established the CSCC "to coordinate, orient, and inform government-wide foreign communications activities targeted against terrorism and violent extremism, particular al-Qaida and its affiliates."[3]

From the moment of its birth, CSCC was a problem child. It was underfunded, its mission was poorly understood, and it became an orphan within the State Department. The National Security Council sought to manage it. The Department of Defense resented it. And Foreign Service officers avoided it. It was originally seen not as an entity that created content, but one that helped coordinate and inform other entities in government about what al-Qaeda was up to on social media. At the time, there was also a fight about where it would be situated at State. Counterterrorism wanted it, so did R. R won, but it was never a perfect fit.

Within the first year, CSCC had grown to about 40 people, with its most visible part something called the Digital Outreach Team (DOT—another awful acronym), which engaged in online debate about violent extremism. About 20 people worked on the team and created content in three languages: Arabic, Urdu, and Somali. Their motto was "Contest the space," and the idea was to target so-called fence-sitters, young men who might be considering joining al-Qaeda. The messaging tried to create doubt in these young men by telling them that al-Qaeda was killing Muslims and that if they went to fight, they were likely to be killed themselves.

The head of CSCC was Alberto Fernandez, a former ambassador to Equatorial Guinea who had also been a U.S. spokesperson in Iraq during the Iraq War. Alberto had fluent Arabic, a dark mustache, and a crafty manner. He was an expert in the history of violent extremist organizations and could tell you how al-Qaeda and Jabhat al-Nusra disagreed about toothbrushing hadiths.

I had first met with Alberto before I was confirmed, to better understand CSCC. He walked me through what they were doing. They seemed very focused on the inside baseball of al-Qaeda politics. He proudly showed me examples of how al-Qaeda's own messengers attacked CSCC online and tried to take down CSCC's Twitter handle. It was clear he thought that being attacked by al-Qaeda was a sign of CSCC's effectiveness. I wasn't so sure.

Alberto mentioned that in spring 2012, they had noticed another organization that had formed in the area, the Islamic State of Iraq and the Levant, which was fighting Bashar al-Assad. (The Levant was the historical region of Syria and the countries of the eastern Mediterranean.) They noticed that ISIS, as he called it, began to increase its influence in rebel-held areas in 2013 through an interesting mix of charity and intimidation. It helped the poor but brutally punished anyone for violating sharia law and was virulently anti-Shia. In early 2013, he said, this organization began warning its followers that the U.S. State Department was trying to sow dissent among jihadis. ISIS was the coming thing, he said.

Bringing Back Our Girls, Slowly

A week later, on April 14, 2014, I got a sense of just how rapid the rapid-response mechanism of CSCC was. Most Americans had never heard of Boko Haram when news organizations began reporting that the group had kidnapped 276 girls from a secondary school in Chibok, a town in Borno State, Nigeria.[4] Boko Haram was an Islamic terrorist group formed in 2002 in northeastern Nigeria. Its aim was to turn Nigeria into an Islamic state under sharia law. According to U.S. intelligence, Boko Haram had formed an alliance with al-Qaeda in the Islamic Maghreb in 2011. Over the past few years, Boko Haram had been responsible for hundreds of attacks, multiple bombings, and thousands of deaths in northeastern Nigeria, murdering far more people than al-Qaeda.[5]

Alberto came to me and said this would be a good opportunity for CSCC to branch out a bit and do some counter–Boko Haram social media and show support for the kidnapped girls. He proposed that CSCC do some quick mock-ups. Great. The next day, CSCC showed me some potential banners. They were poorly designed, not very modern-looking, and quite bland, but what the heck, government wasn't known for its aesthetic sense. I approved them immediately because I didn't want to delay our efforts.

In the meantime, the story had captured people's attention. A hashtag started trending on Twitter: #BringBackOurGirls. It turned into a social media supernova when First Lady Michelle Obama posed for a picture holding up a sign with the handwritten hashtag. "In these girls, Barack and I see our own daughters," she said in a video.[6]

I didn't think about the banners again and just continued to monitor the situation on the ground. Ten days later, Alberto came to see me and said, I need your help on something. What about? Well, he said sheepishly, the banners had not been able to get through the clearance process. What? The Africa bureau had objected to them. We made some changes, he said, and they were approved, but then the Bureau of Intelligence and Research objected to those changes. It was a bureaucratic standoff, and he wanted to see whether I could fix the problem. This was insane. A ten-day-old tweet might as well not exist.

The clearance process was unmistakable evidence that State was a horizontal culture as well as a vertical one. Almost every memo or note or paper that was going from one level to another, or one bureau to another, was subject to the clearance process. Any bureaus, functional or regional, that had a stake in the paper had to "clear" it before it went to the next level. And since they were so protective of their equities, they wanted to weigh in to make sure someone else wasn't treading on their turf. This illustrated another axiom at State: many more people could say no than say yes. A deputy assistant secretary or a special assistant could not initiate policy or even commission an anti–Boko Haram tweet, but they could kill it by refusing to clear it.

Even when things did get through, the clearance process made a mockery of deadlines. It optimized for purity over urgency. Things that I originally expected to take hours would take days; things that I thought would take days would take weeks; and things that I thought would take weeks would take months. And I haven't even mentioned the reclama process. Don't know that word? I didn't either. A reclama— from the Latin *reclamare*, meaning "to cry out in protest"—was a request made through the chain of command to reconsider a decision. So this meant that even after the final decision had been made by a principal and cleared, you could request that it be overturned. To me, it seemed like asking for the referee's call to be reversed after the game was over. At State, the term was used as a verb, as in "you can reclama it." And that's what had happened to the Boko Haram banners—they had been reclama'd again by the Africa bureau.

When Alberto left my office, I picked up the phone and called David Wade, the Secretary's chief of staff, to explain the situation. He had a one-word response: "Jesus!"

The banners were cleared and posted within two hours.

The Ben Cave

There's nothing grand about the West Wing. The offices are small and dark, the hallways narrow, the entrance areas unprepossessing. It's pretty underwhelming. I was there during my first week for my initial meeting with Ben Rhodes. Ben's office was a grotto, a long, narrow cave with no windows. He was adjacent to the Navy Mess, about a 15-second walk from the Oval Office.

Ben was Obama's foreign policy boy wonder, his chief speechwriter on foreign policy, and, in some ways, his foreign policy alter ego—though Ben was later criticized in the press for saying that himself. Ben's official title was Assistant to the President and Deputy National Security Advisor for Strategic Communications and Speechwriting. Everyone at State told me he was my equivalent at the White House, but that was a disservice to Ben. He would become my closest and most reliable touch point at the White House, and from first to last, he was generous and supportive.

Ben is a cool presence. Pretty much all Obama's people were. It's not that he avoids looking you in the eye, but he often looks away or up or down when he is speaking. This seems to be in part because he really does concentrate while he's talking, rather than just rattling off practiced phrases, as lots of people in Washington do. He had already been working for President Obama for five years, and I was the new kid. When you're in government, you look at every new person as someone who can potentially advance or set back your agenda.

He wanted to talk about two topics: the BBG and counter-ISIS. BBG was the acronym for the Broadcasting Board of Governors—the truly dreadful name for what was also known as U.S. International Broadcasting, made up of the Voice of America, Radio Free Europe and Radio Liberty, Radio Free Asia, Middle East Broadcasting, and the Office of Cuba Broadcasting. These legacy media organizations were originally part of the United States Information Agency and then became quasi-independent by virtue of the 1999 legislation, which also created my job.

BBG had a $750 million budget and about 3,500 employees, which made it one of the largest news organizations in the world. But few Americans knew about it. This was in part because of Smith-Mundt, which mandated that it be directed abroad (Voice of America broadcast in more than 60 languages), and in part because it didn't do much journalism that broke through in the U.S. It was also cursed with a contradictory mission: it was government-supported independent journalism. If that sounds strange, that's because it is. Its employees saw themselves exclusively as journalists, but they were also tasked with creating content "consistent with the broad foreign policy objectives of the United States," as its enabling legislation puts it. Hmm, how do you create objective independent journalism consistent with American foreign policy objectives? That's a tough one. Ben said President Obama was interested in U.S. international broadcasting and wanted to see what more we could do with it. "It's a lot of money," he said. The President, Ben added, would like to sit down with me and Jeff Shell, the new chairman of the BBG, and talk about it. Ben said I should get my thoughts together and we'd schedule a meeting.

The other place where Ben thought he could help was counter-ISIS messaging. He supported CSCC, and had an idea on how to enlarge the platform. He said two Defense Department "influence" sites were being disbanded because of budget cuts. His idea was that DOD could essentially hand them over to State, and we would run them and pay for them.

Ben rummaged around his desk and found a glossy brochure about the sites, prepared by the Defense Department. The pamphlet described them as "cost effective, 24/7 influence with proven impact." It felt a little like he was a realtor trying to sell me that dark apartment on the second floor. He explained that their content had to say that they were supported by the Defense Department. Or, if we took them, the State Department. But the only way you'd find this out was if you clicked on the "About Us" link. Here's what the brochure said about that: "Less than 1% of readers click on the 'about us' link. Extremely limited loss of readership due to DoD attribution." Ben said the sites cost almost nothing. How much was nothing? I asked. One cost about $4 million a year to run and the other $6 million.

Ben, I said, that was three times the budget that I had for all of CSCC.

That's a problem, he said.

I wondered why I needed to buy something from DOD. The Defense Department had more people in military bands than the number of foreign service officers. For them this amount of money was just the nickels left on the table.

Welcome to International Broadcasting

As it happened, I had a BBG board meeting that first week. I admit that when I came into the job, I barely knew what the BBG was. Even in my years as editor of *Time*, I couldn't remember ever seeing a Voice of America story or one from any of the other entities. Even the names— Radio Free Europe, Radio Free Asia—seemed like anachronisms, throwbacks to the Cold War. The meeting was at BBG's headquarters in the Wilbur J. Cohen Federal Building, a gloomy 1930s-era building filled with somber New Deal–era murals.

By statute, I was the Secretary's official designee to the BBG board. But I was the first Under Secretary in anyone's memory to actually attend a board meeting. Most of my predecessors had politely ignored

it. When she was Secretary of State, Hillary Clinton told a House committee hearing that the BBG board was "practically defunct in terms
of its capability to tell a message around the world." The Chairman of
that House Committee, Ed Royce of California, described the board as
"dysfunctional."[7] By all accounts, this was a pretty accurate description.
As one board member said to me, it was like the Albanian politburo but
without the handguns. But under the chairmanship of Jeff Shell, the
head of Comcast Universal, the board had undergone a turnaround.
Jeff was a smart, no-nonsense, even-keeled chairman who just wanted
to make things work.

At that first meeting, I did see some snippets of the journalism
from some of the services. It was sober and straightforward, but seemed
old-fashioned and not up to U.S. broadcast standards. The editing was
a little rough, the graphics were poor, and the anchors didn't seem all
that comfortable with teleprompters. I also learned that the way the
BBG "supported" U.S. foreign policy goals was to air "editorials" from
the State Department. It was a neat solution for them. It hived off the
material that supported U.S. foreign policy from news reporting, but it
was also a way of saying to the viewer, Hey, don't pay attention to this,
it's just American State Department propaganda, and we'll get back to
the news in a moment.

One issue in that meeting illustrated the curious relationship
between State and the BBG. The executive producer for the Africa
service did a short presentation asking for $300,000 of R's public diplo-
macy funds to pay for a 15-minute daily newscast in Sango. I nodded
as though I knew what Sango was. Sango, it turned out, was the lingua
franca of the Central African Republic. I was told that the BBG currently
broadcasts to the Central African Republic in English and French, but
not Sango, the language most people speak. They told me that this was
a priority for the National Security Council. I decided in the moment

that I would say yes—that seemed like the diplomatic thing to do—but I said to the table that it was a onetime payment and that in six months I wanted to see some kind of metric showing whether it was working or not. The head of the Africa service looked a little nonplussed at this, I was later told no one had ever asked her for metrics before.

Before leaving, I told Jeff that Ben wanted to organize a meeting for us with the President about international broadcasting.

Choice of America

Ben was as good as his word. Within a couple of weeks after our sit-down, a meeting was on the calendar with President Obama on international broadcasting. Ben told me this was an ideas meeting where, once a month or so, the President called together a group in the Situation Room to brainstorm about one topic. This would be a whole hour devoted to international broadcasting.

Ben said that I should do an overview of international broadcasting, discuss State's role, and mention any other quick observations I'd made since I arrived. Okay.

I got to the White House early and had a few minutes with one of Ben's aides. Let's call him Jaden. Jaden was a State staffer who had been tapped by the NSC to come over to Ben's shop. He had served in Africa and South America. He was sharp and smart, had a goatee and a conspiratorial manner. He mentioned that he was going to be presenting about our response to Russian media. I knew from Ben and others that people at the NSC were concerned about Russia Today, the state-supported news channel that broadcast in the United States as RT. I wasn't quite sure why. One story I heard was that Vice President Biden had turned on his television in a hotel room in Europe and thought he was watching CNN, and then . . . slowly . . . realized . . . it was RT.

Jaden said his presentation was about the idea of the U.S. standing up its own version of RT.

Jaden showed me his PowerPoint presentation: it was titled "The Freedom News Network." The idea was essentially to take the annual BBG budget and create an international U.S. government television network. While I wasn't a gigantic fan of Voice of America or any of the other BBG entities, this plan was, well, *crazy*. The idea that the U.S. government would spend three-quarters of a billion dollars to create content 24/7, find and hire the people to do so, figure out shows and schedules, license content, and get carriage around the world on both satellite and terrestrial TV providers was absurd. I knew there were some Congressmen who were saying we should do this (and in fact, a bill would later be introduced to create the Freedom News Network), and I knew there were some people in government who thought that's what the United States Information Agency had done (they were mistaken), but my overwhelming conviction was that this would do more to hurt America's image than to help it.

And that wasn't even the main reason that it was a dumb idea. The main reason was: don't compete against yourself. No, we didn't have an exact equivalent of Russia Today, but we had CNN and Fox News and MSNBC and CBS and the Discovery Channel and PBS and the National Geographic channel and on and on and on. We had Facebook and Google and Instagram. We had *Game of Thrones* for chrissakes. Someone had earlier mentioned to me that Russia Today got about the same rating in the U.K. as CNN. I went and checked and that was true. But RT was literally the only Russian channel in the top 100 channels watched in the U.K.—and the U.S. had more than 40, everything from Lifetime to the Cartoon Network. I wouldn't trade that for a U.S. version of RT. America's soft power in terms of TV, movies, and pop music far outweighed in influence, scope, and power anything the

American government could create, much less Russia Today. RT didn't have enough viewers in the U.S. to even qualify for a Nielsen rating.

One of the things I'd noticed in government is that people who had never been in media, who had never written a story or produced one, who didn't know about design or graphics, who didn't understand audiences or what they liked, seemed to think it was easy to create content. People had the illusion that because they consumed something, they understood how it worked.

I didn't say much to Jaden about the idea before the meeting began. I had a place setting about two-thirds of the way down the table from where the President sat. Ben was sitting directly to the President's left and spoke first. He very briefly and graciously introduced me. The President said, "Hi, Rick," but in a completely businesslike way. When Ben called on me, I went straight to the nitty-gritty of the State Department's relationship to BBG and why it wasn't working. I mentioned that I was the first PD Under Secretary in memory who had actually gone to the board meetings. That the "editorials" that State did on Voice of America and other services were a waste of time. I made the case that the BBG entities, instead of spending all their time creating content, should actually aggregate U.S. news coverage and present that to foreign audiences. Voice of America should be Choice of America. (That got a couple of smiles.) I mentioned what I used to say about *Time*'s website, which was smaller than those of our big competitors: curate more, create less. If we simply showed people around the world the reporting that American journalists already were doing, we would also get credit for how we cover ourselves. It would be a model. See, that's what the First Amendment is all about. Try it! In short, I was saying pretty clearly, Let's not create a gigantic American-government news network.

When I finished, the President leaned back in his chair, locked his hands behind his head, and went up to 30,000 feet himself. He'd obviously thought about all this and proceeded to engage in a Socratic dialogue, mostly with himself.

"What's the problem we're trying to address here?" he asked.

His answer was pretty simple: we want people around the world to be able to get our point of view on things.

"What is it that we want them to have?"

His answer: "Usable information."

"Who do we want to reach?"

I want to speak to a global audience, he said, but what I'm most interested in is reaching 15 or so countries. We talk about global public opinion, but I'm more interested in public opinion in a few specific places. I want to talk to the man in the barbershop in Istanbul. The young woman teacher in São Paolo. The businessman in Abu Dhabi. The factory worker in Munich. He was frustrated that our image was more negative than it should be.

He conspicuously did not mention Russia. Russia wasn't among the top 15 countries he wanted to reach.

"What are the tools to do that?"

He asked whether we could license or commission local content in those countries. And what's the best content to give them? Is it news or is it game shows or reality TV? He said we needed to do more market research.

I had the sense then—which I would have a number of times while I was at State—that the President had thought more about the issues being talked about than anyone else in the room, knew more about those issues, and had come up with better answers than anyone else. This was both a good and a not-so-good thing.

Ben then called on Jaden. Jaden was backbenching, sitting against the wall, and stood up and sketched out the idea of the Freedom News

Network. He essentially gave the same presentation he had done for me a little earlier. I was prepared to weigh in on this if no one else did.

Everyone could see from the President's body language that he wasn't very taken with the idea. He had twisted himself into a pretzel. He was quiet. He wasn't looking at Jaden. He then perfunctorily asked a couple of very small questions, and then said, Let's move on. It just wasn't an Obama kind of fix. I always hated it when people would say at meetings, "There are no bad ideas." Unfortunately, there are—a lot of them. I wish that just once I had heard someone say, "You know what, that's a really terrible idea."

As I saw Obama again in other similar situations, I came to believe that he was essentially a small c, Edmund Burke kind of conservative. That is, the first thing he did in every situation was to look at whether doing something was actually going to make the situation worse than doing nothing. And often he came to the conclusion that, yes, it would. Plus, he only ever wanted to use as much wrench as necessary to turn the bolt. It was the Occam's razor school of foreign policy: the solution shouldn't be more complex than the problem. Keep it simple. Don't fix things that aren't broken. Don't do dumb stuff. Spending three-quarters of a billion dollars to start up a global U.S. government news network to reach a 24-year-old sitting in a barber's chair in Istanbul was not the simplest solution to the problem.

The president ended the discussion by saying, with a tone of frustration, "We've been talking about this for five years."

PART IV

Information War

Putin's Pulp Fictions

First, there were the little green men.

That's how early news reports referred to the masked men in unmarked uniforms who suddenly appeared in strategic locations around Crimea at the end of February 2014.[1]

On February 27, these units took over Crimea's Supreme Council—its parliament—as well as critical locations like airports and military bases and television stations.[2]

The green men were Spetsnaz—Russian special operations forces. Putin vehemently denied they were Russian troops, claiming instead they were patriotic local militias defending the rights of ethnic Russians in Crimea. How local militias had Russian PKP machine guns, Russian composite helmets, and Russian tactical vests was not explained. These troops were accompanied by digital forces, as Russian internet trolls and bots echoed the message that they were local militias.

At a press conference a week later, Putin was asked if there were Russian troops in Crimea. He said, "No."[3] Putin asserted that "there were no Russian troops in Crimea."

This was an unblinking lie. It was a lie without any verbal hedges or ambiguity, a direct knowing lie on the world stage about one country invading another.

Within days, Putin had engineered the installation of a pro-Russian government. The new council declared the Republic of Crimea to be an independent entity, and a referendum was to be held on March 16 in which voters would choose whether or not to join the Russian Federation.[4] The vote was overwhelmingly in favor of joining.[5] On March 18, a treaty was signed in the Kremlin between Crimea and Russia to formally bring Crimea into the Russian Federation.[6]

The White House condemned the violation of the sovereignty of Crimea and called for sanctions on Russia. In a phone call to Putin, President Obama said that Crimea's referendum would "never be recognized by the United States and the international community" and that "we are prepared to impose additional costs on Russia for its actions." Putin, for his part, told Obama that the referendum was "fully consistent with the norms of international law and the U.N. charter."[7]

Oh, and one month after the initial invasion, Putin owned up to the fact that they were Russian soldiers—without ever acknowledging that he had denied it in the first place.[8] That's Putin's way. Establish a new baseline of reality and never look back.

The context for all this was the months of demonstrations in Kiev that began in November 2013 and culminated in the flight of the Putin-supported president of Ukraine, Viktor Yanukovych, at the end of February.[9] The protests, centered in the neo-Stalinist-style square known as the Maidan, began in reaction to Yanukovych's rejection of a Ukraine–European Union Association Agreement that would have established a free-trade zone. Putin had urged Yanukovych to reject it, and he had.[10] On the Maidan, pro-EU demonstrators carried EU flags and chanted, "Ukraine is Europe."[11] It was the largest gatherings of protesters since the pro-democracy demonstrations of the Orange Revolution in 2004.[12] And that's what spooked Putin—he had long claimed that America was behind these "color revolutions" in the Russian periphery.[13] In 2011, Putin had accused Secretary of State Hillary Clinton of being the invisible hand behind the anti-corruption protests that had rocked Moscow and St. Petersburg that year.[14]

The U.N. rejected the Crimean annexation and referendum, passing a nonbinding resolution affirming the "territorial integrity of Ukraine."[15] The leaders of the G7 condemned "the Russian Federation's clear violation of the sovereignty of Ukraine"[16] and then suspended

Russia's membership in the G-8 and canceled the planned summit in Sochi—a blow to Putin, as the gathering was meant to showcase Russia just before the Russian-hosted Winter Olympics.[17]

Over and over, the President and the State Department reaffirmed that Ukraine's sovereignty and territorial integrity must be respected.[18,19] Secretary Kerry went further. On *Face the Nation*, he said, "It's an incredible act of aggression. It is really a stunning, willful choice by President Putin to invade another country."[20]

I was outraged about Putin's actions. I was particularly incensed by the stone-cold lying and disinformation. We had been monitoring for months how Russia had been claiming that Nazis and fascists were behind the "Euromaidan" protests. What could I do? Well, heck, I was the head of public diplomacy and public affairs at the State Department, and at the very least, *we could tweet about it*. I know that sounds like shooting spitballs at a tidal wave, but it was no small thing at State. I asked that public affairs officers and State staff and ambassadors tweet out the statements about Ukraine that the President and the Secretary had made. Easy, right? But nothing happened.

So, I started to tweet myself, condemning Putin's actions in Ukraine, all the while not getting out ahead of the Secretary or the President. Here's an early one:

> The unshakable principle guiding events must be that the people of #Ukraine determine their own future.

Not exactly fire-breathing words, but it was something.

After I began tweeting, I noticed something I hadn't seen before. I didn't get much reaction from within the Building, but I would get immediately trolled online by dozens of seemingly furious people. Someone named Petrik Krohn tweeted a few minutes later:

The key to the liberation of #Ukraine is understanding that
the US @StateDept = #CIA. #Euromaidan is their anti-
Russian #pogrom.

And then this got retweeted by other Russian-sounding Twitter
handles. This was all new to me. Here are a few others, all of which
were liked and retweeted by one another:

Everyone knows for a long time that the State Department
only deals in misinformation.

The US is the empire of evil and fascism [accompanied by
an image of a bloodied Obama holding a map of Ukraine].

Why is it forbidden to hold protests like the Maidan in the
USA? You are undemocratic and authoritarian.

And the always useful:

Are you a drunk or do you lie deliberately?

In the beginning, there was very little echo of what I was trying
to do within the department. The attitude at State was: the President
has spoken, the Secretary has spoken, the U.N. has spoken—why do
we need to do anything else? Even people who were privately furious about what Putin had done were reluctant to go on social media
and say the same thing. Or even support what the President and the
Secretary had said.

I asked to be furnished with regular tweets. Public affairs sent me
some, grudgingly. Here is one that was sent to me to post, provided, of
course, that EUR cleared it, which they eventually did:

U.S. is closely monitoring developments in #Ukraine.

Putin must have been quaking in his boots.

"A Message to America"

August 2014. The video begins with moody, hypnotic music. White type on a black background: "A Message to America" in English and Arabic. A grainy clip of President Obama authorizing air strikes. Then a cut to a man in an orange tunic kneeling in a vast desert against a darkening sky. Shaved head. Stubble on his chin. A strong, handsome face. He looks straight at the camera.

Looming over him, a tall, slender soldier in black with a balaclava over his head. He is holding a knife and has a gun in a leather clip draped over his shoulder.

Then in a strong voice with an American accent, the man in the orange tunic says:

> I call on my friends, family, and loved ones to rise up against my real killers, the U.S. government. For what will happen to me is only a result of their complacency and criminality.

The microphone in his collar picks up the sound of him swallowing. His voice chokes as he mentions his brother.

> I call on my brother John, who is a member of the U.S. Air Force. Think about what you are doing. Think about the lives you destroy, including those of your own family.

And then:

I wish I had more time. I wish I could have the hope for freedom and seeing my family once again . . . I guess all in all I wish I wasn't American.

Then the man in black spoke. His voice was grim, and his accent sounded as though it could be from East London. With his knife, he pointed to the man in the orange tunic:

This is James Wright Foley. An American citizen of your country. As a government, you have been at the forefront of the aggression towards the Islamic State. You have plotted against us, and gone far out of your way to find reasons to interfere in our affairs . . .

You are no longer fighting an insurgency. We are an Islamic army and a state that has been accepted by a large number of Muslims worldwide. So effectively, any aggression towards the Islamic State is an aggression towards Muslims from all walks of life who have accepted the Islamic Caliphate as their leadership.

So any attempt by you, Obama, to deny the Muslims their rights of living in safety under the Islamic Caliphate will result in the bloodshed of your people.

And then, well, they do not show the gruesome deed. Like the makers of horror movies who understand that the most terrifying act of violence is the one that happens offscreen, they cut to an image of Foley's headless torso lying in the sand, the knife next to him in a pool of blood, a pair of sandals tossed to the side.

The final frame showed a brief glimpse of another American, the journalist Steven Joel Sotloff. "The life of this American citizen, Obama," the man in black says, "depends on your next decision."[21]

It was horrifying and riveting in equal measure. The quality of the video showed sophistication and craftsmanship—a concern with aesthetics and design—like nothing we'd ever seen from al-Qaeda. The makers of this video cared about art direction, light, music, pacing— even the typography of the titles.

For ISIS, this was their Super Bowl ad. It introduced their grisly brand to an audience of millions. Within minutes, ISIS fanboys were tweeting using the hashtag #NewMessageFromISIStoUS.[22] One tweeted a picture of an ISIS flag on a cell phone with an image of the White House in the background.[23] YouTube removed the Foley video three hours later, but it had already gotten hundreds of thousands of views. Highlights from it had been broadcast to millions by every global news channel.[24]

James Foley had been kidnapped in Syria nearly two years earlier. He was a freelance journalist who had been working for Agence France-Presse. He had once worked for the U.S. Agency for International Development in Baghdad. He had written for the military newspaper *Stars and Stripes* while in Afghanistan. He had worked for the news service GlobalPost in Libya, where he had been captured by rebels and held for 44 days. Foley was a young, white American male who could have passed for one of the American soldiers in Iraq. That was the idea. Putting him in an orange tunic was meant to evoke the garb of the prisoners in Abu Ghraib and Guantánamo Bay. ISIS had found their poster boy.

The Foley video transformed what had been an obscure offshoot in the world of Muslim extremism into a gigantic global brand known to billions: ISIS. The black flag. The severed head. It was meant to show them as ruthless, magnetic, messianic, and undeterred by American power. Men in black. Avengers of Sunni Islam. Holy warriors.

The video had an even more practical purpose: it was a recruitment ad for ISIS's extreme army—ISIS's version of the U.S. Marine

Corps' TV ads in the 1980s to recruit "a few good men." After all, ISIS was also a volunteer army that required a steady flow of recruits. Its appeal was both religious and adventurous—if you want to lop off some American heads and go to heaven in the process, come to Iraq and Syria. Violent Islamic adventure tourism. Their proposition was zero sum—join us, or be a *kafir* (an apostate) and die.

This was how most Americans, and most people around the world, were introduced to ISIS, the Islamic State of Iraq and Syria.

But ISIS was not new to CSCC. They had spotted an escalation of ISIS social media in the spring of 2014. ISIS, they informed me, already had a media arm called Al-Hayat, which a couple of weeks before had released an English-subtitled video showing young children breaking their Ramadan fast with ISIS warriors. A week later, to mark the Eid al-Fitr feast at the end of Ramadan, they had released a video that showed a mass execution of Syrians. They mixed the grisly with the G-rated. Less than a month after releasing Foley's execution video, ISIS fighters had started a meme of fighters posing with jars of Nutella. The Nutella was meant to suggest that life in the Caliphate was sweet. It was a double-edged campaign: graphic violence to scare America and the West, and sunny travel ads to recruit foreign fighters.

I pushed CSCC to do more counter-ISIS messaging. They sent me a plan, saying their target audience was "Sunni Iraqis, pan-Arab, and global"—unfocused, but at least they were starting. They launched a series of tweets around themes of brutality, betrayal, and the limits of sectarianism. Here are a few, translated from the Arabic.

> ISIS has betrayed you before, will betray you again.
> @CSCC @ThinkAgain_DOS

> ISIS's barbarism is its only real goal. It has no religious justification. @CSCC @ThinkAgain_DOS

The United States will not assist those who throw their lot
in with ISIS. @CSCC @ThinkAgain_DOS

"Think Again, Turn Away" was CSCC's motto. The tweets got a
bit of traffic, and some responses from digital jihadis accusing CSCC
of being a tool of the State Department. When we pointed out ISIS's
hypocrisy, the digital jihadis pointed out ours. @de_BlackRose tweeted:
"Remember how American arrested and humiliated our brothers in
Iraq," next to a graphic image from Abu Ghraib. CSCC replied: "US
troops are punished for misconduct, #ISIS fighters are rewarded." I'm
not sure CSCC changed the minds of any young men thinking of going
to fight in Iraq and Syria, but it was something.

But tweeting was not going to stop ISIS from executing the other
American journalist they had shown at the end of the video—like a
cliff-hanger in a serial—Steven Sotloff.

Punching Back

Sometimes knowledge can be a barrier to starting something new.

My very ignorance of how things worked at State actually helped
me launch something we hadn't done before.

I had looked around the department and I didn't see any entity
that could push back against all the Russian propaganda and disinformation surrounding Crimea and Ukraine. The European bureau was
reticent—messaging of any kind was just not what they did.

There was one large, wonderful exception to State's social media
passivity: Geoff Pyatt, our ambassador to Ukraine. Geoff was all over
social media: he was tweeting dozens of times a day, not only his own
strong anti-Russian tweets but also regularly retweeting the reports of
journalists and observers who were calling out Russia for its actions.
Pyatt didn't think Russian lies should go unchallenged.

I had a number of conversations with Pyatt, and he encouraged me to do something. I decided to call a meeting with representatives from EUR, PA, PD, and the spokesperson's office to discuss the idea of starting an internal counter-Russian messaging hub. Actually, I didn't quite say that. I said we were going to meet to discuss what could be done about Russian propaganda.

We had the meeting in the big conference room adjacent to my office. I had planned on opening with a discussion of the hub idea, but we happened to have a young public affairs officer from Kiev who was visiting. I thought it might be interesting to hear from him first. He was a burly, bearded, Russian-speaking foreign service officer who had been in Kiev for the past year. Before that, he had spent two years in Moscow. Like so many of the people serving in Ukraine, he was passionate about what he had seen.

"The Russians," he said, "have a big engine. They are working overtime on building a compelling narrative—a narrative that undermines democracy in Ukraine. They say the same things day in and day out. These are the three big lies they repeat again and again:

" 'The protesters are fascists and hate Russia.

" 'Ukraine is historically and emotionally a part of Russia.

" 'America and the West are the source of the instability.'

"You have to understand," he said, "that the Russians are baffled by the protests in the Maidan. They cannot believe that the aspirations of the protesters are genuine. They are incapable of understanding something that is not cynical or purely transactional. They are so utterly corrupt themselves that they don't see how the corruption in Ukraine angered everyday Ukrainians. They project their corruption on everyone else. The idea that people may actually be protesting for individual freedom does not even occur to them. The only explanation is that America must be behind it."

He said the single most important thing for American policy was to make Ukraine a success. If Ukraine fails, he said, that sends a signal to everyone else in the periphery that the West is a fickle partner.

"Right now," he said, making a fist on the table, "we are being out-messaged by the Russians. The Russians don't have a clearance process. They don't feel the need to be truthful. We are too timid and reactive."

This was so much more powerful than anything I could have said. It was the perfect preamble for what I wanted to do. He had made the case for me. But the protocol at all State meetings is that everyone gets a say. Only then can you try to steer toward a conclusion, and that was never simple either.

Someone said we should message to the "Moscow million"—the million people who mattered in Moscow. Someone said we should focus on the Baltics. Someone said we should think about Germany, as the Germans were critical to the success of Europe. A fellow who had once worked at USIA said we used to know how to do counter-Russian messaging.

We were in what I came to think of as the "counter" mode. In Washington, when you're threatened or attacked, the first reaction is always, How do you hit back? How do we *counter* them? This is what you always hear Representatives and Senators say. We need to hit them back even harder. From a bureaucratic standpoint, what this usually means is that whatever you're against, if you put the word "counter" in front of it, you've created an entity to fight it and satisfy the bureaucratic impulse: counterterrorism, counterextremism, counterinsurgency, counterpropaganda.

I wanted to get something going. I said, Let's start a counter-Russian version of CSCC. I said it wouldn't have to create its own content but could be a coordinating entity and aggregate and optimize content from State and everywhere else. (Coordination always ruffles the fewest feathers.) How do we do that? Where do we start? I was looking for volunteers.

Nobody volunteered. Not PA. Not EUR. Not PD.

Someone said—without irony—*We can't do what we know we should do until we hear what the NSC wants us to do.*

And then the public affairs officer from Kiev stood up and said, *Count me in. Count Kiev in. We're all in on this.*

At the end of the meeting, I said that as of today, we were going to form a Ukraine messaging hub or war room. Someone called it the Ukraine Task Force. Not catchy, but at least it didn't have "counter" in the name.

One of the people at the meeting was Doug Frantz, the assistant secretary for public affairs, who reported to me. I'd known Doug a little when he was an investigative reporter for the *New York Times*. Doug approached me with an idea: What if we went directly after Putin's lies? What do you have in mind? I asked. He said we could create a direct rebuttal of 10 statements that Putin had made about Ukraine. I told him, Full speed ahead. Two days later, in coordination with the new Ukraine Task Force, Public Affairs produced a fact sheet called "Putin's 10 False Claims." It began by saying the world hadn't seen such "startling Russian fiction since Dostoyevsky." Here are the first three:

1. **Mr. Putin says:** *Russian forces in Crimea are only acting to protect Russian military assets. It is "citizens' defense groups," not Russian forces, who have seized infrastructure and military facilities in Crimea.*

   The Facts: Strong evidence suggests that members of Russian security services are at the heart of the highly organized anti-Ukraine forces in Crimea. While these units wear uniforms without insignia, they drive vehicles with Russian military license plates and freely identify themselves as Russian security forces when asked by the international media . . .

2. **Mr. Putin says:** *Russia's actions fall within the scope of the 1997 Friendship Treaty between Ukraine and the Russian Federation.*

   The Facts: The 1997 agreement requires Russia to respect Ukraine's territorial integrity. Russia's military actions in Ukraine, which have given them operational control of Crimea, are in clear violation of Ukraine's territorial integrity and sovereignty.

3. **Mr. Putin says:** *The opposition failed to implement the February 21 agreement with former Ukrainian President Viktor Yanukovych.*

   The Facts: The February 21 agreement laid out a plan in which the Rada, or Parliament, would pass a bill to return Ukraine to its 2004 Constitution . . . Under the terms of the agreement, Yanukovych was to sign the enacting legislation within 24 hours . . . Yanukovych refused to keep his end of the bargain. Instead, he fled, leaving behind evidence of wide-scale corruption.[25]

It's not a work of art, but it's pretty darn punchy for a government press release. (I tweeted it out as "Putin's Pulp Fictions.") I can't tell you how unusual it was for the State Department public affairs office—or any government public affairs office—to put out such a document. Usually, we would issue a statement that we were "concerned" about something or, if it was really bad, "deeply concerned." This was something new from the State Department and it actually went viral. It got written about in lots of countries and retweeted thousands of times.[26] "Putin's False Claims" was also picked up by the public affairs departments of the Baltic countries and Germany and many of the countries in what Russia called "the near abroad." They liked it. They thought we were leaning forward. All the Baltic countries wanted more where that came from. A Baltic foreign minister emailed: "When is the sequel?"

The Republic of Fear

Steven Sotloff had worked for me at *Time*. He had been a stringer, someone we could assign stories to on a freelance basis. He had turned up in Libya at the start of the Arab Spring and pitched stories to us. He was soft-spoken but intense. In 2013, he had come by the office in New York and our two international editors, Jim Frederick and his deputy, Bobby Ghosh, tried to dissuade him from returning to Libya and flat-out refused to commission him to go to Syria. It was far too dangerous. I agreed and said Syria was off-limits. Sotloff was young, green, and a little naive.

But he had gone on his own and was kidnapped in northern Syria in August 2013 while reporting on that country's civil war. It was the single most dangerous place in the world for a journalist, as more than 70 had been killed and 80 kidnapped since the beginning of the conflict.[27] The last story he had done for us was a detailed examination of the Benghazi raid. After Sotloff was captured, the senior leadership of *Time*—all of whom I knew well—had reached out to the State Department for help. I spoke to them a number of times but ultimately turned them over to David Wade, the Secretary's chief of staff, who was handling the situation.

For months, Sotloff's family had wanted to keep his abduction quiet. We had supported them in this, as did the White House. But after the Foley video, Sotloff's mother made her own video appealing directly to Baghdadi, whom she called the "Caliph of the Islamic State." "I appeal to you to spare his life," she said. "He's an honorable man who has always tried to help the weak . . . I ask you to use your authority to agree with the prophet Muhammad who said to spare the people of the Book."[28]

Two weeks after the Foley beheading, ISIS issued a new video titled "A Second Message to America." The same executioner, later known as Jihadi John, returns and points his knife at the camera and says, "I'm back, Obama, and I'm back because of your arrogant foreign policy towards the Islamic State . . . As your missiles continue to strike our people, our knife will continue to strike the necks of your people." Kneeling next to him in an orange shirt, with his head shaved, Sotloff calmly begins by saying, "I am Steven Joel Sotloff. I'm sure you probably know exactly who I am by now." Reading from a statement, he said: "Obama, your foreign policy of intervention in Iraq was supposed to be for preservation of American lives and interests, so why is it that I am paying the price of your interference with my life?"[29]

A few minutes later, the video revealed Sotloff's severed head. CSCC did virtually no messaging around the kidnapping and the killing of Sotloff. The reason was that we believed ISIS may have been holding other Americans, and we didn't want to jeopardize their lives. Sometimes there are good reasons for staying silent.

A few hours after American intelligence agencies had analyzed the Sotloff video, President Obama held a press conference in which he said that the videos had "repulsed" the world, but that they "only unite us as a country and stiffen our resolve to take the fight against these terrorists." Ironically, President Obama made his statement from Tallinn, Estonia, his last stop before the NATO summit in Wales, where he would endorse a rapid-reaction force that could deploy quickly in situations like Russia's intervention in Ukraine.[30] He was at a joint news conference with President Toomas Hendrik Ilves of Estonia, who had been one of the European leaders most outspoken on Russian aggression and disinformation. In introducing President Obama, President Ilves first condemned the killing of Sotloff before saying the main issue they would be discussing that day was "Russian aggression." In the same breath, Obama criticized "Russian aggression against Ukraine" and ISIS's "barbarism," saying that we would not be intimidated by either.[31] It was a noteworthy moment, when the two strands of this information war—ISIS and Russia—overlapped. As would become increasingly clear, both Russia and ISIS were engaged in a battle against American influence and ideas and sought to undermine both. America was what the Russians once called "the main enemy" and what ISIS called "the far enemy." We were the foe on which everything could be blamed.

The two horrific beheadings and their accompanying videos and social media put ISIS on the radar of ordinary Americans. We began to get estimates that there were tens of thousands of pieces of social media being posted a day in support of ISIS. Americans were not only outraged, they were worried about their own safety. By fall 2014, national polls showed the highest level of concern about terrorism since 9/11. The beheading videos were a textbook example of effective modern terrorism and information warfare—that is, they had an effect out of all proportion to the deaths of two young men, and the threat ISIS actually represented. Terrorism works because human beings imagine possibilities instead of probabilities. Suddenly, we could see the possibilities on our phones. Social media's combination of immediacy and intimacy made it the most powerful terroristic tool in history.[32]

My office started getting calls from Congressmen asking, What are we doing about ISIS's messaging? How are you *countering* it? After all, CSCC was the single counter–violent extremist messaging entity in the whole federal government—and it reported to me. Mr. Stengel, you need to get on top of this, they said. Several members of Congress told me they believed that social media had itself given rise to ISIS. People seemed to attribute an almost mystical power to the internet. You'd often hear Congressmen say things like, They were converted by the internet. I visited one Democratic Representative who asked me, "Mr. Stengel, can't we just close down that part of the internet where ISIS is?"

Ukraine Deputies

Five days after the meeting that created the Ukraine Task Force, the NSC held a deputies meeting on Ukraine. I was still new to what was known as the DC/PC process. DC stood for Deputies Committee; PC stood for Principals Committee. The latter is presided over by the National Security Advisor and the participants are cabinet members and heads of agencies. The DC is usually led by a deputy National Security Advisor and includes deputies of the cabinet officers—the Deputy Secretary of State, the Deputy Secretary of the Treasury. The idea is that the DC lays the groundwork for the PC. There can be many DC meetings leading up to one PC meeting. This was referred to as the "interagency process." I won't get into the pros and cons of the process now, but DC meetings—at least for me—were a pretty big deal.

The White House was getting ready to impose serious sanctions on Russia. There was concern that the invasion of Crimea was a precedent for what they might do in eastern Ukraine. The hard-liners in the administration saw this as an expression of Russia's age-old desire to expand in order to feel more secure. It reflected Putin's abiding anger about the extension of NATO up to Russia's doorstep. Putin wanted Ukraine to lean east and be a client state of Russia; we wanted Ukraine to lean west and be a part of Europe.

The Ukraine DC was led by Deputy National Security Advisor Tony Blinken. Whip-smart, even-tempered, and with a weakness for very bad puns, Tony ran a meeting that was a model of openness and efficiency—something pretty rare in Washington. The announced purpose of the DC meeting was to consider a new round of sanctions against Russia. Ben Rhodes wanted me to be there to talk about combating the avalanche of Russian disinformation. I had stopped by his office before the meeting to brief him on the Ukraine Task Force.

Geoff Pyatt, our ambassador in Kiev, flew in for the meeting. It was my first time seeing him in person. Geoff looked like how you'd cast an ambassador in a 1950s movie: tall and rangy, with tortoise-shell glasses and a powerful voice. Geoff's principal concern was that Ukraine succeed as a modern, non-corrupt, Western-focused nation. As he said to me one of the first times we spoke, "Ukraine is a nation the size of France in the heart of Europe." If Ukraine did not succeed, he said, that would be a powerful message to all the countries in the Russian periphery that it was not worth the risk to be a partner with America and the West.

Because Pyatt was there, Blinken called on him first. People at the NSC respected Pyatt, which was not always the case with career ambassadors. He began by saying that we were looking at three big problems that were interconnected like Russian nesting dolls. The first was Ukraine itself: it wanted to be part of Europe, which Russia opposed. "Russia's response," he said, "is to try to turn Ukraine into a failed state, or at the very least, what they call a 'frozen conflict.'" The second, he said, was the countries of the former Soviet Union. Russia wanted to send a message to them, especially the Baltics. The message was, "You can't put your chips with the West and America—they will only disappoint you." And finally, there was NATO. Geoff said Putin wanted to undermine NATO and the Atlantic alliance by testing Article 5, the very heart of the treaty, the principle that said if one nation is attacked, everyone must come to its aid. He did not have to mention that the first and only time Article 5 had ever been invoked was after 9/11.

Then Geoff dived into what was going on at the moment. He said things had become even more fragile in the last few days. He said there were "paid Russian provocateurs" in the Euromaidan protests who were creating controversy that was then amplified by what he called "Moscow's incredible propaganda machine." That machine, he said, was in overdrive, telling people that this was not an indigenous protest but a subversive plot by America. "It's important to recognize that what we call Russian hybrid warfare—which Ukraine has been subjected to for two years—is a combination of different things. It's not just the little green men, but it's economic pressure, military pressure, and information pressure. The Russian goal is not to prove its version of the truth; it's to confuse and distract and push Ukraine off track and us off balance."

The actual action being discussed was a new round of sanctions, handled by Treasury. David Cohen was the Treasury Under Secretary for Terrorism and Financial Intelligence. Sober, serious, meticulous, Cohen outlined the actions Treasury was going to take against Crimean companies and individuals. Some of them, he said, had already been approved by the Europeans. But he said there were new players whom we were not that familiar with. He paused and said, "You know, you make these decisions in the moment, and they have decades-long consequences." It was a throwaway line, but one of the best I've ever heard about the effects of what you do in government.

The discussion then shifted toward public diplomacy. Ben mentioned our talk and nodded for me to speak. I said that in conjunction with EUR we were in the process of creating a small task force, essentially a communications "war room," as a way of pushing back on the Russian propaganda machine. We would also seek to reach credible third-party voices with information they could use. This was greeted with general enthusiasm. A couple of people noted that we should work with the intelligence community to make sure we were getting the best information about what was happening on the ground. I said the group was still so new that we didn't have a leader yet, but that we would love to have colleagues from other agencies.

Toria Nuland seconded the idea. Toria was the assistant secretary for Europe and a powerhouse in the Building. She was always forceful about her point of view, and argued in a take-no-prisoners style. She was seen as the principal Russian hard-liner at State. This was in contrast to Secretary Kerry, whom some at the NSC regarded as being a mite too willing to see things from Russia's perspective.

"We need to put out the story on Russian activities," Nuland said. "We need to flood the zone. The intelligence community only gives us a yellow light on this, but we need to get it out there. We need to get out the OSCE [the Organization for Security and Co-Operation in Europe] report. We need to establish facts on the ground. Geoff can't do it alone."

The thing I discovered as the "communications guy" was that everyone's an expert on messaging. People feel they can chime in on messaging in a way they would not about trade negotiations or nuclear disarmament. But there was never much discussion about what in the private sector would be a key concern: audience. Whom exactly do we want to message to? People are very quick to say, Let's counter their message, but no one really talked about whom we counter it *to* or what we counter it *with*. People in government seemed to think that people paid attention to government messaging because it was, well, *government*.

I did suggest whom we should be messaging to. I said we were trying to reach what you could call the swing voters in the Russian periphery, the people in Eastern and Central Europe who weren't quite sure whether they should lean west or east.

But before we figured out what our message would be, we needed to find someone to lead the messengers.

The Dangers of Transparency

CSCC had gone into overdrive in its efforts to counter ISIS's messaging. But folks in Congress and the media couldn't see it. Why? Because CSCC did not create content or tweet in English. From the beginning, CSCC produced social media in three languages: Arabic (the majority), Urdu, and Somali. Not many Americans realized that the lion's share of ISIS's social media was in Arabic. For those in Congress, and many other Americans, it was as though what we did didn't exist, because it wasn't in English.

But, heck, I wanted to be able to show some of what we are doing, and there was a way to do that. CSCC had had plans for a while for what they called the English Language Initiative—a typically government name for something pretty simple: tweeting in English. The idea for expanding into English had been put in motion before I was confirmed. It was a way of giving Americans a window into what CSCC was doing. What was wrong with that? Why not be more transparent?

I had to approve the initiative, and I did.

But there were some things in government for which my natural reflexes as a journalist were all wrong.

I had inherited a longtime foreign service officer as chief of staff. She was bright, experienced, organized, and spoke three languages. But she did everything by the book and always took no for an answer. One night I was flipping through the channels, and came upon the scene in the Godfather when Sonny says he wishes he had a "wartime consigliere." That's what I wanted too.

A friend from State said I know just the person for you, but I don't think you can get her. She introduced me via email to Jennifer Stout, who was then working in legislative affairs at the White House. Stout had been a deputy assistant secretary for East Asian Affairs at State. She reluctantly agreed to meet me for breakfast at a Le Pain Quotidien in Georgetown. She was poised, composed, cool. Skeptical. But when she smiled and said, "I don't have one creative bone in my body. I like managing people and organizations," I knew I had found my wartime consigliere. It wasn't easy for her to leave the White House. It never is. It was only the prospect of coming back to State, which she loved, that made the difference. She was the game changer for me. She understood, in a way I never could, how to make the bureaucracy work for us.

Jen had recently started, and when I told her that I'd said yes to the English Language initiative, she looked at me like I was crazy. Why would you ever want to do that? You know it won't make a real difference to what you're trying to accomplish, she said, and it will make you and CSCC a target for criticism. Her general view was that in order to get things done in government, it was almost always better not to attract attention to what you were doing. I told her she was being silly. I said I *wanted* people to see what we were doing. You'll regret it, she said.

The first CSCC English-language tweets were pretty conventional and highlighted ISIS's violence and hypocrisy, its violation of the Koran and Islamic law. The young contractors who had been hired to do this not only created general tweets, but also directly addressed individual digital jihadis. When someone with the handle @AboudouAbdallah tweeted, "I want to remind you . . . never forget what happens to your 'soldiers' in #Fallujah #Iraq #CalamityWillBefallUS," along with a blurry photo of the burned body of a Blackwater contractor, CSCC responded with a snapshot of Osama bin Laden watching television and asked, "Would you throw away your life for those who hide far away?" The picture was lousy, the graphics were amateurish, and we repeated his hashtag. His original tweet was retweeted only twice before we focused on it, at which point it was retweeted dozens of times.

Some of these digital jihadists were quick, witty, and extremely savvy users of social media. They were much more facile than our own contractors. Observing all this back-and-forth, a user with the handle @AbuOttomon tweeted to CSCC: "Your boss is going to fire you if your tweets don't improve!"

Jen's warning proved true even more quickly than she expected. From the moment we started tweeting in English, the criticism of CSCC escalated. We were tweeting too little. The tweets were ineffective. Why were we tweeting *at* terrorists? While some applauded us for hitting back, most people's reaction was, "Is that all there is?" In fact, we did tweet too little (fewer than 10 a day) and too slowly (it often took us hours to respond). The contractors still had to reckon with the clearance process. For most of them, English was their second or even third language. ISIS's use of the medium was more intuitive. Our tone was priggish and self-righteous. As one analyst wrote, "State's messages arrive with all the grace of someone's Dad showing up at a college party."[33]

What few of us understood at that point was that our opponents— Russia as well as ISIS—wanted us to get into a back-and-forth with them. It validated what they were doing, brought us down to their level, and besides, we weren't as good at it as they were. They won when they got us to respond in kind. We were echoing their narrative.

I'm sure they high-fived each other when that happened. They courted controversy; we dreaded it. And they didn't have a clearance process.

The fact that we were tweeting only a few times a day highlighted something I began talking about publicly: how we were getting beaten on volume in the information war against ISIS. I had started getting briefings from the intelligence community on what ISIS was doing online. I had been told that ISIS and its followers were creating as many as 90,000 pieces of content a day of all kinds. And that was compared with about 350 pieces a day from the entire U.S. government. There were perhaps 100 people all across government who were on social media trying to rebut ISIS's claims, while ISIS had thousands of digital jihadis. Even though the intelligence folks would later scale down this number, I stated using the 90,000 figure and mentioned it to a few newspaper reporters.

My goal was to turbocharge our effort against ISIS, and in Washington one of the best ways to do that is to say you're *losing*. That gets people's attention. No one wants to lose, and even more important, no one wants to be blamed for the loss. "Who Lost China?"—a reference to the Communist takeover of the mainland in 1949—is still a haunting refrain at the State Department. I did a number of early interviews where I was quoted as saying they were out-tweeting us, that we were getting killed on volume, and that they had a vastly larger audience.

In fact, there were good reasons that we didn't really know how much they were doing. It wasn't easy to measure. What was a tweet from a paid ISIS digital jihadi in Iraq—of whom they were maybe a few thousand—and what was a tweet from a 14-year-old boy in Bangalore pretending to be an ISIS warrior? As they used to say, on the internet no one knows you're a dog—or a nerdy teenager pretending to be a bloodthirsty ISIS warrior. In some ways, the idea that there were many thousands of people pretending to be ISIS fighters was more worrying:

part of ISIS's marketing strategy was to get Muslim young people around the world to be sympathetic. If we lost that battle, that would really be a problem. And that was a much harder battle for us to fight.

So, the *New York Times* quoted me as saying that figure, 90,000. As I said, it was a guesstimate, and within a few months, we revised it downward by more than half. Yet for the next year and a half, almost every newspaper and television network that did a story on ISIS's messaging quoted that 90,000 figure, and I don't think one of them ever bothered to check the number with me again, even after it had changed.

I did tell reporters that, just for context, Taylor Swift was retweeted more than three million times a day—so ISIS's collective output of 90,000 was just 3 percent of how often Taylor Swift was retweeted in one day, but no one quoted me on that.

At around this time, I was invited to a Deputies Committee meeting on what we were doing to "degrade and defeat" ISIS, as President Obama had put it. There was going to be a section on messaging, which was why I was there. The meeting was run by Lisa Monaco, who was the Deputy National Security Advisor and the person who briefed the President every morning on terrorist threats. She was smart, cool, deliberate, and often cut through the government jargon with an incisive question. She said that when it came to messaging, we didn't know what worked and what didn't. I agreed, but asked what it was that we were trying to accomplish. I mentioned that I had recently had a conversation with a member of Congress who had asked me, "Mr. Stengel, how many young men did you persuade not to go to Iraq and Syria today?" I know it sounded a bit preposterous, but that was the question we wanted to answer.

We shifted to talking about how to message on ISIS not being Islamic. It was a sensitive subject. The President had said that ISIS was un-Islamic; the Secretary had also. But there was a school of thought that we shouldn't be getting into the religious aspect of this at all. I shared it. At this point in the discussion, Ben Rhodes looked around the room—everyone was white—and said, "Maybe we're not the best messengers for the message we want out there."

Finding the Messenger

You'd think it would be easy to find someone to lead the new Ukraine Task Force. At least I did. I was wrong. Staffing at the State Department is very peculiar. First, almost every job has a two- or three-year time frame. Whether you are a disaster at your job or fantastic, you stay in it for the agreed-upon time commitment. Firing people was just not an option. Thus, it was nearly impossible to pluck people out of their current jobs and put them in new ones. Second, almost every job is filled before it officially comes open. That's because with a year to go on your current job, you start applying for your next one. They call this bidding. Third, it's very hard to evaluate whether people are good or not. Why? Because everyone writes their own evaluations, even though these are attributed to their supervisor. How do I know this? Because everyone on my staff wrote their own evaluation and then gave it to me. Every one, of course, was exceptional.

The other problem with taking on the Ukraine Task Force job was that it was new. At State, *new* was a bad thing. Foreign Service officers had no way of evaluating it in terms of their "career." And they always talked about their career. When I was at *Time* and someone I was interviewing for a job mentioned their career, I made a mental note that perhaps this person wasn't right. I wanted to hear why applicants would be good for *Time*, not why the job would be good for them. At State, I think every foreign service officer I talked to about a job mentioned how it would affect her career. Not whether she would be good at it or whether it benefited the State Department, but how it would affect the arc of her time at State. Really? A job that was new and unconventional was a question mark that most foreign service officers automatically interpreted in a negative way. People asked me, Was it really a job in Public Affairs or EUR? Was it a job for someone in the PD cone? How long would the Task Force be around? I could see the thought bubble over people's heads: "It's not going to help my career."

At first, I looked in what seemed like the most natural place: the European bureau. Was there a Russian-speaker in EUR who was willing to give it a try for a year? The challenge was important and urgent. No one was interested. I looked at our embassy in Moscow and at whether any Russian-speaking PD officers were in any of the R bureaus. No takers.

I brought up my frustration at the daily comms meeting, and people nodded sympathetically. Afterward, Doug Frantz sidled up to me and said, Has anyone mentioned Will Stevens? No. Where is he? I asked. In AF, he said, the Africa bureau. What he was doing there. He said he didn't know but that Will was a Russian-speaker who had been based in Moscow and everyone spoke highly of him. I tracked him down , called him myself, and he was in my office 20 minutes later.

Will was a lanky, fair-haired foreign service officer from Great Falls, Virginia, by way of Brigham Young University. He was working in AF because he loved Africa, but he'd had assignments in Belarus, Turkmenistan, and Israel. He was fluent in Russian and Hebrew. When I started talking about the Ukraine Task Force, he moved so far forward on the couch that I thought he was going to fall off. He said he was appalled by what Russia was doing in Crimea and Ukraine. He said he'd been watching and thinking—these are his exact words—"Goodness gracious, we need to do something!" Will had a traditional FSO pedigree but was anything but standard issue in terms of his willingness to take a chance. I told him what we were going to try to do, and said that I was looking for a leader of the new entity. Was he interested? Yes, he said.

I admit I paused here—I was so used to being turned down. Are you sure? I asked him. Then Will paused and said, "I'm in!" But it wasn't as simple as all that. I had to get him a waiver from the Africa assistant secretary. No assistant secretary wants to lose a good person for a year, because it's almost impossible to find someone else to fill in. I had promised I would fund a number of African public diplomacy programs and give the Africa bureau a temporary replacement, all in exchange for one year of Will.

It was worth it.

Satire Is What Closes on Saturday Night

The two-minute video begins with the sound of ominous drumming and an Arabic voice singing softly in the background. *Nasheed* is the name for this haunting jihadi music, which had become the sound track of Islamic extremism. Then, in white type on a black background, the words "Run don't walk to ISIS Land." The first image is of Abu Bakr al-Baghdadi, ISIS's leader, speaking in Arabic. Then more white type: "Where you can learn useful new skills for the Ummah!" (The Ummah are all Muslims.) And then images of mosques being destroyed with the legend: "Like blowing up mosques." Then brutal images of men being beheaded, shot, or nailed to a cross, and the words "Crucifying and executing Muslims." And then, against an image of dead ISIS soldiers: "Travel is inexpensive because you won't need a return ticket."

This was a video produced not by ISIS but by CSCC. It was a mock ISIS recruitment video, a satire of ISIS's videos. Yes, it was brutal and disturbing—but to whom, I wasn't quite sure. According to Alberto Fernandez, everyone—State, the White House, the intelligence community, and the Department of Defense—had cleared the video. I had not seen it before it was posted, but I'd asked to review it because it had started to generate some attention, almost all negative. A reporter for the *Guardian* had done a "What the heck is this?" link on his Twitter feed, and then the *Washington Post*, the Associated Press, and CNN did stories about the video and questioned what CSCC was doing. Within a few days, it had a few hundred thousand views on YouTube. A monster hit for CSCC, but perhaps not the right kind. I'd urged Fernandez to be more aggressive, take more risks. He had.

No one in government takes the just-as-long-as-they-spell-my-name-right view of publicity. Negative publicity was considered far worse than no publicity at all. The "Welcome to ISIS Land" video was becoming not just an object of public derision but the main thing that CSCC was known for. Suddenly, the same politicians who had been criticizing CSCC for doing too little were now criticizing it for being out of control. The video had put CSCC on the map, but not in a good way. And then the amateur satirists at CSCC became the target of a professional one: John Oliver.

From behind his desk on HBO's *Last Week Tonight*, Oliver introduced a segment called "Ironic Propaganda." Here's how he began: "It seems that everyone has noticed ISIS's viral success, even the U.S. government, because they recently decided that for some reason it would be a good idea to try to beat ISIS at their own game." Cut to a CNN story saying the State Department has produced a new video that "sarcastically tells potential ISIS recruits that they can learn new useful skills by blowing up mosques, by crucifying and executing Muslims."

Cut to John Oliver. Eyes wide. Long theatrical pause.

"*What the fuck are they doing?!*" he said, to much audience laughter.

And then he continued: "The State Department has genuinely created a sarcastic parody recruitment video for ISIS that begins with the words 'Run, do not walk to ISIS Land.' And you are banking a lot on any potential militants understanding that that was sarcasm." Then in a mock imitation of a young would-be jihadi: "'You know what? I was just about to join ISIS and then I saw your very clever video telling me to join ISIS, but using ironic juxtaposition of word and image to suggest that I should actually do the opposite. Just like Chandler in *Friends*, you know. Could we be any more militant? Great stuff! I totally get it. I totally get it.'"

Long pause.

"Ironic propaganda is a dangerous game for a government to be playing," Oliver said.[34]

I had to say that I agreed. The idea that irony—in English—was a way to reach potential fence-sitters seems awfully far-fetched. And if it was for official Washington, well, irony was never a smart Beltway tactic. It was also not clear who the audience was. Not Arabic-speakers in the Middle East. Not unhappy young Muslim men in Europe. Potential ISIS sympathizers in the U.S.? Maybe, although that wasn't part of CSCC's mission. The video had alienated a different domestic audience: the White House, the NSC, the media. The word Secretary Kerry used to describe it was *wacky*. One of our spokespeople had to publicly apologize for it.

I actually didn't think it was all that dreadful. But the idea of government doing irony or satire or parody is itself kind of absurd. One of the simplest things I learned in Washington is that government should do the things it's good at, and only the things it's good at. And satire or comedy or whatever you want to call it is definitely not one of them. When Helene Cooper of the *New York Times* decided to do a story on the fallout from the video, I told her: "Apart from the fact that the U.S. government shouldn't do snark, it's not persuasive. We're not the most effective messenger for our message."[35]

This became one of what my staff started calling Rick's Rules: We don't do snark. I spoke to Fernandez and the CSCC staff and said, Let's just be straightforward, a just-the-facts approach that seemed more appropriate for government.

#Hashtag Diplomacy

Will Stevens proved to be a dynamo. The day after he was cleared for the job, he convened a meeting of Public Affairs, the European bureau, and International Information Programs and explained that he was going to try something new and needed people. He found them.

He did a far better job than I ever could have done in assembling his team. He was like the pied piper of counter-Russian messaging. He found an enthusiastic Indian American public affairs officer who was a Russian-speaker to do social media campaigns. He found a data analytics Ph.D. who was working in International Information Programs to do the metrics. And he found a Russian-speaking Kazakh woman married to a foreign service officer who could manage the team. As a foreign service officer, he knew how to make the pitch to other young FSOs. Unlike most officers, who were reticent when it came to making any kind of political statement, Will was outspoken about what Russia was doing and unafraid to say so on social media. He found others who felt the same way.

The other thing about Will was that he seemed indifferent, even impervious, to the clearance process. He just started putting out content. Most of it was in Russian, so it went under the radar in the same way CSCC's Arabic tweets had. But they got picked up by Russian-speakers. He also started what we called "playbooks" for the bureaus, with sample tweets in Russian and English. He created a toolkit for posts on how to respond to Russian propaganda. His attitude was, Let's see what works. In some ways, Will's actions mirrored those of the Russians, who had much more leeway than we did to be aggressive on social media. Will also started probing something he had first seen in Russia some years before: the use of trolls and bots. One day at the computer in my office, he showed me how it worked. The instant the Task Force used certain keywords—"Crimea," "Ukraine," "sanctions," "Maidan"—the bots went into action and were instantly tweeting nasty stuff about the United States and the State Department.

Will explained to me that what the Russians were doing on social media around Crimea and Ukraine was what Putin had been doing domestically for years. The motherland was always the first of Putin's concentric circles of importance. And what worked at home, they used abroad. They used the same strategy externally that they did domestically: push back on any negative narratives while creating their own narrative that has nothing to do with reality. Their playbook posited that their opponents are fascists, everyone picks on Russia, and it's all the U.S.'s fault. Will said that the messaging they were doing in the periphery about Crimea and Ukraine was still a small fraction of what they were doing domestically. Much of that was on VKontakte— usually known just as VK—the Russian version of Facebook based in St. Petersburg that every Russian with a smartphone was on. In Russia, Facebook wasn't banned, but it was frowned upon by the authorities, and it was often used by the opposition and protesters. What Facebook is for the domestic American audience, VK is for the Russian audience. Inside Russia, Facebook was regarded as the platform for critics, protesters, and liberals.

One of the first things that the Ukraine Task Force did was start a hashtag: #UnitedforUkraine. We used it to tweet out support for Ukraine, respond to Russian actions, and retweet credible voices and partners. To start it off, we tweeted photos of various State Department figures holding up a sign that said #UnitedforUkraine, starting with the State spokesperson Jen Psaki. I did one as well. We had Secretary Kerry tweet out the hashtag from his account, which he had recently started and which already had hundreds of thousands of followers. I suppose this now seems like the usual kind of thing organizations do, but in the spring of 2014 it was pretty radical for the State Department.

> @JohnKerry. As POTUS said: US & allies will keep
> standing together #UnitedforUkraine & its ppl as they
> chart a democratic course.

The hashtag got more than 10,000 likes and retweets in the first 48 hours. For State, that was pretty darn impressive. I don't know exactly who coined the phrase, but people in the media started calling what we were doing "hashtag diplomacy." It wasn't meant as a compliment; it was used a little scornfully. That contemptuous attitude was nearly universal. Here's the lead of a story from *Mashable*:

> As Russian troops amass along the Ukraine border and take
> over military facilities in the Crimea region, the United
> States has distanced itself from any boots-on-the-ground
> intervention. The U.S. won't send troops or weapons, but it
> will send hashtags.[36]

The smart-alecky tone was pretty standard. But, heck, I loved the phrase—#hashtag diplomacy was the future! And did these journalists and the American people, for that matter, really want us to send American troops to eastern Ukraine? I didn't think so. Besides, I was in the business of bytes not bullets. The only weapons I had were digital. These stories tended to quote retired diplomats who had spent their careers writing long turgid cables back to Washington. *Mashable* quoted one as saying, "I don't know what effect a hashtag is meant to have. What's it going to do?" As though an old-fashioned diplomatic démarche delivered to the Russian embassy was a better idea.

But then something else happened. The Russian Foreign Ministry picked up our hashtag and essentially tried to hijack it. They did a few dozen tweets and then enlisted the Russian foreign minister, Sergei Lavrov, who tweeted:

> @Lavrov. Our US counterparts must compel the acting officials in Kiev to bear responsibility for current situation #UnitedForUkraine.

That's how sophisticated the Russian government was on social media. And how *nimble*. The Russians got their foreign minister to co-opt a State Department hashtag. They responded quickly, and understood the mechanics of Twitter.

Our spokeperson, Jen Psaki, quickly replied:

> @statedeptspox. The world stands #UnitedforUkraine. Let's hope that the #Kremlin & @mfa russia will live by the promise of hashtag

Well, then the phrase "the promise of hashtag" started getting roundly mocked in the Twitterverse. Senator Ted Cruz tweeted:

> @SenTedCruz. Note to the State Department: "The promise of a hashtag" isn't going to make Putin pull out of Ukraine.

This one by Geoffrey Skelley was my favorite.

> @geoffreyvs. Once more unto the hashtag, dear friends— once more.

We also started a #RussiaIsolated hashtag, which was meant to show how sanctions were hurting the Russian Federation. But then Russian embassies around the world started appropriating it with positive messages about Russia. They were better at playing our own game than we were. They were faster, cleverer, and more entrepreneurial, and had many more troops on the digital battlefield.

I noticed that a Russian sympathizer on my Twitter feed had commented, "Hashtags are diplomacy by other means."

Exactly! Hashtags *are* diplomacy by other means. Digital ones. And the fact that it was getting so much attention delighted me. Not everyone in the Building was happy. EUR was conspicuously silent. But Secretary Kerry seemed to enjoy it. The Secretary often used to say that war was the failure of diplomacy. Much better to be exchanging tweets than Tomahawks.

The Secretary Is on the Line

On a Saturday morning, about a month after Putin had annexed Crimea, I received a call from the State Department operations center saying they had the Secretary on the line. Only it wasn't Secretary Kerry, my boss, but former Secretary Hillary Clinton. I knew, liked, and admired Clinton. When I was editor of *Time*, I'd traveled with Secretary Clinton to Oman, Afghanistan, and Libya and we'd done a cover story on her called "The Rise of Smart Power."[37] I'd seen her not long after I'd agreed to join the State Department—but before it was publicly announced—and she'd warmly encouraged me.

I assumed she was calling belatedly to say congratulations. When she came on the line, I said something bland about how nice it was to hear from her. But there were no niceties or small talk from her end. She launched right into it: "Rick, Russia is winning the information war on Ukraine and elsewhere and we need to stand up a much stronger and more robust counter-Russian messaging machine. They are outcompeting us in places that are extremely important, like Germany. They are repeating lies over and over, just like in the Soviet days. But they're doing it on 21st-century platforms."

And then she paused, and said, "The State Department is still issuing press releases while Putin is rewriting history!"

Whoa. In the cartoon version of this, I was holding the phone about a foot from my ear. She was blistering. I hardly said anything as she continued describing how the Russians, ISIS, the Chinese, and the Iranians were spending billions of dollars on media. This is a global information war, she said, and we're losing. She told me that while she was Secretary, she had sent a communications team to London to do counter-Russian messaging on European time and found that we were outgunned by the Russians. She said we should respond to Putin's lies the way Media Matters does when it exposes what she called "right-wing" disinformation. If we don't want to respond to everything directly, we should form alliances with nongovernmental organizations and other media groups to get the truth out. Specifically, she said that we should help push out the story of Putin's personal corruption, the enormous bribes he and his family had taken, and the coterie of crooked oligarchs who kept him in power. That would crack his image and undermine his influence and power.

"All of this," she said, "will make the President's job easier and the Secretary's—they shouldn't have to carry all the water on combating disinformation themselves."

Mrs. Clinton knew a lot about Russian disinformation. She had been on the receiving end of it. In 2011, hundreds of thousands of demonstrators gathered in Moscow and across Russia just before local parliamentary elections chanting, "Putin is a thief" and "Russia without Putin." These were the first large-scale demonstrations during

Putin's decade in power, and they threatened to break up his ruling coalition. At Putin's direction, the Russian authorities had deployed battalions of riot police to contain the protests and also orchestrated pro-government counterdemonstrations. By all accounts, Putin had been rattled by the scale and fury of the protests. His party, United Russia, would suffer significant losses in the election. When the election was over, Putin directly and personally accused Secretary Clinton of inciting the protesters.

"She set the tone for some actors in our country and gave them a signal," he said at his annual state press conference in 2012. "They heard the signal and with the support of the U.S. State Department began active work." He then talked about the election itself. "I looked at the first reaction of our U.S. partners," he said. "The first thing that the Secretary of State did was say that they were not honest and not fair, even though she had not received the material from the observers." In fact, her first comments came after a highly critical preliminary election report had been issued by monitors.[38]

For the rest of her time in office, and beyond, Putin seemed to reserve a special animus for Mrs. Clinton. The Russians in general and Putin in particular are sticklers for what in diplomacy is called "reciprocity." He would eventually find a time and place to retaliate against her.

When she paused for a moment, I managed to mention that we had formed the Ukraine Task Force and we had already started in a small way to rebut Russia's narrative.

"You will be obstructed by Public Affairs, as I was," she said. "They are too cautious, too afraid of making mistakes. We need to do much more, and you cannot let the old ways of doing things stand in your way." She added that the Defense Department and the intelligence community would be better partners for both counter-Russian and counter-ISIS messaging and that I should investigate that.

"Rick, I will help you in any way I can, privately or publicly, talking to the Secretary or the President. Please use me. It really needs to be done!"

And then the phone call was over. No farewell—she was off to the next call. I sat and thought for a while. So many of the things I was beginning to think, she had articulated. She had been there before, that was clear. She seemed to have a deeper understanding of what Russia and ISIS were up to and what I was up against at the State Department than any of the principals I was dealing with. And she was much more aggressive about it than any of them. I felt encouraged to have her as an ally on the outside, but I was still looking for allies on the inside. I felt I also needed to get out of Washingon, to head out to the Middle East and the Russian periphery—to see what was happening on the ground. After all, that was where our real audience was.

PART V

The Battle
Is Engaged

A Coalition of the Unwilling

On September 10, 2014, President Obama gave a prime-time Oval Office address to the nation about ISIS. Within a few weeks of the beheadings and reports of ISIS's advances in Iraq and Syria, concerns about the threat of ISIS had risen to the top of opinion polls. People were anxious. Obama needed to address the issue directly.

"Let's make two things clear," he said, "ISIS is not Islamic. No religion condones the killing of innocents. And the vast majority of ISIS's victims have been Muslim. And ISIS is certainly not a state." The principal threat, he said, was to Iraq and Syria, but if left unchecked, the terrorists could pose a potential risk to the United States. He cited the 150 military air strikes the U.S. had made against ISIS in Iraq and announced an increase of 475 American soldiers in Iraq to help support Iraqi and Kurdish forces with training, intelligence, and equipment.

"Secretary Kerry," Obama continued, "was in Iraq today meeting with the new government . . . And in the coming days he will travel across the Middle East and Europe to enlist more partners in this fight, especially Arab nations who help mobilize Sunni communities in Iraq and Syria to drive these terrorists from their lands."[1]

I didn't see the actual speech because I was with Secretary Kerry in one of those cavernous C-17s the military uses to fly into Baghdad. Baghdad in summer is an oven. We had arrived early in the morning and the temperature was already over 100 degrees. When you step out of the plane, you're met by that baking gasoline smell of a war zone. Bagram Airfield had the look of something that was built in a hurry and then immediately started decaying. We were ushered into a building where we were blasted with air-conditioning set to 63 degrees. We all put on protective vests and helmets for the helicopter trip to the Green Zone to meet the new Iraqi prime minister, Haider al-Abadi.

When the President had asked Secretary Kerry to put together a military coalition against ISIS, Kerry asked me to come along on his trip to talk to our Arab allies about what we could do together to counter ISIS propaganda. I also wanted to get a sense of how ISIS was perceived on its home ground and what we could learn for our own messaging effort back home.

We had flown overnight to Amman, Jordan, on the Secretary's plane, a retrofitted Boeing 757 that was built about 20 years ago but seemed much older. It felt cramped and a little dingy. The traveling staff sat in the middle section of the plane, where there were four or five rows of business-class seats. In front of that was an open seating area for "the line," the State staff who process all the information going to and coming from the Secretary. They're the nerve center of the department. Next to them was a table where the Secretary's personal staff sat, including his reliable body guy, Jason, who was the only person on the plane—and at State, for that matter—who was taller than the Secretary. At the back of the plane was diplomatic security. They are the Secret Service for the State Department, and at their best, they combined the brawn of the Secret Service with the knowledge of foreign service officers. The reporters—about a dozen of them—sat in the rear of the plane, mostly in coach-class seats.

The Secretary's private cabin was tiny—and seemed even tinier when he was in it. He had to hunch over to get inside, and I can't imagine he was able to stretch out on that small bed. Once on the plane, the Secretary was immediately out of his suit and into a pair of jeans and a Yale hoodie. The atmosphere changed too: it was more relaxed, more intimate, more clubby. When you traveled at State, there was always a sense that you were where the action was, that the world was revolving around what was happening on your trip. Sometimes that was even true.

*   *   *

We met Abadi in a nondescript building in the Green Zone that looked like it had once been an airplane hangar. The usual arrangement of seating in the Middle East: two big, high-backed chairs for the Secretary and the prime minister at the end of the room, and then two perpendicular rows of smaller chairs on either side for their respective delegations. A cup of tea on everyone's side table. And a small bowl of dates. Abadi is squat, bullet-headed, friendly—a fireplug. First greeting of Kerry to Abadi: "Hey, man, how are you?" From the outside, the Secretary can seem aloof and patrician; up close in diplomatic situations, he's warm and regular guy–ish. Abadi brightened and relaxed.

Abadi spoke quietly but forcefully. He called ISIS a cancer. "This is *our* fight," he said. "And it's a very hard one." It was one of the first times that I'd heard an Arab leader say that it was their battle, not our's, and it was powerful. In the U.S., people were always asking what were "we" doing about ISIS, as though it was entirely America's problem. It was consoling to hear a Muslim leader say, No, it's ours.

Abadi had one of the hardest jobs in the world. He was replacing Nouri al-Maliki, the relentlessly pro-Shia prime minister who had lost the trust of everyone in Iraq. We knew that we probably couldn't defeat ISIS without the support of the Sunni tribes, and the tribes would not support us unless they saw that Abadi was different from Maliki.

I had been briefed about how our public diplomacy efforts were working in Iraq. The answer was dismally. American popularity in Iraq was in the single digits. More than 9 in 10 Iraqi Sunnis thought the country was going in the wrong direction. A majority of Iraqis—Sunni and Shia—actually thought that the U.S. had created ISIS. I asked one intelligence officer why this was. He smiled and replied that most Iraqis say, "We have seen what you are capable of when you invaded us, and the fact that you are not doing it to them must mean that you are on their side." I wasn't sure that any messaging effort could fix that.

The Secretary pulled me over and introduced me to Abadi, telling him I was the person who would be in charge of our messaging. Abadi gave me a look that seemed to say, Good luck with that.

Our next stop was Jeddah, Saudi Arabia.

On the way to the plane, the Secretary grabbed my arm. "I don't think we should be talking about religion," he said. "Give me some language to say." And then he was off. I agreed.

On the trip to Jeddah, I batted out something short and colloquial and printed it out on the plane's printer.

> I don't claim to be an expert on Islam, but I know this—at
> its heart, Islam is a religion of peace and tolerance. And ISIS
> is a perversion of that vision.

At the airport in Jeddah, I handed him the note as he got off the plane. He glanced at it before putting it in his pocket. The Secretary was met by Prince Saud al-Faisal, the aristocratic Saudi who was the world's longest-serving foreign minister—he had been in the job for four decades. Dressed in an immaculate *thawb*, Prince Saud was bent and spoke in a hoarse whisper. His English was perfect—he went to Princeton—but he spoke exclusively in Arabic. At a brief press conference at the airport, Saud said ISIS had nothing to do with Islam.

Secretary Kerry—without notes—echoed Saud's comments and then gave an almost perfect recitation of the two sentences I had handed him about Islam. The Secretary was the best I've ever seen at quickly absorbing some language and then saying it as though it had just popped into his head.

The Saudis were hosting a meeting for us with the ministers of the Gulf Cooperation Council, plus Turkey, Egypt, Lebanon, and Iraq. The

GCC was an old-line organization of the Sunni states we had worked with for decades. We were in a beautiful white palace, with rich marble floors and hallways overflowing with Saudi men in white *thawbs*. The only women I saw were in our delegation. Inside the main room, at an enormous, rectangular wooden table, Kerry and Saud welcomed everyone. I was seated next to Jon Finer, the Secretary's deputy chief of staff. Jon had come to State from the NSC when Kerry started. A Rhodes Scholar and a former foreign correspondent for the *Washington Post*, he was young, supersmart, and deeply knowledgeable. Within the Building, he was sometimes referred to as "the Secretary's brain." This was said not with derision but with respect. Kerry was wonderfully unselfconscious about relying on his expertise and advice. Often the Secretary would call out, "Hey, Jon, come over here and explain this."

In the room, the Secretary said we must collectively end ISIS's terrorism. He said, We're going to talk to you about what each of you can do. Each foreign minister then spoke. The Egyptian foreign minister said that ISIS offers an ideology of hate. The Jordanian foreign minister said we need to broaden our commitment to fight all kinds of terrorism, not just ISIS. This was echoed by the UAE minister, who said, Let's not let this opportunity go to waste.

When everyone had finished speaking, the Secretary turned around and motioned for me to stand up. He said, This is Rick Stengel, he was the editor of *Time*—you've all heard of that—and he's going to be working with all of your countries to figure out how we message against ISIS. They nodded, and I could see some of the backbenchers take note.

As they began to get down to details, I went out to meet some of the communications people from the Gulf Cooperation Council. They were polite but reticent. For us, ISIS still felt new. And we knew them only on social media. The Arab ministers knew them more intimately.

I mentioned the idea of forming a messaging coalition to complement the military coalition we were creating. They were not against it. It was the first of many times that I felt our allies wanted America to take the lead yet didn't necessarily think we knew exactly what we were doing. That was the American foreign policy conundrum in a nutshell.

When we left Jeddah, I mentioned to Finer the idea that we should form a messaging coalition. He must have mentioned it to the Secretary, because on the flight back, I heard from my staff in Washington that we were given a "tasker" by the Secretary. In the words of the email I got from my staff: "S tasked R with paper that talks to: (a) ongoing activities and planning by the R family in the fight against ISIS, and (b) additional resources that will be brought to bear in this effort."

I banged out something on the plane. In the memo, I said I had already started working on a counter-ISIS messaging coalition. In truth, I didn't really know what that even looked like. I knew I had to enlist our Arab allies, and I mentioned that I would try to recruit media executives in the region, but I had no idea if any of it would work.

Every Battle Is Won or Lost Before It's Fought

My first question before visiting was: KEY-ev or Keeve? I'd noticed that some people pronounced Kiev the way most of us learned it—two syllables, with the accent on the first, KEY. But many of the people in the European bureau said, "Keeve," with a long *e*. It turns out that in Ukrainian, "Kiev" is pronounced as one long syllable. Saying it that way did show solidarity with Ukrainian nationalism, but it did sound a wee bit pretentious. I stuck with KEY-ev.

I was keen to visit Kiev. I had by then given a million and a half public diplomacy dollars to the embassy there to help with everything from bringing in new public affairs officers to buying more copy machines. I wanted to get a sense of whether Kiev felt like a city at war. What did the actual information battlefield look like? For that same reason, I was also going to Latvia. Latvia and the rest of the Baltics were the front lines of the Russian information war. As with Ukraine, they had been under an information assault for decades.[2]

The first thing we did after arriving in Kiev was to take a tour of the Maidan led by one of the local guides who had sprung up since the old regime had been toppled. Independence Square itself—*maidan* is the Ukrainian word for "square"—is a vast, twisting space punctuated by elaborate fountains (all of them dry and pockmarked by bullets) and surrounded by neoclassical Stalinist buildings. The square had already become a kind of living museum to the protest—we wended our way through the fantastical barricades that looked like massive junkyard sculptures composed of metal, wire, blankets, bicycles, concrete, and a rainbow of colored ribbons. We paid our respects to the monument for the Heavenly Hundred, commemorating the protesters who had died in the struggle. Our guide, a young man wearing a jumble of military fatigues, seemed intent on pointing out where every bullet had been fired by troops that were then loyal to the former president, Viktor Yanukovych, who had fled to Moscow.

We stopped to chat with a young university student who told us with a shy smile that she had always fainted at the sight of blood, but during the protests she volunteered to care for the wounded in one of the Maidan's makeshift hospitals and never faltered. Now, she said, she had seen enough blood for a lifetime, and was focused on creating a truly democratic Ukraine. Like so many people I would talk to in Ukraine, she possessed a patriotism that seemed lit from within.

Outside the Maidan, it seemed to be business as usual in Kiev. It's a gorgeous city with winding cobblestone streets and baroque-style buildings. When we went downtown, it was teeming with young, stylish people going about their business—contrary to Russian propaganda that Kiev was in chaos and not functioning. It did feel like a city on a war footing in one sense: people seemed to have an urgency and intensity about what they were doing.

My first meeting was with the new government's acting information minister. One of the things that has always separated the U.S. from so many other nations is that we don't have an information ministry. To American ears, it sounds like something out of *1984*. In authoritarian countries, the information ministry's job is suppressing information, not disseminating it.

The acting information minister was a bantam-size fellow with enormous glasses. He was nervous and high-strung. I told him that I wanted to help Ukraine compete with the Russian narrative. What can we do? That opened the floodgates, and the minister began to ask me a series of questions. What is a press release? How do press conferences work? Is there a difference between a briefing and a press conference? What is the difference between "on the record," and "off the record," and "on background"?

I was a little taken aback. These were Communications 101 questions. It was apparent that the new Ukrainian leadership knew almost nothing about media. They needed a great deal of help. No wonder the Russians were having their way with the narrative.

I could have stayed there all day answering his questions, but that wouldn't have accomplished much. I said I would see if I could get someone from the Public Affairs staff at the embassy to come around and talk to his people. I told him that he could really benefit from hiring an American communications consultant who knew all this stuff cold. The idea that there were professional communications experts for hire seemed to come as a revelation to him. Certainly, the old regime had known; former president Yanukovych had spent millions on the American media consultant Paul Manafort.[3]

The next day we went to Riga, the capital of Latvia. The Latvians were a lot more sophisticated about Russian disinformation than the Ukrainians. Riga is a graceful, 800-year-old city that opens onto the Baltic Sea to the west; to the east, the country shares a border with Russia. Like the other two Baltic states, Lithuania and Estonia, Latvia was part of the Russian empire from the 18th century until the Russian Revolution in 1917, when it became independent. It was occupied by the Soviet Union at the beginning of World War II, invaded by Germany, and then reoccupied by the Soviets in 1945, remaining a part of the Soviet Union until 1991. Schools in Latvia were still bilingual: instruction was in Latvian and Russian.

That first day I had lunch with a senior Latvian official in the defense department who specialized in cybersecurity. We ate in a sunny private room at an art nouveau–style restaurant on a canal. He was natty and compact, with a shaved head and a goatee. He spoke fast, fluent, Slavic-accented English.

"Russia yearns to be a great power again," he said. "They are trying to re-create the multipolar sphere-of-influence world of the 19th century. They see what they call the *blizhneye zaruezhe*—the near abroad—as their sphere of influence. They feel they have the right to do whatever they want with all the countries of the former Soviet Union.

"What does Putin want?" he asked, and then answered his own question. "He wants to destabilize Ukraine. A destabilized Ukraine gives him more control. Like us, Ukraine had a 50-year occupation from 1940 until 1991. Now it feels like 1940 again. But Russia destabilizing its neighbors," he said, "is a 300-year-old problem. Russia feels most secure when its neighbors feel least secure. Putin has been waging an information war here in the Baltics for years. Remember, there is one very big difference between Ukraine and the Baltics. The Balts are in NATO, and Ukraine is not. He absolutely hates the Balts being part of NATO. He has never been comfortable with the Baltics not being part of imperial Russia. Remember, Russia is a zero-sum power. There's no win-win in the Russian language. It's we win, you lose."

I asked him about Russian propaganda and disinformation.

"Russian propaganda is brutal. They don't even pretend to be objective. They are creating an alternative reality. They lie shamelessly. And they do not care if they are caught in it. They just create another lie. You Americans care about being caught in a lie"—and here he smiled. "They don't. That's a handicap for you. During the Cold War, there was some allegiance to reality. No more. The idea is to use disinformation to make your opponents do what you want them to do short of violence. This has been going on since Sun-tzu. Remember what he said? Every battle is won or lost before it starts. Russia has put the communication and information piece at the core of its military efforts. The kinetic has become secondary."

He paused for a moment. "You Americans dropped the ball in the 1990s after the Wall came down," he said. "The Russians created television stations throughout the periphery. But it wasn't just about the Russian language; it was about the content, and the content is good. They learned how to make good television—game shows, talent contests, reality TV. People like them. People here watch the Russian-language channel, and then when the news comes on, they don't change the channel. That's the idea. They watch *Russian news*."

The food was delicious but he'd barely had any. His tour of the waterfront was humbling. "So, what can we do?" I asked him. He didn't have great answers. He wanted us to support Latvia's counter-messaging efforts. Done. Second, he said, you have to try to create an awareness in the public—not only in Ukraine but elsewhere—that Russia was trying to influence their opinion. People cannot see influence operations, he said. You need to tell them about it. I mentioned that we had started the Ukraine Task Force, which he knew about. But he was skeptical. He didn't trust us Americans to really understand what was going on.

"You're not as suspicious of the Russians as we are. Nor as experienced. You Americans are naive. You don't think anyone lies to you. At the same time, you must learn not to take the bait. You can't react to every bit of disinformation. You can't overreact to every one of Putin's lies, or anyone's. You need your own narrative and you need to stick to it. We can't fight propaganda with propaganda because then we become what we are fighting. We value truth. That's the difference."

Lines of Effort

John Allen seemed unsuited for civilian life. This was literally true in one sense: his civilian suits were too large and boxy for him, decades out of style. But it was also true in a broader sense: even in a civilian suit, he still seemed to be in uniform. Allen had retired the year before as a Marine Corps four-star general. He was built for command: compact and sturdy with a deep baritone that you could imagine directing troops on the field of battle. Earlier in September, President Obama had named Allen as Special Presidential Envoy for the Global Coalition to Counter ISIS. Along with Secretary Kerry, he was assembling the military coalition of allies as well as leading the different strands of the U.S. mission—what he called the "lines of effort" (LOE)—to combat ISIS.

I was sitting in Allen's spare, undecorated office on the seventh floor of the State Department. The only individual touch was a large whiteboard that he liked to scribble on while talking. I'd just gotten back from the Middle East a couple of weeks before with a new appreciation of how difficult the messaging effort would be—especially outside the U.S. We were all still in the "how do we hit back" mode. But things had moved quickly since my memo to the Secretary on starting a messaging coalition. The White House had asked me to be the co-lead of line of effort 5, "Exposing ISIS's True Nature" (I joked with Allen that ISIS was already doing a good job of it). I was happy about this but not entirely sure what it meant. John was leading the whole enterprise, and he began by telling me how important the information battlefield was.

"This is a lot more than putting warheads on foreheads," he said with a grim smile. "The information war is the ultimate battlefield. That is where the whole game is. On the military battlefield," he said, "the measurement of victory is physical space. On the information battlefield, the measurement is time. When I was commanding, I always said that the information sphere is the only one where I can react with the speed of light, and the result can last forever."

From the moment Allen had started, he was on the road recruiting countries to be a part of the anti-ISIS coalition. He said he had spent half his life preparing for wars and the other half fighting them. He had fought against al-Qaeda and the Taliban when he was deputy commander of U.S. Central Command and commander of U.S. Forces Afghanistan. He had nurtured the Sunni Awakening in Anbar. He understood the double pull of Sunni grievance and the call to Sunni greatness. But he saw ISIS as different in kind and degree from al-Qaeda. They had greater depth and cohesion than al-Qaeda, he said. They were the military wing of Sunni Islam. He saw that their self-declared Caliphate was a beacon to young Muslim men around the world. Very few in government understood this, and almost no one in the media. I had seen ISIS's appeal on my trip to the Middle East, though it was still anathema in America to admit that ISIS had any attraction whatsoever. For many young Sunni men, they were _cool_. They looked cool. They had a cool flag. ISIS were magnetic. They were seen as winners.

Someone had called them the Muslim version of the Baader-Meinhof gang from the 1970s and '80s. Already more foreigners had gone to fight for ISIS than went during the whole Russia-Afghanistan war. But what was truly revolutionary about them, Allen said, was that they understood the information battlefield.

General Allen wrote the name ISIS in big letters on the whiteboard with an arrow pointing to the right. Then he posed a series of questions: What happens after we destroy ISIS on the military battlefield? Will they really be defeated? They will fragment, he said, and turn to the informational battlefield to counterattack. "The military part is the least of it," he said. "We need to win on the information battlefield."

I asked him how he saw my job in practical terms. On the whiteboard, in handwriting that was pretty close to indecipherable, he jotted down his three-part messaging strategy.

1. Shape the reporting before the event.
2. Get third-party validators organized in advance.
3. Jam the opposition's media.

Allen believed that you could plan your information campaign in advance. We should have what he called "products on the shelf," that is, information products that go out at the same time as or even before battles.

Finally, he talked about analytics. Analytics was a mantra for the military. But he said there was only one statistic he was interested in: a decline in the number of foreign fighters. That was their lifeline. If we cut off the supply of foreign fighters, we would suffocate them.

What Allen understood is that in the age of social media, the idea that history is written by the victors was an old-fashioned notion. History was being written in the moment in 140 characters. What was new about ISIS—and Russia—was that they were writing the history before the battle, shaping the victory narrative before there was a victory. We talked about Russia, and he said that in this case Ukraine was the center of their information battlefield, the way Iraq was in the case of ISIS. Both Russia and ISIS, he said, wanted to topple the information hegemony and moral authority of the West. They were allies in that, he said. But with ISIS, he said, you can't kill your way to victory and you can't message your way to victory. You have to do both.

We talked about difficulties in forming the international messaging coalition. We were in agreement that we needed the Sunni nations, but he raised an eyebrow when he talked about getting them on board. Be patient, he said.

We talked for an hour, much of the time about line of effort 5. At the end, he said, See you Saturday. He had called a rare Saturday meeting for the leads of the different lines of effort to hash out a collective battle plan. It was at the National Counterterrorism Center (NCTC) in McLean, Virginia, near Tysons Corner.

The National Counterterrorism Center was one of those government entities created in the wake of 9/11.[4] It grew out of the idea that the intelligence services weren't coordinated in a way that could have prevented the attack. NCTC was meant to connect the dots. The meeting was belowground in a vast room with a giant U-shaped table. Many backbenchers were at the sides. Allen sat at the top, and arrayed around him were the leads of the different lines of effort.

General Allen opened the gathering. The man doesn't need a microphone. ISIS, he said, "is a learning and adaptive organization." That's what sets them apart from al-Qaeda. ISIS's brand is that they are the savior of the Sunnis and that Sunni Islam was under attack by the West. The problem, he said candidly, is that most Sunnis see their leaders as weak and corrupt, and they're right. This will not be fixed until Sunni Islam finds leaders who can bring it into the 21st century. He saw the military stage as a three-year battle and said that we needed to eliminate ISIS's "safe havens" and prevent them from "regenerating." He talked a lot about analytics and measures of performance ("LOEs will need to develop MOPs"). He ended by talking about my line of effort, saying that social media has been a tool that has enabled them to increase recruitment. We needed to see if social media could be used to reverse that.

When it was my turn, I began by saying the U.S. must help build a messaging coalition that complements the military coalition. We need to do it across our own government as well. I said that while ISIS had done a pretty good job of exposing their true face by themselves, we would highlight their savagery and hypocrisy through key influencers. I mentioned that I would soon be heading back to the Middle East to find local partners and would appreciate any help or suggestions.

The meeting was really too big to accomplish much. In government, any meeting with more than a dozen people was mostly for show. This one turned out to be an everybody-stands-up-and-says-his-piece type of meeting. The folks sitting on the side were from State, the intelligence community, and the military. The military folks would stand up and ask a question. The intelligence folks would clarify a point with data. But when the State Department people would stand up, they'd always begin their questions or comments with the words "I think."

General Allen was trying to do something often talked about in Washington but rarely done: he was attempting to organize a "whole of government" effort to degrade and destroy ISIS. I'd heard the phrase often. But the meeting illustrated how hard this was to accomplish: the different lines of effort were actually not hooked up. They were operating independently of each other and managed by people from different agencies and bureaus who felt ownership of their respective

LOEs. Assembling our internal coalition was going to be just as complicated as putting together our external one.

About midway through the morning, the lieutenant general who was sitting next to me leaned over and whispered, "I know how to defeat ISIS."

"Really!" I said, "How?"

"Get them involved in the interagency process."

I did my best not to laugh out loud.

You Have Your Truth—We Have Ours

If you really want to experience animosity toward Russia—"hatred" might be a more accurate word—go to Lithuania. Lithuanians feel perpetually threatened by their aggressive neighbor to the east. They are longtime targets of Russian disinformation and regard us as amateurs. But, all the same, they want our help in countering it. And that's not all they want; they want something much more substantial: tanks! American M1 Abrams tanks with American soldiers in them. Almost everyone I spoke to said, Your tanks are the only thing that will prevent the Russians from doing here what they are doing in Ukraine. Don't you understand that Putin wants to break up NATO? Lithuanians are not fans of American humility.

I was visiting the charming and gracious city of Vilnius. Vilnius was founded in the 12th century, and it has been entangled with Russia in one way or another ever since. I had returned to the Baltics to see how Russian disinformation was working in the periphery. The truth is, I'd fallen in love with the Baltics and Ukraine. My first stop was Lithuania, and then I would go to Latvia and Ukraine.

I had also come because I had authorized $500,000 for a program in Lithuania to train Russian-speaking Baltic journalists in investigative journalism. One of the practical things we could do to combat

Russian disinformation was to train journalists who could report on it. The Baltic journalists would be visiting newsrooms in the U.S. over several weeks. We hadn't announced the program yet, but just before my trip, someone else did: Sputnik, the Russian state-sponsored digital news service. Their story, "US Puts Up $500K to Fight Russian Media in Baltics," said that I had "raised alarm over the specter of a supposedly monstrous Russian Propaganda Machine."[5] Nice. It also said that the program was masquerading as a journalistic endeavor but that it was actually an attack on Russia. And what did the State public affairs team say in response to explain our program and defend the profound importance of independent journalism to democracy and freedom? "The spokesperson of the U.S. Embassy in Lithuania refused to comment on the launch of the project."

I was meeting with a Lithuanian colonel in the basement of a government building in Vilnius. I'd never seen such large epaulets before. They looked like wings on his uniform. The colonel was in his mid-thirties, tall, angular, precise. "We've lost our state to the Russians twice," he said, "in 1793 and 1940—each time without firing a single shot. Russian soft power conquered Lithuania two times. It eroded our will to resist. We lost both times without fighting."

The colonel explained that in 1940, after the Hitler-Stalin Pact, the Soviet Union gave Lithuania an ultimatum that it form a pro-Soviet government and admit Russian troops. Lithuania succumbed—and Russia began the gradual Sovietization of Lithuania. The Lithuanians call the period after 1940 "the Occupation." It lasted until the fall of the Berlin Wall, and then in 1991, Lithuania became the first of the former Soviet republics to declare its independence. But Russia sought to maintain another kind of control.

"Putin first mentioned 'soft power' in a speech in February 2013," the colonel said. "But the Russians have been weaponizing information for a long time. One of their battlefields is history. Since 1991, the Russians have been trying to rewrite Lithuanian history. They say the Lithuanian kings were actually Belorussian. They say the east of the country belongs to Belorussia and the west to Russia. They say that Klaipeda, our third-largest city, does not belong to us because it was a gift from Stalin after World War II. This is what they do—they try to manipulate history to show the Russian narrative as supreme. The parallels with what they did in Crimea are clear and dangerous. Why would they start an information war if they aren't planning a real war? Russia's message to us right now is, We're not going to invade you, but if we did, no one would defend you. Putin wants us to think that Article 5 is not worth the paper it is written on."

One of the things drummed into your head if you're a diplomat is that when you go to Europe—and especially to the Baltics—you say, over and over, "Our commitment to Article 5 is ironclad." ("Ironclad" was the preferred adjective, but "inviolate" was also acceptable.) Article 5 is the commitment that all NATO countries will come to the aid of any NATO country that is attacked. The idea, especially in countries like Lithuania, is not to waver an inch because, well, they get nervous. And who can blame them? Russia, with an army more than 100 times the size of Lithuania's, was right next door. But what many feared was that Putin would put our "ironclad" commitment to the test. Would we honor Article 5 if he sent Spetsnaz troops into Lithuania, or Latvia, or Estonia? The question Putin had posed in his soft invasion of eastern Ukraine was essentially the same one: Will you go to war over this? It was the question that Secretary Kerry had asked one morning at the 8:30: "Are we really willing to go to war over Ukraine?" The answer, thus far, from the President on down was no. But what Russia was doing in Ukraine was not a full test of Article 5, for the simple reason that Ukraine wasn't in NATO. The Lithuanians, like the Latvians and

Estonians, saw what Russia was doing in Crimea and Ukraine as a trial run for what it might try in the Baltics.

I mentioned that after leaving Lithuania, I was going to Latvia to talk to some Russian journalists in exile about how to compete with the Russian narrative. The colonel said that was a good thing, but that I should be aware that Russia had already successfully exported its skewed view of the world to the region. "Russian channels here are plentiful and cheap. Russia subsidizes the cost of their programming, particularly entertainment programming. This is all part of Putin's soft power initiative. American programming is attractive, but it's too expensive for us. We can't get Netflix or HBO. Ninety-seven percent of people here get their news from TV. Only 6 percent of Lithuanians are ethnic Russians, but 60 percent of people here can speak Russian, especially older people. Russia is targeting that large Russian-speaking audience. There's no Russian-language alternative to Russian state programming. There's Lithuanian state TV, but that's in Lithuanian. Among Russian-speakers"—and here he paused—"there's a nostalgia for Soviet times. It was spartan, but clear and orderly."

He knew about our training program for Russian-speaking jour-nalists and I mentioned *Current Time*, a Russian-language news broad-cast started by Voice of America, which we had spurred them to create. "It's not as good as what the Russians do," he said with a smile. "But it's a lot better than what we had before—which is nothing.

As I was leaving, he said: "But remember what the Russians say: You have your truth; we have ours."

With Putin closing down much of independent media in Russia, there had been an exodus of Russian journalists. I had talked often about how we ought to support their next chapter, whatever it was. A number of those independent Russian journalists had ended up in Latvia's capital,

Riga, where three of them had started a Russian-language website called Meduza. I met with them at a beautiful art nouveau–style café in the center of town.

They were young and enthusiastic, and there was a sense that they had already been through a lot. Of the three, only one spoke good English, and that's because he and his family had left Russia when he was 13 and moved to Minnesota. He had an earring in his left ear and a short-cropped beard and joked that at least the weather was better here than in Minneapolis. After college, he had moved to Moscow and worked for the independent broadcaster TVS. When TVS was shut down by Putin, he had come to Riga. Let's call him Alexander. He spoke really fast.

"Russia's message is about the relativism of everything," he said. "The relative truth of the two sides in Ukraine. The relativism of the West. A plague on both your houses. All your houses. Don't believe anyone. The Cold War was ideological. Today, the Russians don't have a view that they are trying to persuade you of, just that everything is relative. Nothing is better than anything else." As the Russian journalist Peter Pomerantsev once said to me, "It's not an information war; it's a war on information."[6]

"Look, I was raised in America," Alexander continued. "If Americans could experience what Russian state media says about the U.S. on a daily basis, they would be outraged. That America is a lowdown, hypocritical society. The essence of Russian propaganda is 'It's America's fault.' There is no problem in the world too small to be blamed on the U.S. Maybe once there was some grudging admiration for America, but no more. It's just animosity and resentment. That comes from Putin and goes all the way down."

I asked about the diaspora of Russian journalists and whether they could make a difference against the onslaught of Russian propaganda. He shrugged his shoulders. "There are a lot of us," he said. "And we want to push back against the Russian narrative." I asked how safe it was for them, even here in Riga. He smiled and they looked at one another. "We're fine," he said.

As I was leaving, I mentioned that I was going to Ukraine. One of his colleagues said in English that was not as fast as Alexander's but just as passionate, "You must understand, there is hybrid war here in Latvia, but real war in Ukraine."

My last stop was back in Kiev. This was the ostensible public diplomacy reason for my trip: the opening of America House.[7] America House was a modern example of what were known as "American Spaces," a Cold War–era program of State Department–operated venues that showcased American culture. America House, an attractive two-story residential building in central Kiev, had been wonderfully restored. It was meant to be a place where Ukrainians could come to learn about the U.S. but also attend events that supported a democratic and free Ukraine. The whole thing had cost a few million dollars, and I had given them a considerable amount of that. I was the "deliverable" for the opening and got there early and met the U.S. and Ukrainian staffers, who were young and excited.

As usual, there were a succession of speakers. I was the last. I began by saying, "Ukrainians have suffered at the hands of the two most monstrous totalitarian regimes of the 20th century—the Nazis and the Soviets. The rich soil of Ukraine had been host to more human misery than almost anywhere else on the planet. America House is a symbol of our commitment to the people of Ukraine. We want more than anything to see a successful, vibrant, democratic Ukraine, and we will help in any way we can."

I kept my remarks short. There was no air-conditioning, and I could see the crowd was a little warm. The speaking had already gone on too long. When I finished, a young public diplomacy officer introduced a brother and sister of Ukrainian ancestry from Milwaukee. They appeared to be in their early twenties, and both had dark, lank hair and didn't really look the crowd in the eyes. He had a guitar. He played a few opening notes, and then they began to sing the Carpenters song "We've Only Just Begun"—very, very badly. I would never ever say that I have a good ear, but I'm pretty sure it was the single worst rendition of any song I've ever heard in public. They were out of tune, introverted, unfriendly. The crowd shifted a little uneasily, but the Ukranians were too polite to do anything but pretend to listen.

Here I was, the chief marketing officer of the United States of America, the country of Beyoncé and Taylor Swift, of Kanye West and Katy Perry, the country of hip-hop and Hollywood, of music videos and iTunes, and we had just spent hundreds of thousands of dollars on this wonderful venue in a country that was essentially at war with our principal adversary in the world, an adversary that was trying to use its own soft power to subvert democracy and freedom, and somehow, for the final act of opening night, the public diplomacy staff had managed to find the two least talented, least inspiring Americans in Kiev—though they did genuinely seem to be of Ukrainian extraction.

The Gray Zone

Tysons Corner, in Fairfax County, Virginia, which lies along the Capital Beltway about 15 miles west of downtown D.C., is a "census-designated place," a term devised by the U.S. Census Bureau to define somewhere that is not a city, town, or village, but has a lot of people in it and functions kind of like one. Tysons Corner may not have a mayor, but it does boast dozens of corporate headquarters. Some corporations, like Capital One and Booz Allen, are well known, but many are the anonymous, blandly named companies that deal with the Defense Department and the intelligence community. They are housed in unmemorable office parks with sleek but unostentatious buildings that have acronyms but no names or logos. Their corporate branding is no branding at all.

I drove out to one of these corporate headquarters not long after getting back from Ukraine, for a seminar on Russian hybrid warfare. It was run by the Defense Department and had about 50 officials from State, DOD, CIA, NSC—the usual suspects. The meeting was in an enormous double-basketball-court-size room with a 100-foot ceiling and long tables laid out on three sides with a giant screen in front. Like most of these seminars, this one had a facilitator, and the one we had that morning was an American colonel who combined the bland, ingratiating manner of the role with a deep knowledge of the subject matter.

At the beginning, the colonel put on the big screen George Kennan's definition of "political warfare," as outlined in his famous 1948 Policy Planning memo:

> Political warfare is the logical application of Clausewitz's doctrine in time of peace. In broadest definition, political warfare is the employment of all the means at a nation's command, short of war, to achieve its national objectives. Such operations are both overt and covert. They range from such overt actions as political alliances, economic measures, and "white" propaganda to such covert operations as clandestine support of "friendly" foreign elements, and "black" psychological warfare.[8]

"That's a pretty good definition of Russian hybrid warfare," the colonel said. "And it's as true today as when Kennan wrote it." The modern Russian notion of hybrid warfare, he said, comes from what he called the Gerasimov model. Valery Gerasimov, he said, is the Russian general who is Putin's favorite military intellectual. Gerasimov is the father of the idea that in the 21st century, only a small part of war is kinetic. Modern warfare, he has written, is nonlinear with no clear boundary between military and nonmilitary campaigns. The Russians, like ISIS, merged their military lines of effort with their information and messaging line of effort.

The colonel then outlined the "Selected Terms" that flashed on the screen. "The Gray Zone," he said, encompassed "conflicts that fall outside the war-peace duality." "Frozen conflicts" were wars that never quite end, which makes their territory difficult to govern. He mentioned what the Russians had done in Abkhazia and South Ossetia as examples of frozen conflicts. "The information domain," he said, included cyberwarfare, propaganda, and deception. Russian actions in this realm, he said, were always accompanied by the "persistent denial" of those same operations. Any action on the ground always starts without any declaration at all. Crimea, he said, was a textbook example of Russian hybrid warfare: the Russians first seeded the terrain with propaganda and disinformation; they "invaded" with unmarked and unidentified troops; they denied the existence of those troops; and they took over the means of communication.

He said our term "disinformation" was in fact an adaptation of the Russian word *dezinformatsiya*, which was the KGB term for black propaganda. In the old days, disinformation involved placing a false story (often involving forged documents) in a fairly obscure left-leaning newspaper in, say, India or Brazil; the story was then picked up and echoed in Russian state media. A more modern version of *dezinformatsiya*, he said, was the campaign in the 1990s that tried to suggest that the U.S. had invented the AIDS virus as a kind of "ethnic bomb" to wipe out people of color.

In addition to Gerasimov, the colonel said he wanted to talk about two other theorists of modern Russian information warfare:

Igor Panarin, an academic and former KGB officer; and Alexander Dugin, a philosopher whom some called "Putin's Rasputin." Panarin sees Russia as the victim of information aggression by the United States. He believes there is a global information war between what he calls the Atlantic world, led by the U.S. and Europe; and the Eurasian world, led by Russia. He believes American hybrid warfare led to the collapse of the Soviet Union. He claims the color revolutions in Eastern Europe and the Arab Spring were products of American information warfare. He sees the same hand behind the protests in Russia in 2011. Of course, he says that the Euromaidan protests in Ukraine were an anti-Russian information campaign orchestrated by the West. He regards Russia's actions in Crimea and Ukraine as the first step in countering the Western information hegemony. All these beliefs, the colonel suggested, were shared by Putin.

Alexander Dugin—the colonel showed his picture on the big screen: long hair, long beard, piercing eyes; he actually looks like Rasputin. Dugin uses the term "net-centric warfare" for what he sees as a new military line of effort. Russia, he believes, needs to offer a symmetric response to the American information war. He has advocated putting the best Russian minds on addressing this challenge. "He has a particularly Russian vision of history," the colonel continued. "He says that while the 20th century was a titanic struggle among fascism, communism, and liberalism, in which liberalism won out, in the 21st century there will be a fourth way. Western liberalism will be replaced by a conservative superstate like Russia leading a multipolar world and defending tradition and conservative values." He's also predicted, the colonel says, the rise of conservative strongmen in the West who will embrace these values. Part of Putin's strategy, Dugin has said, is to back regional strongmen so that they are Putin clones. Erdoğan in Turkey. Orbán in Hungary. Xi Jinping in China.

Dugin supports the rise of conservative right-wing groups all across Europe. He has also formed relationships with white nationalists' groups in America. He had done two Skype lectures for white nationalist groups in the U.S. Dugin believes immigration and racial mixing are polluting the Caucasian world. Rolling back immigration, he says, is one of the key tasks for conservative states. He preaches the importance of the survival of white culture. For many American white nationalist and supremacist groups, Russia is, as David Duke once said, the "key to white survival."[9] Dugin has said all truth is relative and a question of belief; that freedom and democracy are not universal values but peculiarly Western ones; and that the U.S. must be dislodged as a hyperpower through the destabilization of American democracy and the encouragement of American isolationism.

The facilitator then introduced our first speaker, a major who had been recently posted in the Baltics. He was the sort of person you might shake hands with and then not recognize an hour later. He was slender, with glasses and neatly combed brown hair. He had a calm manner that camouflaged a lot of energy. He paced back and forth while he talked.

"We in the West," he said, "like stability. We like organization. We like international order. We like predictability. You know who doesn't? Vladimir Putin. What Putin likes," he said, "are failed states and chaos and so-called frozen conflicts. He likes disorder. Frozen conflicts are havens for criminal groups and terrorists. Putin likes that. He is trying to create a frozen conflict with Ukraine so that, in the end, he turns Ukraine into a failed state."

The major paced from left to right. "Putin likes the countries on his periphery to be unstable," he said. "The more unstable those nations are, the more comfortable he feels. It's not just Ukraine; it's Lithuania, Latvia, Estonia, Moldova, Azerbaijan. He wants all of these countries to be off balance, and he wants them not to look to or trust the West. He wants them to look to Russia."

I rarely mentioned it at the State Department, but I had met Putin and spent several hours with him in 2007. We had made him Person of the Year at *Time* because he had, as I wrote, "brought Russia back to the table of world power." But also because of something more mundane: he had agreed to an interview. I had talked to Henry Kissinger before going, and he had said to me, "You will be surprised at what little effort he will make to charm you."

In fact, Putin was an immensely frosty presence—cold air seemed to emanate from him. The official interview took place at his dacha outside Moscow. He was five hours late. The interview almost ended as soon as it had begun, as our first question got the year of his birth wrong. Putin became irritated and complained about the error. I apologized for our mistake, and he calmed down.

It was in that interview that Putin talked passionately about how the end of the Soviet Union was "the greatest tragedy of the 20th century." After the fall of the Soviet Union, "25 million Soviet citizens who were ethnic Russians found themselves beyond the borders of new Russia . . . their historical motherland without any economic means." He asked, "Is that not a tragedy?" While he seemed fatalistic about it, the subtext of everything he said indicated that what he wanted to do most of all was put the Soviet Union back together again. He derogated American exceptionalism, said NATO was an anachronism, extolled Russia as a beacon of free speech, complained that Americans think Russians are savages who "just climbed down from the trees," and talked about how Russia never supports candidates in other people's elections.[10] From first to last he seemed angry, and much of his anger seemed to come from resentment of the United States, as though all of Russia's disappointments—and his own—were caused by America. He said America interfered in Russia's affairs, but Russia did not interfere in the U.S.'s. It was a cornerstone of Russian policy, he insisted, that nations should not interfere in other nations' affairs.

Russia's annexation of Crimea, the major said, was extremely popular. While we in the West saw this as a violation of another nation's sovereignty, he said, "Russians see Crimea and Ukraine as part of Russia from time immemorial. Putin always points out that the Russian Orthodox Church was born in Kiev. Internally, Putin played it perfectly. Annexing Crimea was a way of changing their narrative. People saw it as restarting Russian history after the breakup of the Soviet Union. He was showing Russian strength on the world stage. Russia was acting like a superpower again. It fit all his narratives."

Ukraine, the major said, is not as easy as Crimea. He can't do to Ukraine as a whole what he did to Crimea. "It is too big, too diverse, too European. What he can do, though, is try to make it so dysfunctional that people will yearn for the Russian father to hold it together. That's what he's doing in eastern Ukraine. He has his fifth columnists there. The loss of the Donetsk and Luhansk regions of Ukraine deprives Ukraine of almost 20 percent of its GDP. It is putting Ukraine in a downward economic spiral. He wants Ukraine to fail. That would be a success for Putin.

"This sounds strange to Western ears," he said, "but Putin and Russia's leadership do not believe the West's model of secular modernism will inevitably win. Putin hates this Western rules-based order that we talk about. He sees Russia as a counterpoint to the Western order and has positioned it as a conservative alternative that challenges the Western order. He sees the West as weak and undisciplined and decadent. He is using his information operations to accelerate the decline of the West.

"When it comes to messaging," he said. "Nothing much has changed. The Russian are better at this than anyone. They've been working on it as a part of their conventional warfare since Lenin. We knew this during the Cold War and we responded. Our work during the Cold War was a whole-of-government effort. Today, there's nothing like that. We do operations well. We do tactics well. We have lines of effort, but no strategy."

It was humbling. The Russians had been thinking and writing about information war for decades. It was embedded in their military doctrines. There seemed to be an analogy between failed states and disinformation: Putin wanted failed truth. In the grand scheme of things, it was easier to disrupt things than it was to keep them together. And all Putin wanted to do was disrupt, upset, sow chaos. Putin's strategy seemed more thought-out than anything we were doing or even contemplating. I had talked with military colleagues who believed that information war should be part of U.S. military doctrine and that there ought to be information-warfare specialists and officers. But that was still a long way off. The idea that our little counter-Russian messaging group was going to tip the balance was ludicrous.

We're Not the Audience

I never knew Jack's last name. Or even whether Jack was his real first name. I doubt that it was. Jack was a senior intelligence officer whose specialty was violent extremism and terrorism. He was my lead intelligence briefer on ISIS. Jack was about five feet seven and always impeccably tailored in a muted way—shirts and ties with subtle patterns that perfectly matched. His skin was olive, and his salt-and-pepper hair was always neatly combed and parted. He was never agitated in any way.

Every week, he would bring together a few intelligence analysts to brief me on ISIS. The sessions involved a combination of services, but always the CIA and the National Counterterrorism Center, with which we worked on counter-ISIS messaging. At the beginning of my time at State, I'd had an intelligence meeting every week. There was a lot of interesting stuff—the background of an uprising in Chile, an intercepted call between a foreign minister and an industrialist, the origins of right-wing parties in Europe. It was like having a classified newspaper that I could peruse. But it felt random. After a couple of months, I asked to have briefings that focused on the two things I really wanted to know about: ISIS and Russia.

My early sessions with Jack concentrated on the differences between al-Qaeda and ISIS. The intelligence community knew a lot about the theological disagreements between the two groups, the distinctions between Salafism and ISIS's ideology. There was a debate as to whether ISIS was truly religious or not. The intelligence folks saw it primarily as a terrorist organization whose leadership consisted of brutal former officers under Saddam Hussein who were true believers but used Islam as a convenient cover. But I wasn't a theologian; I wanted to know how ISIS worked as a messaging entity and how it differed from al-Qaeda in that regard. Why was ISIS so much better?

Jack was succinct. "Al-Qaeda was centralized," he said. "ISIS is a distributed network. Al-Qaeda is Yahoo. ISIS is Google. Sometimes ISIS's audience is us; mostly it's not. They have a variety of audiences. Sometimes it's the moderate opposition. Sometimes it's potential fighters. But they are smart about information warfare. They video themselves killing people and show that before they invade a town. They want the towns to open their doors to them and they do. That's information warfare."

What set ISIS apart from al-Qaeda was the declaration of the Caliphate. That, he said, got the attention of Sunnis around the world. Al-Qaeda had never wanted actual territory. "Al-Qaeda was an idea," he said. "ISIS wants to be a state. Al-Qaeda said every Muslim had to reconsider coexistence with the West. ISIS said there can be no coexistence. It's been less than a century since the end of the last Caliphate. That's yesterday to them." Jack said someone referred to ISIS as Sunni Zionists, and it's a pretty apt description. They believe the Caliphate should be the home of all Muslims. The idea of the Caliphate is like a Club Med for Muslims, a place where they can take their children, where women can meet a husband.

The recent fall of Mosul, an Iraqi city of more than a million people, he said, was a huge blow to the Iraqi government and a significant victory for ISIS. ISIS fighters were outnumbered by as much as 20 to 1 by Iraqi security forces. He said it completely confirmed their narrative. Their victory was accompanied by thousands of tweets by both ISIS itself and ISIS fanboys. And, he said, don't expect the people of Mosul to turn on them—they see ISIS as brutal; they don't see them as corrupt. They see the Iraqi government as corrupt *and* brutal. Iraqi Sunnis, he said, fear Iranian Shia militias more than they fear ISIS.

Remember, Jack said, most of the content they create is not for us; they have different audiences. The violent stuff—the beheadings—that's for the West. To scare us. But, he continued, they adhere to Islamic law in not showing the actual beheading itself—that would be *haram* and in violation of the Koran. Most of their content is in Arabic, and it's for other Sunni Muslims in the Middle East and for potential recruits. We think we're the target. We're not.

ISIS's other enemy, he said, is the Shia. "ISIS says true Islam has been besmirched by the West. But for them, the even greater threat to Islam than the West is the Shia. They see the Shia as trying to create their own Caliphate—a Shia crescent, they call it. America is the far enemy; the Shia are the enemy up close."

He urged me not to discount ISIS's appeal. "For foreign fighters," he said, "this is the good war. Assad is killing more Muslims than anyone else. For them, it's like the Spanish Civil War was once for us. We shouldn't underestimate their appeal to regular Sunnis. They are the bad guys, but to Sunnis, they are *our* bad guys. They are fighting the people who have humiliated us for aeons."

"In classical Islam," he said, "there is the House of Peace, Dar al-Islam, which is the Muslim countries; and the House of War, Dar al-Harb, which is the West, the realm of the unbelievers. Because of globalization, the two houses are much more mixed than ever. ISIS sees this as a threat to Islam."

U.S. officials often argued that ISIS wasn't truly Islamic. Jack was skeptical about us saying who was a Muslim and who was not. CSCC had moved more toward promoting Muslim clerics who were anti-ISIS. But even using clerics was tricky, Jack said. For ISIS, when established, government-supported clerics—especially Saudi imams—came out against them, it only confirmed their narrative of how oppressive Sunni states were trying to repress them and true Islam. ISIS was the underdog. Jack was always dubious about what we gained by messaging against ISIS. Our own campaign against ISIS, he said with a smile, was probably their best recruiting tool.[11]

Question More

The Ukraine Task Force continued to enthusiastically push back against Russian propaganda on social media. Will Stevens was indefatigable. It felt like our efforts had gained some momentum. Every week, I saw the metrics of what they had done, and their engagements, shares, and traffic were all growing.

One day I was going over the statistics with one of my specials, when he said, You should be watching Russia Today. Why? I asked. You've become one of their punching bags, he said with a smile.

There was a monitor in the center of my office on a side table, and I switched the channel from CNN to RT. Over the next few days, I saw what he was talking about. Along with their regular pillorying of Jen Psaki ("Psaki's 10 Most Embarrassing Fails") and Toria Nuland (they incessantly referred to the Russian-hacked phone call in which she had said, "Fuck the EU"), I would see my picture on the screen, with the announcer talking about Under Secretary of State Stengel's "Russophobic" behavior and my enthusiastic embrace of anti-Russian propaganda.[12] Alluding to my years as editor of *Time*, RT described me as being part of the "chorus of Russian-hating Western media." They played a clip of me saying, at a BBG board meeting, how "sophisticated Russian messaging was on social media. Which is something that we should own." Ever since I had started speaking out and tweeting about the Russian annexation of Crimea, I had become part of their regular cast of State Department villains.

I had first noticed RT in 2013 when I saw bus shelter ads for Larry King in midtown Manhattan, but I didn't know what it was. I was still editor of *Time*, and I remember thinking, Oh, Larry King has landed at some obscure cable channel called RT that I'll never watch. I didn't know what RT stood for—or if it stood for anything at all. I was like the consumer who didn't realize that KFC was short for Kentucky Fried Chicken.

But now, in 2014, RT had been rebranded by Russia's annexation of Crimea. Russia's actions in Crimea and Ukraine had made RT "must see" television for me, and frankly, it was a revelation. First of all, it was *entertaining*. RT resembled a low-rent Fox News with fewer blondes, more conspiracy-theorists, and a pro-Kremlin disposition. It used all the traditional tricks of good tabloid TV: attractive anchors, colorful graphics, wacky guests, sensational chyrons ("Is America the world's biggest terrorist?"), and ominous music. Its motto was "Question more," and the whole tone was conspiratorial, antiestablishment, sly. The station's attitude—reflected by every anchor, every "correspondent," every guest—was, *Things are not what they seem.* They covered the Occupy Wall Street movement as if it were a Vietnam-era protest. They treated the Jade Helm military exercise in Texas as a harbinger of martial law. They did dramatic coverage of police violence against African Americans. They had a show hosted by Julian Assange, whose first guest was the leader of Hezbollah.

I got to know their tricks and tropes. Their guests were "experts" without expertise, pundits from organizations with names that sounded similar to those of legitimate organizations (they had someone from the International Relations Council, for example—the reputable one is the Council on Foreign Relations), and "academics" from universities that you'd never heard of. They had a bench of regulars who claimed 9/11 was an inside job, that AIDS was an invention of big pharma, and that the "Zionist financial-industrialist complex" was behind every war on the planet. I turned it on one day to see how they were covering an anti-Putin march in Moscow, and they were showing a documentary about racism in America.

The annexation of Crimea and Russia's incursions into Ukraine were a constant subject. RT was enthusiastically pro-Russia. Every host and anchor praised Putin's dynamic leadership and accused the U.S. of fomenting discord in Ukraine. On one show, someone identified as an "ex-US intel officer" accused the U.S. Agency for International Development, the National Endowment for Democracy, and George Soros of instigating a coup in Ukraine.

When Russia Today was launched in 2005, Vladimir Putin himself said its mission was not only to provide a fair image of Russia around the world but also to "break the Anglo-Saxon monopoly on global information."[13] Yes, that is an actual quote from Putin at the launch. Putin tapped a 25-year-old reporter and producer named Margarita Simonyan to be the first head of Russia Today. She was sharp and combative, understood TV, and spoke excellent English from her year as a State Department–sponsored high-school exchange student in Bristol, New Hampshire. It was as if Fox's Roger Ailes were reincarnated in a 25-year-old Russian woman from the Black Sea. Like Ailes she understood something basic about the infotainment industry: the controversy machine always trumped the reality machine.

Russia Today was ambitious and had an estimated annual budget of $300 million. In addition to the American-based English-language service, they started an Arabic service and a Spanish one. They also had plans for a French one. They also launched a radio and online service called Sputnik.[14]

In 2009, Russia Today rebranded itself as RT. The idea was to focus less on Russia, and become more of an international broadcaster along the lines of the BBC. At the time, Simonyan said, "Who is interested in watching news from Russia all day long?"[15] The American service became more international and more U.S.-focused. They launched advertising campaigns in print, online, and on air. They had ads on CNN. One ad plastered on New York City bus shelters featured an image of George W. Bush in front of the "Mission Accomplished" banner with the headline "This Is What Happens When There Is No Second Opinion."[16] As Simonyan said at the time of RT's relaunch: "No one shows objective reality. The Western media are not objective, reality-based news services. People don't believe you anymore."

I asked for some research on RT and an intelligence briefing. No surprise, but RT grossly exaggerated the size of its audience. RT claimed it had a global reach of 700 million people across more than 100 countries, including 85 million in the U.S. This was a classic marketing ploy—yes, it could reach 700 million people if every person in the world who could potentially access RT did so. In the U.S., RT's audience was too small for Nielsen to measure, meaning fewer than 30,000 people a day actually tuned in. The NSC had been impressed that RT had more than a billion page views on YouTube, way more than CNN. Yes, true, but more than 80 percent of their top 100 videos showed natural disasters, violent crimes, or horrific car accidents. By far, their most popular video was the dazzling footage of the meteor that landed in the Russian Urals in 2013.[17]

I had taken to mentioning some little tidbit from RT at the 8:30, and I could see the Secretary get steamed about it. One day he said, We need to do something about it. I fed his speechwriters some lines about RT, and when Kerry took the unusual step of speaking at the top of the State Department's regular briefing to give Russia a stern warning about Ukraine, he also accused Russia of masterminding a disinformation campaign around Ukraine led by Russia Today.

> In fact, the propaganda bullhorn that is the state-sponsored Russia Today program has been deployed to promote President Putin's fantasy about what is playing out on the ground. They almost spend full time devoted to this effort to propagandize and to distort what is happening or not happening in Ukraine.[18]

In reaction to Kerry's condemnation, RT requested an official response from the State Department substantiating his claims. The Secretary asked me to write a State Department blog post—we called it a "DipNote"—that would censure RT for what it was doing and try to explain the difference between journalism and propaganda.

My blogpost—"Russia Today's Disinformation Campaign,"—argued that the state-supported media entity was a key player in Moscow's global propaganda campaign. I wrote that as a former editor of *Time* I understood the difference between news, opinion, and propaganda.

> Propaganda is the deliberate dissemination of information
> that you know to be false or misleading in order to
> influence an audience . . . Opinions, however odious, are
> defensible speech in a way that false claims are not. RT is a
> distortion machine, not a news organization . . . And when
> propaganda poses as news, it poses real danger and gives a
> green light to violence.

I affirmed that the United States had no intention of taking RT off the air the way Moscow had ended the broadcasting license of Voice of America. Even RT's propaganda, I said, was protected by the First Amendment.[19]

Within hours, Margarita Simonyan responded with a post of her own. This was accompanied by a three-minute video calling me a "state-supported propagandist."

> Mr. Richard Stengel, the US Under Secretary of State who
> wrote such an impassioned "takedown" of RT in the US
> State Department blog, did get one thing right. Propaganda
> IS the deliberate dissemination of information that you
> know to be false or misguided. And boy, does Mr. Stengel
> make a valiant attempt at propagandizing, because anyone
> would be hard-pressed to cram more falsehoods into a
> hundred words.

Ms. Simonyan went on to fact-check my assertions, and did an excellent job of it. Indeed, her refutation of my claims is more nuanced than my original argument.

The reason you're seeing citations of sources right here, in the text, is so that it cannot be labeled as another "propaganda" piece full of RT's own "false" reporting. Or does Mr. Stengel consider all media organizations that report inconvenient facts that challenge his reality to be propaganda outlets? It is very disappointing that a person of his position knows so little of the reality of the situation in Ukraine, but it certainly explains a lot about the state of US foreign policy.

Facts are facts, Mr. Stengel. It's too bad you can't get your own straight.[20]

Touché. Her takedown of my takedown made me rethink my definition of "propaganda." "Propaganda" is not necessarily false information; it can be factually correct information trying to promote a point of view. In fact, using factually correction information to promote a point of view was not a bad description of public diplomacy.

Secretary Kerry had tweeted a link to the piece saying, "Important read from U/S @Stengel—sets record straight on disinformation."

As ever, there was a flurry of posts by Russian trolls. One tweet, from someone named "Avas Oblomov," caught my eye.

@JohnKerry @Stengel. The electric chair is waiting for you both and your president

Nice.

A Modest Proposal

I got a note from John Allen asking me if I was willing to jointly host a "ministerial" with him in Kuwait. I was still getting used to all the diplomatic terminology, and I wasn't quite sure what a "ministerial" was. So I asked Jen, my chief of staff.

"It's a big f------ deal, that's what it is," she said.

She explained the different categories of international meetings. There are the leader meetings, like NATO summits and the U.N. General Assembly, which are for heads of state. At the next level down are ministerials, which are for foreign ministers and foreign secretaries. Then there are sub-ministerials, which include director-general–level meetings; and below that, the working-level staff meetings.

With the President's imprimatur, General Allen had invited the ministers from all the countries we wanted to join the anti-ISIS coalition, including all the Gulf states and our other Middle Eastern allies as well as NATO countries. He said that as cohost, I could use the meeting to recruit other countries to be part of the messaging coalition.

My plan was to make a couple of stops in the Middle East before going to Kuwait. I wanted to get a better sense of Middle East media and how amenable they might be to helping with counter-ISIS messaging. In Dubai, I would meet with the leadership of the big Arab news channels, as well as the UAE's deputy foreign minister, before going to Kuwait City for the ministerial.

Dubai is the largest city in the United Arab Emirates. It is also the most relaxed and Western of Arab cities. The clubs and hotels serve alcohol, and most women do not wear a veil. On my second night there, I had dinner with the head of a Middle East news channel in one of the city's towering glass boxes. We ate in their boardroom at an absurdly long table; fortunately, we were seated across from each other in the middle rather than at either end. It was just the two of us, but we had half a dozen waiters and endless courses of food. Bahz, as we will call him, was in his 40s, wore a beautiful bespoke pin-striped suit, and had a warm smile. His English was colloquial and perfect.

"Arab TV has undergone a transformation," he said. "In 10 years we've gone from a few dozen channels to over 1,000. And these 1,000 channels collectively lose $5 billion. Why is that? Because they are subsidized by governments and billionaires. But even so, there is a giant fight over mindshare. You should know that there has been a relative decline in the popularity of American content. Before, there was no choice. Only American movies and TV. But now, there are Turkish soap operas. There's Bollywood and Nollywood and Lebanese dramas and Jordanian shows—there are even Russian game shows and reality-TV shows."

Then he switched to news. "Here's the problem with Arab news media. It thrives on conflict. Wherever there is conflict, we amplify it. Al Jazeera is the most watched, but only trusted by half. It is the Qatari Muslim Brotherhood channel and the channel of the street. Al Arabiya is the Saudi channel, and Sky News Arabia is the UAE channel. What most people watch and still trust are the state-run channels, Egypt 1, Jordan TV, LBC in Lebanon. They are still depended on."

What I wanted to talk to him about was how his channel and the others covered ISIS. From all the research we had done, we thought most of the Arab channels depicted ISIS in a neutral way. I told him that we thought the coverage needed to be tougher.

"Ah, well," he said, and here his tone changed. "Let me ask you a question. What are you doing about Syria and Iran? Those are the real problems in the Middle East. ISIS is just your unfinished business in Iraq. You're attacking them now because two Americans had their heads cut off. Assad has killed tens of thousands. In Iraq, you put Malaki in charge, and he crushed the Sunnis and let in Iran. Iran is trying to create a Shia Caliphate. This coalition you are forming, fine. But it will not have the support of the people in the Middle East. They see the U.S. as the cause of the problem, not the solution."

It was a broadside. I listened and did not attempt to rebut him—even if I could have. I'd heard this refrain from every person I talked to during the trip. I don't think one person mentioned to me the Israeli-Palestine conflict, which the Arab world once saw as the heart of the problem in the Middle East—and Americans still did. The rise of ISIS and Islamic extremism made the Israeli struggle less central, while the calamity of the Syrian civil war had pushed the problems of Palestine to the margins.

On my final afternoon in Dubai, I visited the Ministry of Foreign Affairs to see the official who Washington could help in creating the messaging coalition. Let's call him Dr. Ahmed. The ministry was in the center of Dubai, in a towering modern building with a light-filled atrium. I knew that thousands of people worked there, but I barely saw a soul in the lobby. I was ushered into Dr. Ahmed's immaculate office, which didn't seem to have a piece of paper in it anywhere. Dr. Ahmed was wearing a pristine white *thawb* and had a stubby beard and a twinkle in his eye. His soft brown loafers were made by Tod's.

I was planning to launch into what we were doing to counter ISIS and our plan for a messaging coalition, but Dr. Ahmed was one step ahead of me. He knew about General Allen and the lines of effort. He knew that I was leading the messaging effort. He knew a lot of things. He told me he would be glad to help, but first he wanted to paint a picture for me.

"You Americans are winning but losing," he said, with a hint of a British accent. "You are winning on the battlefield but losing the ideological and the information war. It's a bit of a paradox, you know. Even when you win on the military battlefield, that just feeds ISIS's information war. Look, they say, the Western bullies are crushing us. You will always be Goliath. I'm afraid"—and here he smiled—"you are never going to be seen as liberators."

He was candid about the problem. "We need to do more. This is an Islamic problem, not a Western one. But not everyone wants to help," he said. He asked me about CSCC, which he also seemed to know about. I said it was a work in progress.

"You know, it does very little, and what it does is not good. It's clumsy. There are Sunni clerics with more than a million followers on Twitter. You don't even register compared with them," he said.

We started talking about the ministerial that would take place in two days. I wanted to get his thoughts and enlist his help. But he was lukewarm about the meeting; he thought that the right people wouldn't be there and that the Arab countries weren't eager to help us. But I could see he wanted to help me. He leaned forward in his chair. "Why don't you call together a steering committee on how to message against ISIS? It would be the U.S. and a few Arab allies. The purpose is to figure out a social media strategy." Then he paused. "Don't try to make it too broad. Don't make it too ambitious. Keep it small."

This was the first of many times when Dr. Ahmed would propose something for me to do for which he didn't want any credit. He laughed and said that in the Arab world, no one wanted to raise his hand in class. Give this a try, he said, and I will help you.

The ministerial was to be held at a downtown hotel in Kuwait City. I got in the night before and found the hotel had upgraded me. The hotel manager, a short and friendly Kuwaiti, led me up to a gaudy and over-the-top suite: tons of pillows and gold leaf. He urged me to pick up a copy of the hotel magazine sitting on the marble coffee table. On the cover was a picture of a young woman in a black gown addressing the Harvard commencement. "That's my daughter," he said. She had been the valedictorian, and her speech was about the need to build civil society in the Middle East. That was American soft power.

The Kuwaitis are sticklers for courtesy. A delegation came to fetch General Allen and me in the morning and escorted us to the ballroom. Yes, this was a "ministerial," but there were no actual foreign ministers coming. Then, this morning, the Kuwaitis got word from the Emiratis that Dr. Ahmed was indeed coming. This caused a stir because Ahmed *is* a minister, and suddenly the other Arab delegations started beefing up their delegations with higher-level officials.

By the time we sat down, it was perfectly organized. Forty of us were seated at a giant U-shaped table. Every delegation but ours wore *thawbs* and keffiyehs. General Allen opened the proceedings. He greeted everyone thus: "Highnesses and Excellencies." I couldn't help smiling, but no one else did. At first, I thought he was being ironic, but there's not much irony in diplomacy. As I was to learn, it was a very useful way to begin. With all the names of foreign dignitaries one had to learn, the best shortcut was simply to nod your head and say, "Your Excellency." Even if the diplomat did not have the rank that merited "Your Excellency," no government official in human history has minded being called that.

General Allen was a natural diplomat. He complimented all the Arab nations on what they had already done to help in the fight against ISIS. He was careful to say neither that it was "our fight" nor that it was "your fight"—but that it was a struggle that engaged anyone with any sense of morality or religious belief.

Our co-chair from Kuwait had the opposite of John's booming voice: he spoke in a barely audible mumble. I glanced over the day's agenda; I saw that every category recapitulated every other category. This is how most diplomatic gatherings are structured. Everyone gets a chance to speak on every subject.

When the co-chair finished, he began calling on the representatives of each nation attending. Each delegate had a prepared text that he read regardless of what the agenda item might be. When it came my time to preside and call on speakers, I did exactly the same thing. That's diplomacy.

I spoke at the end of the first section and told everyone we had a few simple goals: to enhance cooperation in the messaging space, to support the coalition, and to amplify third-party voices. I said that while not everyone would necessarily be able or willing to contribute to the military coalition, everyone could contribute to the messaging coalition.

One problem was that each of the Gulf states had a slightly different reason for disliking ISIS and didn't subscribe to one common narrative. Moreover, they all disliked and feared Iran a whole lot more than they did ISIS. And while ISIS's popularity in the Gulf was in the single digits, American popularity wasn't all that much higher, about 20 percent. Diplomats are politicians too.

Dr. Ahmed arrived about an hour and 15 minutes late. Big entourage. He came over and greeted me with a big smile and a theatrical hug. He then leaned over and whispered into my ear, "Let us do a 15-minute pull-aside at the break." Pull-aside is diplomatspeak for a private talk.

At the end of the morning session—at which he spoke briefly— there was a half-hour break. We trooped up to Ahmed's room which, for size and opulence, put mine to shame. He sat down on an elaborate couch and patted the space next to him. He launched right into it. "I have a modest proposal," he said. What did I think of the idea of a joint U.S.-UAE counter-ISIS messaging hub? "We would build it and pay for it, and you would contribute some staff. We could do it in Abu Dhabi, and we could launch it in a few months. It could then be expanded to a select few of the coalition, but not everybody.

"What do you think?" he said.

Well, I loved the idea. And in very undiplomatic fashion, I told him so.

What I learned and came to appreciate about Dr. Ahmed in particular and the UAE in general was that they wanted to get things done and didn't care about who got the credit. Strike that—they didn't actually want to get the credit. In many ways, they were the opposite of the U.S.: we always wanted the credit even when we didn't do the work. Ahmed wanted to do the work and give us the credit. He called it the *U.S.*-UAE hub.

What excited me about this is that it could be a model for how we could do all our counter-ISIS messaging. If we were not credible messengers, let's partner with those who were. The idea that the American voice had to be paramount was American narcissism. The new hub would work with CSCC. It would take some of the burden off our own messaging. If, as my military colleagues liked to say, it took a network to defeat a network, this would be our way of creating one.

Within two days of getting back to Washington, we had a concept note for what we called the *UAE*-U.S. counter-ISIS messaging center.

My Bad

I was a relative latecomer to Twitter. When I was at *Time*, I barely used the platform. But at State, I fell in love with Twitter. I saw its power as a tool for public diplomacy. You could have a conversation with people all over the world. I urged all our ambassadors to get on Twitter and to make sure that as many people as possible were on it at posts. Everyone at State should be a foot soldier in the global information war. Every day, my specials produced a number of tweets that I would choose from. Of course, they were State Department tweets so they were pretty mild, but it was something.

I would also tweet on my own, especially on weekends. As I mentioned, I had started using the #UnitedforUkraine hashtag. I was home one Saturday evening and had just read a couple of stories about how the Russians were misleading people about the crash of Malaysia Airlines

Flight 17. MH17 had been shot down while flying over eastern Ukraine, killing all 298 passengers and crew. It had been hit by a Russian Buk surface-to-air missile fired from an area controlled by Russian-backed separatists.[21] Our own intelligence plus open sources suggested that the Russian military had supplied the missile to the separatists, who had most likely shot down the plane in error. In fact, a leader of the separatists had posted on VKontakte, the Russian version of Facebook, that his forces had shot down what they mistakenly labeled a Ukrainian military plane.[22]

But the Russians had embarked on a disinformation campaign to shift the blame anywhere but on themselves. A story by the Russian State News agency RIA Novosti quoted an eyewitness as saying the plane had been shot down by Ukrainian fighter jets.[23] A Russia Today story quoted a Spanish air traffic controller in Kiev named Carlos who also said the plane had been shot down by the Ukrainian air force.[24] (No other news organization could find Carlos.) Russian outlets even promoted a wild conspiracy theory that the plane had been a U.S.-created decoy loaded with explosives and dead bodies so that America and the West could accuse Russia of being behind the shoot-down. Russia's messaging approach was like the old Soviet artillery strategy, to fire *tous azimuts*—a French expression meaning to shoot in every direction all at once. Their goal was to confuse, not convince.

I was irritated by what I had been reading and grabbed my iPad and composed a tweet. I thought we were not outspoken enough in indicting Russia for what was an act of mass terrorism. On my iPad I tapped out: "Critical for a full, credible and unimpeded intl investigation of crash. Urge Russia to honor it's commitment."

I've always believed in copy editors, and the *Time* copydesk would have caught my mistaken use of the contraction *it's*. If only that had been my sole mistake! Anger and Twitter are a dangerous combination, especially for a government official.

After I had written out the text, I went to put in the hashtag #UnitedforUkraine. On Twitter, as you type in a hashtag, the service uses autofill to give you options. I started typing #Unitedfor . . . I was still pretty new to Twitter and didn't really understand autofill or that there might be other #Unitedfor hashtags besides the one for Ukraine. In fact, there were a number of such hashtags, but I wasn't paying attention and just hit the first one that came up: #UnitedforGaza.

So, I tweeted out what I'd written above with the hashtag #UnitedforGaza. I didn't think any more about it until I started getting dozens and then hundreds of angry responses. Many of them alluded to my editorship at *Time*, where I had, occasionally, been accused of being biased against Israel.

Sadegh Gorbani (@GhorbaniSadegh) tweeted:

> Deputy of @JohnKerry & Time's veteran Rick @Stengel tweeted #UnitedForGaza in apparent goof (the tweet is still there).

Mr. Aye Dee tweeted:

> I don't think this is explicit enough, why not go full throttle and simply go all out by saying #IStandWithHamas.

Sandy (@RightGlockMom) replied:

> Wow, cat's out of the bag, eh? Thousands of screen captures, no doubt. (Go back to Time).

As the complaints started coming in, I thought I needed to do something and then, well, I compounded the error. I tweeted:

Earlier tweet with wrong hashtag was a mistake. My bad.

Well, that provoked a torrent of replies, some of them highly amusing. Rachel Ward (@RachelWard301) replied:

"My bad." That's something a 12 yr old would say. Shameful that you represent this country.

Someone who called himself Rabbi MacBones wrote:

He says "my bad" like we are chillin' on the corner.

I did let Jen know about it, and she said, Just don't do anything, *please*. That was her usual advice in a crisis. Her attitude was, Anything you do is likely to make it worse.

The online furor was accompanied by a bunch of news stories that took delight in my mistake. The *Washington Times*: "'My Bad': State Dept. Official Apologizes for #UnitedForGaza Tweet."[25] The piece said, "Twitter users weren't buying Mr. Stengel's apology." *The Forward*: "Oops! Rookie Diplomat Rick Stengel Sorry for #Unitedfor-Gaza Tweet."[26] Twitchy: "'What a Jackass.'"[27]

And then there was Breitbart News:

A senior member of the U.S. Department of State tweeted his support for Hamas on Sunday, but after a barrage of complaints he soon deleted the tweet and apologized for his unwise action, saying it was just a "mistake" and that he accidentally tweeted the "wrong hashtag." . . . It is especially hard to believe Stengel's retraction in light of comments from his boss Secretary of State John Kerry, who was heard slamming Israel this weekend for its acts of self defense.[28]

Within minutes, my mistake had become fodder for all manner of Russian trolls and bots. It was a swarm. The Ukraine Task Force had gotten up to 30 or 40 tweets a day—Russian trolls and bots did that in a minute.

In a small way, the dustup over my tweet was a model for how the Russians operated. The point wasn't really to mock a mistake or an individual, it was to divert attention from the actual issue: Russian culpability in the shooting down of a civilian airliner. I don't think I saw one tweet, in the back-and-forth over my mistake, that had anything to say about how Russia had been responsible for the murder of 298 innocent people. That was their goal all along. Mission accomplished.

Blundering On

Early one morning in the winter of 2015, not long after the "#UnitedforGaza" incident, I was awakened by a call from David Wade, the Secretary's chief of staff.

"CSCC tweeted that Austin Tice was dead," he said.

Austin Tice was a former Marine captain turned freelance journalist who had been kidnapped in Syria in 2012. He had worked for McClatchy, the *Washington Post*, and CBS.[29] He had been one of a handful of Western journalists on the ground in Syria. We didn't know where he was. We didn't know whether he was alive or dead. Americans held hostage abroad were a deeply sensitive issue. It was mainly handled by the NSC, but the Secretary and his chief of staff had taken a deep interest.

"The family is very upset," David said. I told him I would call them once we got it sorted out.

Here's the actual tweet CSCC sent on New Year's Eve:

> Entering 2015, taking time to honor some of terror's many victims and their families—RIP.

The problem was, it included a picture of Austin Tice.[30]

I got a quick update from intelligence folks that nothing had changed with Tice's status. Apparently a contractor had repurposed a tweet about those whose lives had been disrupted by extremism and converted it to a tweet commemorating victims. The first thing we needed to do was tweet out an apology. I asked a staffer to draw one up. It was simple and straightforward. A little clumsy, but fine. Let's get it out.

But I hadn't reckoned with the clearance process. The email in which I received the 140-character text of the apology had more than 30 names on it, almost all of whom felt some need to weigh in. It had been cleared by the Middle East bureau, by public affairs, by consular affairs, but legal had balked. They were objecting to the use of Austin Tice's name, arguing that it would make the department liable. Well, we'd made a mistake, and it seemed like a clear call to me. (I knew a little bit about liability in publishing.) I told CSCC to post it and that I would push through the objections.

Only once the apology was posted did I feel comfortable calling the Tice family. I had been told that Austin's mother was emotional about the mistake. I got the father, Mr. Tice. He said his wife was too upset to come to the phone. I apologized for the mistake, said that it was inexcusable and that people at State were upset about it. He was calm and gracious. He said he'd seen the apology and was grateful for it. He said he believed that his son was still alive and that he appreciated the support of the department. He wondered whether mistakes like this were due to the bureaucracy. I wondered whether he'd ever worked in government.

It was another reminder that not only was CSCC outnumbered, outgunned, and often outwitted by the digital jihadis, but we often were our own worst enemy. We—and I mean government—were just not very good at this kind of thing. There's an old saying in journalism, "We're faster than anyone better than us, and better than anyone faster." CSCC was slower and worse.

What we also realized by this time was that ISIS was a distributed network. Like the Russians, they had numbers and scale. And like the Russians, they seemed to get a few themes from their central media office. Our intelligence as well as open sources like the Brookings Institution estimated that there were 3,000 to 5,000 hyperactive digital jihadis who were responsible for most of ISIS's social media.

It was also around this time that Alberto Fernandez, the head of CSCC, told me that he would be retiring. I had originally asked him to stay on for an extra year. I hadn't had much choice. When we had posted the job and asked for résumés from the State Department—an organization of more than 50,000 people, nearly 15,000 of whom were foreign service officers—we got exactly one applicant. One.

But now, CSCC was ramping up and getting a lot of attention from the NSC. We had a chance to bring in someone who could take the organization to the next level. When we posted the job, the personnel system didn't do much better. There were a handful of names, only one of whom was interested in interviewing for the job. She was a retired foreign service officer who didn't speak Arabic, didn't have much experience in the Middle East, and said she had never been on

Twitter. I reached out to a number of foreign service officers I thought might be a good fit. Everyone had the same reaction. CSCC was still an unknown, a possible detour, or even a dead end.

From the beginning, the NSC had not been happy with CSCC's leadership. And now that Fernandez was leaving, they had a candidate to replace him—Ben Rhodes's candidate, a young guy who had worked for him named Rashad Hussein. He seemed like a dream choice: a Muslim American lawyer who was born in Wyoming, who had worked at the NSC on counterterrorism. He was also an envoy to the Organization of Islamic Cooperation. And he was a *hafiz*, the Arabic term for someone who had memorized the 6,236 verses in the Koran.

I had long thought that having a Muslim-American lead CSCC was a good idea. When I talked to Hussein, he was eager for the job. He said he would be a great ambassador for CSCC around the world. As an Arabic-speaker and a *hafiz*, he could talk to religious leaders and political ones. He would build up the messaging coalition. He talked about how he wanted to create a future for his two young children in a world that did not have such a hateful group. He said he wouldn't rest until the battle was won. He got the job.

Recalibrating on Russia

I talked a fair amount about the Ukraine Task Force in the 8:30 meeting. I talked about it enough that one day Secretary Kerry said he'd like to visit it and give an "attaboy" to the folks working there. That didn't happen every day at the State Department. I knew the staff would be excited, but I also told the Secretary that while we were up against a large problem, the Task Force was a very small operation, about 14 people sitting in front of laptops in a gray windowless office in the bowels of the State Department. No problem, he said.

For the most part, Secretary Kerry stayed in Mahogony Row on the seventh floor. He had his own elevator from the parking garage to his office. That morning, we had a guide to take us to the Task Force office, as I didn't want to get us all lost. I briefed Kerry while we were walking—skipping a bit to keep up—and, as ever, he was a quick study.

At that time, Kerry was engaged almost every day in talking to Russian foreign minister Lavrov about Ukraine and Crimea. Kerry's view of Putin and Russia was nuanced. I've mentioned that people at the White House saw Kerry as being "soft" on Russia, to use a phrase from the Cold War. They thought he was a little too eager to talk to them. But Kerry thought that it was possible to be tough with the Russians and still talk to them. It's not that he wasn't frustrated by their intransigence and deception; he just thought that you'd get more from them if you treated them the way they wanted to be treated—as a great power—even if they weren't one. When President Obama pointedly described Russia as a "regional power," that was the ultimate insult to Putin.

At the 8:30, Kerry often expressed frustration with Russia and Putin. He thought they were never straight with us. But he was able to empathize with how Putin saw the world. I remember him once saying that almost every time he met with Putin, Putin would bring up the same things: the expansion of NATO to the east, beyond what NATO had originally envisioned; the deployment of missiles and the stationing of American troops in NATO countries. These nations are on my border, he would say. How do you expect me to react? Putin always maintained that the West took advantage of a weakened Russia after the fall of the Soviet Union.

When it came to Russia, Kerry thought that there were those in the State Department and at the White House who undermined his efforts. I remember him once saying in exasperation at the 8:30, "We can't have more than one foreign policy on Russia in the Building."

When we got to the Task Force office, he walked into the center of the drab windowless space. Folks were sitting around the wall in front of laptops. For the staff, seeing the Secretary up close was not something that happened every day. Not something that happened *ever*. For them, the seventh floor was like some impossible Mount Olympus that was hidden in the clouds. He had a relaxedness and an informality in small groups that most of them probably had not experienced either. His enthusiasm was palpable.

He said he just wanted to come down and commend everyone. "Rick talks about you all the time," he said. "We need to fight back in this information war." When he said that, he actually pumped his fist. "We need to be proactive in our messaging," he added. "Not just reactive. This problem is not going away, and we will need to grow this." Even though he erred on the side of being diplomatic with the Russians, he understood that we needed to be pushing back in other ways. He knew better than anyone else that the Russians always worked on two tracks with us: undermining the U.S. and talking to us at the same time. And then he started to ask questions in a kind of reportorial way. How many tweets did we do a day? How many did they do? How do we measure the effectiveness of what we're doing?

Will Stevens thanked the Secretary, and like the good leader that he was, called on different members of the team to answer the Secretary's questions. It was definitely a shot in the arm.

They needed it. What I hadn't told the Secretary when we were walking there was that Will's tenure was ending. We had him only until he began his tour in Moscow. He was leaving just when the Task Force was beginning to get the hang of it.

I told Will that if he wanted to break out of his Moscow rotation and stay here to run the Task Force, I could make that happen. But he was eager to head out to Moscow. Going to Moscow was like journeying to the heart of darkness. That's where he wanted to be.

*   *   *

In the weeks after Will left, a lot of the energy went out of the Ukraine Task Force. They posted less on social media. They took fewer risks. Will's energy and refusal-to-take-no-for-an-answer style helped compensate for the reticence of the European bureau and Public Affairs. But as soon as he left, they began pushing to take it over. It's a kind of truism at State—bureaus wanted to control anything that they saw as being in their lane. EUR seemed more interested in having the group support its policy efforts, while Public Affairs wanted oversight on anyone doing any messaging.

Finding Will had been difficult in the first place. I didn't see anyone there who seemed right to take his job. I didn't want to lose any momentum, but at the same time, it would be valuable to pause to figure out how to institutionalize counter-Russian messaging at the department. I'd recently heard one of my colleagues use a favorite military expression: if you're falling, turn it into a dive. Maybe I shouldn't fight EUR and PA, but collaborate with them. If they owned it, they might invest in it.

I went to see Toria Nuland, the assistant secretary for Europe, to talk about it. I suspected that if the group was to be under EUR, she would be more committed to it. She was. The plan that we cobbled together was to rename the Ukraine Task Force the Russia Information Group and find a smart, aggressive person from EUR to run it. Lo and behold, we seemed to have that person sitting right in front of us. Ben Ziff was a public diplomacy deputy assistant secretary whom I had worked with for a while. He was smart, bluff, and passionate about the Russian threat. When he started talking about Russian disinformation, I thought I could see smoke coming out of his ears. The idea was that with someone from EUR running it, the group would get more collaboration from embassies in the region.

Toria's notion for the Russian Information Group was similar to what we were evolving toward with CSCC: to focus more on third-party content and credible voices. It would build on what we had in place—always a good strategy at State. The Task Force was already doing policy playbooks and creating communications toolkits. The new group would also do infographics and other material that partners could use. Again, picking up learning from CSCC, the idea was to do less of the scorching anti-Putin content and more of the straight, just-the-facts stuff that would still offer a contrast with Russian disinformation.

We also wanted to increase the number of Russian-language spokespeople around the world and in Washington. Having spokespeople who knew Arabic had proved valuable in counter-ISIS messaging. It gave us credibility. Now we needed more Russian-speakers. The Russia Information Group would also bring together strategic comms people from our European partners, NATO, the Organization for Security and Co-Operation in Europe, the U.K., France, and Belgium, to coordinate messaging. They would partner with our public diplomacy workshops to help journalists on the periphery. All sensible stuff.

But it was also an acknowledgement of reality: we were small and our adversary was large. We were the guerrilla force, not a role the U.S. government is very good at. Russia's state-supported messaging apparatus was larger and more organized than ISIS's—and even more sophisticated. It was also, paradoxically, more hidden. Direct support for ISIS was a pretty obvious giveaway for someone online. ISIS was a criminal organization. The Russians disguised their content. They adopted personas. They created faux organizations. They tried to sound like Americans. They hid behind the First Amendment.

Once we had negotiated how the groups would work, Nuland and I sent a memo to the Secretary called "Combating Putin's Information

War." It outlined everything that the Russia Information Group would do and ended this way:

> We cannot—and should not—attempt to go head-to-head against Putin's multi-billion-dollar media machine. Our current strategy supports initiatives that are achievable with additional or existing resources, while simultaneously building synergy with allies and partners to create a smart and strategic counterweight to the Kremlin's pervasive and well-resourced disinformation network.[31]

I suppose you could say we had the courage to be modest. No grand schemes. It was a lesson in how to get things done at State: through partnerships, coordination, guidance. It wasn't sexy, but it was reality.

What's in a Name?

Senator Ted Cruz's face came across the television screen in my office. "The President and his administration," Cruz bellowed, "dogmatically refuse to utter the words 'radical Islamic terrorism.' You cannot defeat an enemy if you refuse to acknowledge what it is."[32]

It was February 2015, and we were preparing for the White House Summit on Countering Violent Extremism—a three-day meeting convening local and international partners on what the White House called "community-oriented approaches to counter hateful extremist ideologies that radicalize or incite to violence." In other words, the President wanted to show the nation that he was fighting ISIS and domestic terrorism, but he didn't want to call them Islamic extremists or radical Islamists. Whatever. Fine.

Because of my role in leading the messaging line of the counter-ISIS coalition and CSCC, I was one of the speakers and would also moderate a panel of representatives from Arab countries. It was a good chance to advance the idea of the messaging coalition and introduce our Muslim allies to Rashad Hussein, CSCC's new head.

In the run-up to the summit, the media devoted far more time to why the President didn't use the words "Islamic terrorism" than to the actual problem of Islamic terrorism or violent extremism or radical Muslim extremism or whatever the heck you wanted to call it. Every day, my office received some press query about why wasn't it called a Summit Against Muslim Extremism? Isn't that what it is? Fox News was having a field day. Not only were people lambasting the administration for not using the term, but a few Republicans were going further. Senator Lindsey Graham: "We are in a religious war with radical Islamists. When I hear the President of the United States and his chief spokesperson failing to admit that we're in a religious war, it really bothers me." So helpful. This is precisely what ISIS wanted American politicians to say, and what our allies did not want.

It would be hard to claim that the President was ignoring the problem: he had used the words "Islam" and "Islamic" and "terrorism" and "terrorist" thousands of times. He just didn't put the words "radical" and "Islamic" and "terrorism" next to each other in that order. Despite the verbal conniptions, the reason for it was pretty simple: our Sunni Arab allies, whom we needed in this fight, abhorred the phrase, believing it blasphemed a whole religion. We were bending over backward to show, as the President put it many times, "We are not at war with Islam." The Bush administration struggled with the same lexical problem and came up with the same phrase: "violent extremism."

I stuck to the party line—and didn't say "Islamic terrorism"—but I also felt it wasn't a big deal either way. It often seemed to me that the cost of the President's twisting himself into a verbal pretzel was greater than the benefit of mollifying our Arab allies. I'd had more than enough evidence already that Muslims in the Middle East thought we were anti-Islam whether or not we used the term "Islamic extremism."

The summit was originally a State Department–sponsored event, and nominally it still was, but once the White House saw a need to show that the President was engaged on this issue, it was 100 percent big-footed by the NSC. The White House was more concerned about the potential for domestic terrorism and pivoted the summit toward homeland matters. That wasn't in my lane. But when the White House throws a party, everyone wants to be there. I was keen that CSCC and our efforts at counter-ISIS messaging get a little love. But it was out of our hands. Even though I paid for the transportation and hotels for all the delegates, the White House managed the event down to the number of minutes each speaker had and what font was on the place settings: Helvetica.

At the time, I was in a bit of hot water. A *New York Times* preview piece about the summit had focused on CSCC. It was part of a wave of stories about how we were getting beaten on social media. The story, "U.S. Intensifies Effort to Blunt ISIS's Message," explained how we were evolving CSCC. Right at the top, the story quoted me as saying, "We're getting beaten on volume, so the only way to compete is by aggregating, curating, and amplifying existing content." Unobjectionable. But the quote that got everyone riled up was this one: "These guys aren't BuzzFeed; they're not invincible on social media."[33] Within the State Department, particularly in Public Affairs, and at the NSC, there was a sense that I was trivializing the problem by comparing ISIS to a website that featured listicles like "15 Poop Horror Stories That Will Make You Feel Better About Yourself." But folks in government didn't realize what a juggernaut BuzzFeed was: almost 100 million monthly users and billions of views across all its platforms.[34] If ISIS—or Russia—was as savvy online as BuzzFeed, then we'd really have a problem.

I had a role on the second day giving short remarks and moderating a panel on counterextremist messaging. Secretary Kerry would
introduce me. There were to be four panelists. The guidance I got from
the White House consisted of how long I should speak (4 minutes), a
script for introducing each of the panelists (2 minutes each), and strict
instructions on how long each panelist should speak (not more than
12 minutes). There were also scheduled "interventions," which was
the term for selected audience members who would speak for no more
than 3 minutes each. In fact, moderating these panels was not actually
moderating: it was adhering to a very detailed set of stage directions
that eliminated any possibility of spontaneity.

Ben Rhodes was writing the President's remarks. I had been in
regular contact with him, and he knew pretty much all that was going
on with CSCC. At an event like this, the President's remarks are treated
like the 10 Commandments. Ben added two things. First, the President
plugged the U.S.-UAE messaging hub. "That's why the United States
is joining, for example, with the UAE to create a new digital communications hub to work with religious and civil society and community
leaders to counter terrorist propaganda," Obama said. I didn't know
this was going to be in the speech. I was sitting next to Dr. Ahmed, and
he leaned over to me and whispered, "Now we really have to do it!"

And second, the President himself announced that Rashad Hussein would be the new head of CSCC.

So many people came up to me afterward to either congratulate
me or ask, "How did you swing that?"

These summits, by their very nature, weren't designed to accomplish
anything. They were about inviting our friends and allies to Washington
and making them feel included. They were about giving everybody a
chance to shine. Everyone got a trophy.

The summit presented another opportunity. So many of the members of the messaging coalition were coming that I decided we should have a messaging meeting. Our Muslim partners were chuffed that Hussein was the new head of CSCC. While CSCC was a management challenge here in the U.S., it was a shiny model for our Arab and European allies. So many asked me, How can we start our own version of CSCC? In fact, we started regularly sending people from CSCC over to our allies to help them figure out how to start their own messaging centers. It became the template for what we were doing with the UAE.

But even with the summit and CSCC's new leader, our allies were still reluctant to step up on the messaging front. Some of it was feeling uncomfortable about social media, and some of it was that they didn't want to stoke the ire of Sunnis who were secretly sympathetic to ISIS. Dr. Ahmed told me to be patient, and then said with a smile, "Maybe you should have hired someone from BuzzFeed, eh?"

Petulance as Policy

I loved talking to exchange students.

They were the most delightful and inspiring aspect of soft power. Exchange students were the clearest, most immediate—and happiest—return on the money American taxpayers were spending on public diplomacy.

Educational exchanges are in fact the largest item in the public diplomacy budget, the biggest single one being the Fulbright Scholarships at $400 million. There were dozens of other programs and many thousands of students.

One of the programs was FLEX (Future Leaders Exchange), which Congress created in 1992 after the breakup of the Soviet Union. The idea was to foster better understanding between the former Soviet republics and the United States. Every year, the State Department offered scholarships for high school students from Armenia, Azerbaijan, Estonia, Georgia, Kazakhstan, Kyrgyzstan, Latvia, Lithuania, Moldova, Montenegro, Poland, Serbia, Turkmenistan, Ukraine, and Russia— which had the single largest number of students. These young people would learn about America, and their American high school classmates would learn about, say, Baku or Belgorod. More than 20,000 high school students from these nations had come to study for a year in the U.S. since it was started.[35]

FLEX was precisely the sort of program that quietly pushed back on Putin's anti-Western, anti-American narrative. Students from Russia and the Russian periphery experienced America firsthand, and got a sense of what it means to be a citizen in a democracy. And, yes, maybe some of these values would rub off. Reality would displace disinformation.

The FLEX students were one of the first groups I spoke to at State. My talk was in the Dean Acheson Auditorium, a grand theater that seated about 1,000 people. There were about 350 FLEX students who were finishing up their stay. I never liked giving formal talks standing behind a podium—even though that was the State Department way. I usually wandered about with a handheld mic. Instead of making opening remarks, I began by asking them questions. How many of you are in the United States for the first time? An overwhelming show of hands. How many of you wish you could stay longer? They started laughing and clapping. So I started calling on them.

A boy from Turkmenistan who had been in South Carolina said he didn't want to miss the rest of his high school's basketball season.

A young woman from Romania who was staying in Michigan said she'd always wanted to go to an American high school prom and now she would miss hers!

Then I began to ask them specific questions about their stay.

What surprised you most about America?

Lots of hands.

A girl from Poland who had stayed in California said that from all the American movies she had seen, she had been afraid she might get shot! Lots of laughter and applause at that.

A girl from Georgia stood up and said she had stayed at a high school in—yes—Georgia! She said she'd had a lovely time but was dismayed at how no one there had ever heard of her Georgia.

A young man from Serbia who had spent his year at school in nearby Virginia said that at lunchtime, he was surprised that all the black students sat together, the Asian students sat together, the cheerleaders sat together, and oftentimes—his voice grew quieter—he would sit by himself.

One thing that always surprised them was the freedom of American media. Some of them expressed amazement and even alarm at the criticism they saw of President Obama. How could that happen? He's your president!

Another observation that always came through was the generosity and warmth of their American host families. The students often referred to their host families as their moms and dads and brothers and sisters and spoke about how their moms had learned to cook their favorite dishes and their dads had carpooled them to dances.

A few days later, I was sitting in my office in the late afternoon when I got a call from Evan Ryan, the assistant secretary for Educational and Cultural Affairs.

"The Russians have just canceled their participation in the FLEX Program."

"What?" I said. "Why?"

She told me that there had been an issue with a 17-year-old Russian boy who was staying with a family in Kalamazoo, Michigan. She said he didn't want to go back to Russia—which we told him he had to do—and he'd run away. She was just learning about it herself, and she said her understanding was that the boy was gay and didn't want to go back to Russia, where he faced persecution. But, she said, everyone assumed the cancellation was a reprisal for American sanctions against Russia.

"Why hasn't there been any press about this?" I asked.

She said there had been—in Russia. We had apparently been trying to protect the privacy of the boy and his host family while the Russian media had gone to town on how the U.S. was holding the boy hostage and endangering the welfare of a child. The Russians understood that if you frame the story, you create the narrative.

I quickly got hold of the Russian media, which all had pretty much the same version of the story. The headline of the TASS story is a good summary of the rest: "US Gay Couple Illegally Adopting Russian Child Is Reason for Pullout from FLEX—Official."

The TASS story implied that the boy had been suborned by a gay cabal. It said the boy's mother flew over to plead with her son to return home, and the meeting was held in the presence of two lawyers who were of "nontraditional sexual orientation." Another Russian newspaper quoted the Russian official in charge of children's rights as saying that the boy moved in with a couple "and they gradually developed—how can I say this carefully—close friendly relations."[36]

As I began to investigate, I saw how the Russian media had cleverly manipulated the narrative for their own domestic audience. People at State had talked to the boy's lawyer, Susan Reed, of the Michigan Immigrant Rights Center, who said the boy was gay and experienced persecution in Russia. She said she had been reticent with the press because she did not want to violate the boy's privacy. "I felt I had no right to talk about anyone's sexual orientation except my own," she later said. Contrary to the claims in the Russian press, she declared that she was a practicing Catholic, was married to a man, and was the mother of two children.[37]

She said the boy ran away because he did not want to return to Russia. He contacted the Michigan Immigrant Rights Center, which was where he'd met her. According to Reed, the boy's mother, whose trip was paid for by the State Department, was able to meet with her son privately at least twice. Meanwhile, officials from the Russian embassy in Washington came to meet with Reed and the boy. At that meeting, Reed told the *New Yorker*'s Masha Gessen, "They were there to intimidate us and intimidate our client with possible criminal prosecution." The officials asked the young man to leave the room at one point because they said that the Russian language did not have a politically correct term for homosexuality.[38]

The story generated indignation in Russia, where it played perfectly into many of Putin's themes: the arrogance of America and its belittling of Russia; the decadent and homosexual lifestyle of the West; the use of American soft power to subvert Russian culture. Canceling the program aligned with a number of Putin's recent acts, including his 2012 decision to ban all adoptions of Russian children from the United States. Putin did not like the perception of a rich and powerful America adopting orphans from a poor and enfeebled Russia. Russia had recently kicked out the United States Agency for International Development, which had spent hundreds of millions of dollars since the end of the Cold War helping Russia fight tuberculosis and HIV. Russia had closed dozens of our American Spaces, which were libraries where Russians could come and read American literature or just study.[39]

The cancellation fit into a pattern of official Russian homophobia. In 2013, Russia passed a law, supported by Putin, banning what it called "propaganda of nontraditional sexual relations." The law makes it illegal to equate heterosexual and homosexual relations, and fines anyone for providing information about LBGT organizations or rallies.[40] The law created a spike in young Russians seeking asylum in the U.S. Our own embassy in Moscow had sent us a summary of a documentary then being heavily promoted on Rossiya 1 state TV, called *Sodom*. It was about how the gay rights movement was causing "the collapse of family values in the West."

For Putin, canceling FLEX was both messaging and policy: scrapping it reaffirmed his anti-Western policies and was a tool in his global information war against America and the West. He had weaponized student exchanges. The cancellation also had an immediate effect on the 220 Russian students who had been accepted for the following year.

Suddenly, we had to figure out what to do with those slots and the $5 million we had earmarked for them. I had an idea.

My notion was both practical and symbolic: all the money and the places should go to Ukraine. I spoke to Evan about this and she was all for it. But the State bureaucracy at ECA and EUR thought it ought to be more measured. We could give half to Ukraine students and designate the other half for students from Georgia, Moldova, and Armenia.

Deal.

Our policy became our message.

Business as Usual

I had not planned on attending the next counter-ISIS meeting in Paris. It was June 2015, and I had just been in London for the so-called Small Group, the 24 nations of the more than 60-nation anti-ISIS coalition. But then Secretary Kerry had a bicycle accident in the French

Alps—where he was for the Iran talks—and broke his right femur. It sounded nasty. Tony Blinken stepped in for Kerry and asked me to be his "plus-one." We'd been told the Secretary was going to participate by phone, even though he was in a hospital in Boston awaiting surgery. I imagined he was going to be a little groggy.

The difference between the London meeting and the Paris meeting was that ISIS had taken the city of Ramadi, the capital of Iraq's Anbar province, delivering a serious blow to the military coalition.[41] People were rattled. Everyone had decided that the main theme of the gathering was going to be "It's not business as usual."

At the spectacular Salon de l'Horlage at the Quai d'Orsay in Paris, Laurent Fabius, the French foreign minister, opened the meeting by saying, "It's not business as usual." As he was talking, I saw a mouse skitter across the beautiful parquet floor and then dash behind the draperies. Every foreign minister then repeated the same phrase.

In fact, it was very much business as usual (including the mouse).

It was so much business as usual that the original agenda had not even been revised to reflect the loss of Ramadi. No one wanted to change anything other than to say that it wasn't business as usual. And barring a new strategy, government officials always say the old strategy is working.

Kerry, even though he was not there, was the only dissenter. A large speaker was set up in the center of the long, grand table. Suddenly, the Secretary's voice boomed from the speaker. He sounded intense, the opposite of groggy. "The coalition is still the best hope of defeating ISIS," he said. "Obviously what happened in Ramadi is a setback . . . We need to renew our efforts."

When I got back to Washington, I wrote a one-page information memo for Kerry. Because they are short, less than two pages, information memos go directly to the Secretary without needing to be cleared.

I was frustrated when I wrote it and it is perhaps a little more candid than most such memos. Here is some of it:

> You have undoubtedly heard about Paris from a military and ministerial perspective. Let me tell you about it from the messaging angle: The coalition doesn't communicate well internally or externally.
>
> The two are related, but I will begin with the internal. There is still no mechanism for the small group to communicate internally. Yes, there is a messaging working group—the United States, the UAE, and the UK—but this has not really come together. The UAE is reticent, the Brits are overeager, and the working group structure is confusing . . .
>
> When it comes to the external message, our narrative is being trumped by ISIS's. We're reactive—we think about "counter-narratives," not "our narrative." The external message of Paris, which was summarized in the press as "stay the course" and "the strategy is working," was not well received, at least by the media. We prepared a playbook going into the meeting for interagency use and by the partners, which said the meeting was not going to be "business as usual." This was not reflected in the meeting itself or its outward messaging. From the outside, it mostly seemed exactly like business as usual.[42]

I wrote it quickly, and when it was done, I asked my assistant, Kathy, to send it up to the Secretary. It had to be retyped and formatted in the prescribed way. Even though it did not have to be cleared, it had to go through "the line" and the Secretary's office.

At the 8:30 that morning, I mentioned that I had sent up a memo about the Paris ministerial. A few perfunctory nods. A day later, I passed Tony Blinken in the hall on the seventh floor, and he mentioned that he'd read the memo and thought it was strong. I thanked him. People should read it, he said. They would.

Early Saturday morning, my speechwriter Nate Rawlings emailed me telling me to look at the *New York Times*. In government, people always communicated bad news in a completely neutral way. If, say, your dog was run over, you'd get a message saying, "Have you seen your dog lately?"

What's up? I replied.

"Look at the front page," he said.

There it was, below the fold: "ISIS Is Winning the Social Media War, U.S. Concludes."[43]

Here's the top of the story:

WASHINGTON—An internal State Department assessment paints a dismal picture of the efforts by the Obama administration and its foreign allies to combat the Islamic State's message machine, portraying a fractured coalition that cannot get its own message straight.

The assessment comes months after the State Department signaled that it was planning to energize its social media campaign against the militant group. It concludes, however, that the Islamic State's violent narrative— promulgated through thousands of messages each day—has effectively "trumped" the efforts of some of the world's richest and most technologically advanced nations . . .

The internal document—composed by Richard A. Stengel, the State Department's under secretary for public

diplomacy and public affairs and a former managing editor
of Time magazine—was written for Secretary of State John
Kerry after a conference of Western and Arab officials in Paris
this month on countering the Islamic State.

The piece went on to say that we were in the process of expanding
CSCC and that in September I'd accompanied Secretary Kerry to the
Middle East, where we'd started building a communications coalition.
It also quoted a measured response from State spokesman John Kirby,
that the memo "acknowledges what we've made clear in the past: We
must do a better job at discrediting ISIS in the information space."

Online, the piece had a small icon saying: "State Department
Memo on the Islamic State Group." If you clicked on the icon, you
actually saw a PDF of my entire memo, which meant that whoever
leaked it had sent a photo of the whole document or even slipped a
paper copy of it to the *New York Times*. And this all happened *before*
Secretary Kerry had even seen it.

It's a strange feeling to be the victim of a leak. It's a little like
discovering your house has been burglarized. I felt sick to my stomach.

Leaks are also a type of weaponized information; I had been the
victim of information warfare by someone on my own side.

I first sent a note to the Secretary's chief of staff, David Wade,
alerting him to the leak and apologizing for it. I sent a similar note to
Tony Blinken. I felt particularly bad about the cheap shot I'd taken at
the UAE and the British. I sent notes to Dr. Ahmed and UAE's ambassador to the U.S., Yousef Al Otaiba, as well as my British colleagues. I
let General Allen know.

What else did I need to do? This was also a gift to ISIS in the
messaging realm. The leader of the U.S. government's anti-ISIS messaging operations had said we were disorganized and outgunned. The
digital jihadis were already tweeting about it. What especially bothered

me was the timing. ISIS's messaging was down, and anti-ISIS messaging was increasing. I had been thinking we needed to start shifting the narrative—enough of the "still losing the information war" stories!—but here was a leaked memo by me that seemed to confirm the "we're losing" story line. Heck, the headline implied we were losing the information war. (Weren't editors tired of such headlines?) As I had started to tell people, it wasn't ISIS versus the U.S.—it was ISIS versus the entire Muslim world. It's not whether we're winning, but whether mainstream Muslims were winning.

One thing the *Times* story did not tell you was how curious this leak was. Leaking was obviously an occupational hazard of being in government, and there had been prominent leaks from within the State Department before.[44] In 2012, a top secret cable from the U.S. ambassador to Afghanistan, Ryan Crocker, was leaked to the *Washington Post*.[45] But cables, even though they were classified as secret (and an information memo is not), would go through many more hands than mine had. Information memos to the Secretary are not passed around digitally. The Secretary's office prints out physical copies and then delivers them to those on the distribution list. So someone had to either receive an original copy or take a digital picture of the memo in order to give it to the *New York Times*.

Of course, you can't help trying to figure out who leaked the document. I wasn't even sure of the motive. Who would benefit? Who was it meant to hurt, besides me? Well, it would hurt the coalition, and the Emiratis and the Brits, but I didn't think that someone at the State Department would risk leaking something in order to do that. Most internal leaks come from people who are upset that someone is straying onto their territory, or territory they covet. A lot of people and bureaus were involved in what was known as CVE, "countering violent extremism." There was the NSC, of course; there was the counterterrorism bureau; and then there was J—the bureau for Civilian Security, Democracy, and Human Rights.

I prayed that no one thought that I'd leaked it. You always wonder whether people might think you did it. After all, I'd been a journalist, I was familiar with the leaking subculture, and people probably thought I was a grandstander. Oh, well. Perhaps someone leaked it to make it seem like I had leaked it? Kremlinology is not unique to the Kremlin.

The general consensus in my front office was that someone from J—the bureau for Civilian Security, Democracy, and Human Rights—leaked it. They seemed the most competitive with us about who would own counterextremism. They were generally seen as a poorly run bureau with a lot of unhappy people.

The story and the memo got picked up everywhere but seemed to get the most attention in the Middle East. It was well covered in the Gulf newspapers, all of which seemed to highlight how lackluster our efforts had been. UAE's *National* called the memo "hugely dispiriting."[46] ISIS fanboys retweeted the local stories and enjoyed pointing out the disarray of the coalition.

It was annoying, but one reason it didn't arouse an even bigger fuss is that it confirmed the prevailing narrative. It wasn't the man biting the dog; it was, We're *still* losing.

One unintended consequence of the leak was to make me seem like a truth-teller. In the end, it was once again evidence that we seemed to spend as much time fighting ourselves as with our adversaries.

General Allen called me after he got my email. He said two things. First, "Welcome to the big leagues." I laughed. And then he said, "I hope you're taking notes."

Why? I said.

"Because this is the first time we've tried to control information as part of a military operation, and there's a book in that."

Holding Fire

The Russia Information Group had been a going proposition for a few months. It was a pretty representative group of people from across the State Department, including folks from Public Affairs, Public Diplomacy, International Information Programs, and of course EUR. Ben Ziff was leading it and he reported to me and Toria Nuland. I saw it a little like the old structure at Time Inc.—Ben was like the managing editor of the publication and he reported to the editorial director of the company. I had spoken at one of the earliest meetings to say it was Ben's show and I just wanted them to be proactive and to help coordinate responses across State. I met with Ben every other week to get a sense of what was going on, but otherwise I was hands-off. That was very much the State Department way, but it didn't make me entirely comfortable. I wanted to get my hands under the hood a bit, as I had with Will Stevens. Instead, I would get weekly reports like this:

> The team had their highest-level of engagement on Twitter
> in the last three months with 230K+ impressions yesterday.
> This was largely the result of live-tweeting (and Embassy
> Kyiv retweeting) A/S Nuland's remarks at the American
> Enterprise Institute.

I wanted to see if they could be a little more entrepreneurial. In October, after a 15-month investigation, the Dutch Safety Board was planning on releasing its final report on the shoot-down of Malaysia Airlines Flight 17.[47] We were pretty certain it would confirm what Secretary Kerry had said a year earlier: that MH17 was shot down by a Buk surface-to-air missile launched from the separatist-controlled territory in eastern Ukraine. In other words, the Russians were to blame.

I told Ben at our regular meeting, Let's put together a messaging plan. There was still a long weekend before the report was due. But the Russians were undoubtedly preparing as well. The day before the report was to be released, the Russian state-owned maker of Buk missiles held a press conference to say that the missile that hit the airliner was no longer in use by the Russian military. Russian Channel One interviewed a Kremlin defense analyst who said, The Americans have satellite photos of everything; why don't they have photos of this? Classic Russian whataboutism. That same day, Putin's spokesperson, Dmitry Peskov, said that the Dutch authorities had ignored information presented by the Russians. Classic Russian poisoning the well.

The report was released that Tuesday morning. I had a busy day with back-to-back meetings, plus I was speaking at the Atlantic Council in the afternoon on "Countering Misinformation" and had an interview with the *Wall Street Journal*. I'd asked my specials to keep me posted on what the Russian Information Group had done. Periodically, I'd check to ask whether we had done anything. Nope. Around lunchtime, one of my specials reported that the NSC had said that morning, Don't do anything until we do something. I knew that foreign service officers would abide by that. In the afternoon, the NSC released a statement saying that the report was "an important milestone" and that "our assessment is unchanged—MH17 was shot down by a surface-to-air missile fired from separatist-controlled territory."[48]

State public affairs followed with something similar. Mark Toner, the deputy spokesperson, issued a statement saying, "We welcome the important findings of the Dutch Safety Board in its final report on the shooting down of Malaysia Airlines flight MH17."[49]

At the end of the day, I combed through the social media of embassies that were affected and the European hubs for something. Nothing about the false claims from the Buk manufacturer. Nothing about the false assertions from the Kremlin spokesperson. Nothing about any kind of disinformation. Nothing but the press release from the NSC and public affairs.

It was disappointing.

I decided to speak to Ben.

Ben was apologetic and frustrated himself. He said the NSC didn't want anyone to get out ahead of them. Then, after the NSC, the State spokesperson was next in line. By that time, he said, it was six hours late.

Let's take a step back, I said.

Okay, he said, here goes. You also do counter-ISIS, right? Yes, I said. Well, Ben said, that's what we know how to do. The machinery of State and of DOD and the intelligence community has been focused on terrorism and terrorist narratives. It sounds odd to say, he noted, but the Russia stuff is new to people. We haven't done it since the end of the Cold War. We've lost our institutional memory. We have hundreds of Arabic-speakers and barely any Russian-speakers. We don't have an agreed-upon counter-Russian narrative like we do against ISIS. We don't know what, if anything, DOD is doing, what the intelligence community is doing. We're in the dark.

So, what should we do?

Ben was not keen to create content, and he was realistic in saying that it wasn't State's strength. He said he'd like to work more closely with our missions abroad and with public affairs officers in the field. He said he wanted to give those officers more room to move. To try to see what they would do.

He mentioned working with civil society groups and pro-democracy groups. Also good. Credible voices. Not our voice. Fine, too. I just wanted a little more that was in our voice as well.

I wasn't sure what to do. In my old life, I would have ordered up stories and social media. I couldn't do that now. There were too many different lines of authority, too many different equities. Let's face it, I had two content shops that weren't really producing much content.

*   *   *

A few days after the MH17 report came out, I sent an email to Jen Stout, my chief of staff.

> I just feel that neither the anti-ISIS stuff or the anti-Russia
> stuff is moving fast enough. I'm sure you must be sick of
> me comparing things to my old world, but if both of these
> things were projects in my old life, I would say that neither
> of them are even off the ground yet.

I felt like all the work we had done was basically for naught. I couldn't quite figure out how much was my fault; how much was due to the institutional ways of the State Department; and how much was the nature of the challenge that we were up against. I chided myself for not being more hands-on. But there were all kinds of impediments to that too, including the fact that it wasn't really my job. In truth, CSCC and the Russia Information Group were a tiny part of the public diplomacy portfolio. In terms of spending and resources, together they represented about 2 percent of my entire budget. They occupied about 60 percent of my time.

There were some other institutional impediments. One of them was the Privacy Act. Passed in 1974, the Privacy Act established a code for how the government collects, maintains, and uses information about individuals. It was passed in the wake of the Watergate abuses when Congress wanted to be more rigorous in defining how federal agencies collected and used information on Americans. It was meant to balance the government's need to maintain information about citizens with the citizens' right to be protected from invasions of privacy. But the law had an unintended effect for what we were trying to do. For both our counter-ISIS and our counter-Russian efforts, we needed to be able to harvest information about the internet trolls and bots that we were up against. The problem was something called PII, personal identifiable information—pretty much any kind of information that identifies an individual. That information was protected by the Privacy Act. Harvesting PII of an American citizen was a violation of the law. State legal affairs had decided that anything CSCC or the Russian Information Group tried to do to identify bad guys would also violate the Privacy Act. As result, it was like we were driving at night without any headlights.

Legal did not even allow us to use Twitter's own analytics, or Facebook's. These were services that any private citizen could use for free. Each time we tried to set up an in-house analytics department or tried to bring in an outside contractor, we got a big fat no. Even within the intelligence community, there seemed to be little information on Russian disinformation. When I asked intelligence officials why, they'd shrug and say they were frustrated as well. I raised this issue a number of times with Secretary Kerry, who said he would break through the logjam. And both CSCC and the Russia Information Group sent up to the seventh floor any number of action memos, which I signed off on, but nothing was ever approved.

The Right Path

In government, deadlines always seemed elastic. Things almost always took much longer than expected. But the new joint messaging center in Abu Dhabi was a fantastic exception to the rule: the Emiratis had created and constructed our joint counter-ISIS messaging center three months earlier than we'd been promised. From concept to execution and launch, it had been only five months. Ambassador nominations took longer than that.

One big reason the center got done so quickly was Muhammed, Dr. Ahmed's deputy, whom he had put in charge of the center. Muhammed was young, no-nonsense, and hyper-capable. Like so many Emiratis, he had studied in the U.S.—in his case at American University in Washington, D.C.—and he went about his task in a quiet, focused, self-effacing way. About a month before the center was due to open, Muhammed called me with his sole request: "We need a name," he said. If the name had been left to the State Department, it would have been something like, the Joint UAE-US Anti-ISIS Messaging Center, with the unpronounceable acronym JUUAIMC. But Muhammed was a step ahead of me. What do you think of the name *Sawab*? he said. In Arabic, he explained, it meant "the right way" or "the right path." The Sawab Center.

I liked it. The Sawab Center it was.

Both Muhammed and Dr. Ahmed were keen for me to be there for the launch. As was true in pretty much all governments, a new endeavor couldn't officially begin until a principal arrived to cut the ribbon.

I was also keen to go to show our own folks how partnerships with our Arab allies could produce results. Our international counter-messaging strategy was now based in part on creating such hubs with our Arab allies. We would create a network to fight a network. The Sawab Center would become Exhibit A in that strategy. We were also talking to the Jordanians, the Malaysians, and the Nigerians.

I flew overnight to Abu Dhabi. Even though the Emiratis had always been very discreet about Sawab, it was located in a modern glass-and-steel high-rise in downtown Abu Dhabi overlooking the harbor. "The Sawab Center" wasn't listed on the building's directory. It was hidden in plain sight.

The elevator took us to a high floor and let us out on a sleek, open modern office space that looked like a combination of a state-of-the-art newsroom and a military situation room. There was an enormous screen in the center—about 8 feet by 20 feet—with a few chairs and desks in front of it. Standing around were a couple of dozen young Emiratis, men wearing keffiyehs and the long white robes the Emiratis call *kanduras*, and women in hijabs and black abayas. Most of the women wore blue jeans underneath.

Muhammed stood in front of the screen and welcomed everyone. It was very informal and obviously not a press or public event. It felt like a family gathering. There was a sense of shared purpose. Muhammed introduced Dr. Ahmed as the godfather of the center. Dr. Ahmed joked that they had chosen the location with the best views in town. The Emiratis had put together a terrific video about Sawab, featuring charts and graphics about what ISIS did online and how Sawab would combat it. When it came my turn to speak, I mainly thanked Ahmed and Muhammed and said what a spectacular job that they had done. I said Sawab was a model of how we could work together to create something that was better than anything we each could have produced alone. I said how proud I was of our joint creation and that it symbolized how President Obama liked to conduct foreign policy, in collaboration with our allies.

Afterward, I chatted with a few of the young Emiratis who worked there. Quiet and earnest, they were anti-ISIS techies—a very heartening combination and one that we hadn't really cracked at State. We needed our own digital anti-jihadis. I spoke to a young Emirati woman who had been a computer science major at an American university in the Midwest. She talked about what a setback ISIS's ideology was for women. She said that people in the West did not seem to understand that Arabic women can be devoutly Muslim—and wear a headscarf—and still be for women's rights. She smiled and called herself a "hijabi anti-ISIS feminist."

State's only commitment was to supply one senior foreign service officer, and I thought we had hit the jackpot with our choice: Ali Baskey. Ali had been one of my original special assistants and had just come from a stint working for Ben Rhodes. Ali was fluent in Arabic and had impeccable judgment. He had been there for a month already, and we talked a little about what he had seen. Ali confided that the Emiratis were pretty nervous. I said every media launch is pretty scary. He told me they wanted every tweet cleared by him. I said I hoped that was a temporary state of affairs; if we had to clear every tweet, we would certainly lose the information war! He laughed and said they just needed to get the hang of it.

They wanted to start slowly, with about a dozen tweets a day. In fact, that first day, they went from zero followers to 4,000, which isn't bad. Not Katy Perry numbers, but pretty good for a government-run anti-ISIS Twitter account. The launch made the front pages of all the Emirati newspapers and got pretty good coverage throughout the Gulf. Some of that was because it was a good news story at a time when everything else seemed pretty bleak.

I was scheduled to leave at 3 a.m. for an overnight flight back to Washington. Dr. Ahmed had invited me to his *suhoor* dinner, which is the very late meal that people have before going to sleep at dawn during Ramadan. (*Iftar* is the break-the-fast meal at sundown.) I explained that I was leaving on the 3 a.m. flight, and he said, Perfect, you can go straight from *suhoor* to the airport. We ate at one of Abu Dhabi's glittering hotels where Dr. Ahmed had a large, private room off the main ballroom. It was the middle of the night, but the ballroom was filled with hundreds of festively dressed people dedicated to eating and having a good time.

I wasn't terribly hungry, but Dr. Ahmed had ordered a seemingly endless series of courses. He was keeping a close eye on me and making sure I sampled everything. We talked a bit about Sawab, and he said, You should feel very good about this. It's new and has never really been done before. He nodded at the water pipe—the hookah—that was standing next to the table. Let us smoke to celebrate, he said. You've smoked from a hookah before? he said. I said yes, and I think it was the only time I ever lied as a State Department official. The waiter brought out a selection of flavored tobaccos. He mentioned that Dr. Ahmed liked apple. The remaining choices were: banana, cherry, lemon-lime, and cinnamon. I chose cherry. They put on a new mouthpiece, and Dr. Ahmed warned me not to inhale. I didn't inhale, but the amount of smoke that floods your mouth can be overwhelming. I tried not to cough. That's diplomacy.

For Whom the Bell Trolls

Fifty-Five Savushkina Street, St. Petersburg. An attractive four-story limestone building, about 40 years old, in a quiet section of the city. No signs, no name, no shops on the ground floor. No reason to remember it, which was probably the reason it was selected. Every morning at precisely 8:55, dozens of young Russians hurry into the building. They could be office workers, and in a way, they are.

Fifty-Five Savushkina Street is a troll factory. It is registered to the Internet Research Agency, a shadowy Russian company that seems to do everything from creating sock puppets to practicing cyber vandalism. Every day, in two shifts, a few hundred young people spend their time writing blog posts, tweets, Facebook posts, VKontakte posts, and much more. They work in open rooms of about 20 people with three editors, who vet posts and levy fines. Trolls often work in teams of three, with one posting a complaint and the others weighing in with supporting posts. English-language trolls were paid more than Russian-language trolls. They all signed nondisclosure agreements and were paid in cash. It is indeed a factory; they manufacture thousands upon thousands of pieces of pro-Russian, anti-American content a day.[50]

The Internet Research Agency was the Sawab Center on steroids. Sawab had cost $20 million to create and was publishing a dozen carefully monitored tweets a day. Even across all the U.S. government, we were creating perhaps a hundred pieces of content that pushed back on Russia. The Internet Research Agency was creating hundreds of pieces of fake and misleading content an hour. Like a digital marketing agency, it operated across the entire social media ecosystem. The whole enterprise is financed by a tycoon who is an ally of Putin's.

I learned about the Internet Research Agency because I continued to see all kinds of curious posts on my Twitter feed, especially on hashtags affiliated with the Russia Information Group. They were angry, profane, ungrammatical, with very poor spelling. There were Twitter "eggs" that were following thousands of people and had never tweeted. There were similar eggs that had tweeted thousands of times and followed no one. I'd asked for briefings from my intelligence folks and also read excellent open-source articles from several independent Russian publications, including Novaya Gazeta, MOI Region, and the Russian news site MR7.ru.

MR7.ru had actually published documents smuggled out by IRA employees. They ranged from overarching guidelines about posting (amount, frequency, use of keywords) to talking points about the news of the day (protests on the Maidan, American policy toward Syria) to a glossary of internet slang. The guidelines offered a blueprint for what the workers did and how they did it.[51]

One document describes their job this way:

> TROLL. The purpose of the troll is to produce a quarrel which offends his interlocutor. It is worth remembering that trolling is not writing articles to order. It is a deliberate provocation with the goal of ridiculing your opponent.[52]

The first thing workers needed to do, according to one of the memos, was to create online personas, sometimes called "sock puppets." These personas are meant to look and sound like real people. They have names and photographs. They "like" other people's photos and comments and statuses. Workers are meant to have multiple social media accounts—one memo said they should each have at least three different Facebook accounts. There are also specific guidelines, for example, for posting pro-Russian material in the comments sections of Fox News, Huffington Post, Politico, and the Blaze. The guidelines suggest that these identities should mix political opinions with more mundane posts about things like music or movies or "the owner's social life."

One of the personas used in a document to illustrate how the process works is named "Natalya." "Natalya" has a blog, a Twitter account, a Facebook page, a Google+ profile, and a VKontakte account. "She" is interested in "art, psychology and all that happens in the world." She writes about doing a manicure at home, about how she enjoys *Fifty Shades of Grey* parodies, and about Facebook getting rid of the "feeling fat" emoji. But she also expresses vehement political opinions: that America is behind the protests in Ukraine; that the protesters support Nazi fascism; and that the new Ukrainian government is hopelessly corrupt.[53]

Each day, the workers are given "themes." These are basically talking points about what's happening in the news. They also are supplied with a list of sample tweets, comments, or posts on subjects like Ukraine, Putin, the United States, and the EU. Here are a few.

Ukraine
The news from Ukraine is becoming sadder and sadder.
The country is in a state of deep crisis.

No wonder Russia was worried. Ukraine is indeed coming under the influence of the West and the United States.

The West took advantage of Ukraine and sparked a conflict between Ukraine and Russia

Putin

Putin's policies have a positive effect on Russia. Our country is flourishing despite the sanctions.

The president of the Russian Federation is the only leader who always looks for a peaceful solution to every conflict. The US is ready to fight in every scenario.

With such a leader as the president of the Russian Federation, we do not worry about anything! Putin is the greatest diplomat of our time.

The Middle East and ISIS

ISIS is completely the project of the United States and it simply got out of hand.

The US is at war in Iraq, at war in Syria. When will the US withdraw itself from the Middle East?

Soon Syria will become a desert. Thank you, United States, for creating terrorists. What a bunch of shitheads!

The USA

US policies are aimed at achieving a unipolar world. They are ready to destroy any country to achieve their goal.

The EU and NATO act on the orders of the United States. Because of this, Europe cannot establish relations with Russia.

The internal problems of the United States are violence, terrorism, obesity—but they try to teach the whole world how to live! The only thing America ever gave the world was Coca-Cola and that turned out to be poison.[54]

The troll factory also created phony Ukrainian news agencies that put out fabricated stories that were pro-Russian and anti-American. They understood that anything called a "news agency" would have credibility, especially with people who didn't look at its provenance. "The Kharkov News Agency" was allegedly based in Ukraine but was actually housed at 55 Savushkina Street. It featured headlines like "The United States Is on the Threshold of Economic Collapse."[55]

I found one area especially disconcerting. There was a special section on the United States that had very specific guidance about issues that were classically liberal ones: gun control, civil rights, police violence, and privacy. Here are some of them:

> The massive proliferation of weapons, and the
> accompanying mass shootings, crimes and violence in
> America. Firearms are in half of American families, with the
> average number of units being 4. Gunfire and massacres are
> constantly flaring up in America.

> Excessive force by American policemen. If twenty years ago
> a suspect could count on a lawful investigation, now when
> people are arrested they are routinely beaten and killed.
> The police are equipped with the latest military hardware
> and use it as an apparatus of repression rather than
> defending constitutional rights.

> The total surveillance of US citizens by the intelligence
> services. Thanks to Edward Snowden, it became known
> that the NSA monitors every third member of American
> society and on a daily basis the NSA collection system
> intercepts and records 1.7 billion telephone conversations
> and electronic messages.[56]

It was sobering. They were equal-opportunity offenders. They supported liberal causes and conservative ones. There was no particular through-line or ideology in their messaging other than to stir up dissatisfaction and grievance in the audience. In the same day, they created social media that said immigration was polluting America and that racism was keeping down African Americans.

They highlighted the protests in Ferguson, Missouri, around the shooting of an unarmed black teenager. The guidance said to refer to Ferguson at every opportunity in discussing racism in the U.S. My intelligence briefers put this in the context of the Soviet Union's long history of spotlighting racism in America, going back to propaganda posters about the Scottsboro Boys in the 1930s. It was a particular focus of Russian propaganda during the Cold War when the Russian press focused on protests against school integration in the South. The idea was to discredit the American system and accuse the U.S. of hypocrisy when it was preaching democracy abroad. The classic Russian Cold War retort was "But you lynch Negroes."

After one information session, I asked my main Russian intelligence briefer about what we could do. She was young, a Russian-speaker, and philosophical about disinformation. She shrugged her shoulders. Not because she wasn't concerned about it, but because the dark genius of disinformation is that it worked a little like double-bind theory. If you engaged disinformationists—which is what they wanted—they won; if you did not engage them, they won. They tapped into prejudice and ignorance and grievance. They weren't so much creating resentment as aggravating it. Yes, facts mattered, but since they did not really engage with the world of facts, it didn't have much of an effect. At the end of the day, she said, they didn't acknowledge that empirical facts even existed. Their goal was to persuade everyone else of that, too.

PART VI

Disruption

Making _____ Great Again

On June 16, 2015, my special advisor on counterextremism, Haroon Ullah, and I were at Los Angeles International Airport, coming back from a workshop we had organized for Hollywood writers, producers, and executives to meet content creators from the Middle East. It was the inaugural event of a series we had put together with the Annenberg Foundation Trust at Sunnylands. We had spent two days at a hotel on the beach in Santa Monica talking about how to create a counter-ISIS narrative in the Middle East. One of the Middle Eastern producers had suggested developing an animated feature film starring a Muslim superhero who wiped out ISIS.

As we were walking to our gate, we stopped in front of a wall of television monitors. CNN was showing Donald Trump gliding down the escalator at Trump Tower in New York to announce that he was running for president. As a lifetime New Yorker who had observed Trump for decades, I had been certain that he was not going to run, that he was simply flirting with it as he had done many times before in his quadrennial ritual of self-promotion.

It was a curious place to have a presidential announcement: a garish marble lobby that seemed cold, corporate, and awfully far from the cornfields of Iowa. It was as though he couldn't be bothered to find a place that was more "presidential." Or maybe he thought it was. In fact, he began by mentioning that the other candidates didn't have great venues for their announcements. "It's great to be at Trump Tower," he said. "I can tell you, some of the other candidates, they went in, they didn't know the air conditioner didn't work. They sweated like dogs," he said. "How are they gonna beat ISIS?"[1] Not a terrible question, but certainly an unusual beginning to a presidential-announcement speech.

What got the most attention was his line about Mexicans: "They're bringing drugs. They're bringing crime. They're rapists." But I was more curious to hear what he had to say about ISIS and Russia. First, ISIS.

> Islamic terrorism is eating up large portions of the
> Middle East. They've become rich. I'm in competition
> with them. They just built a hotel in Syria. Can you
> believe this? They built a hotel. When I have to build
> a hotel, I pay interest. They don't have to pay interest,
> because they took the oil that, when we left Iraq, I said
> we should've taken. So now ISIS has the oil, and what
> they don't have, Iran has . . . Iran is going to take over the
> Middle East, Iran and somebody else will get the oil, and
> it turned out that Iran is now taking over Iraq. Think of
> it. Iran is taking over Iraq, and they're taking it over big
> league. And we have nothing.

Well, putting the non sequiturs aside, and I have no idea what he meant about ISIS building hotels in Syria, if that is what he meant, but the thing that struck me was that he, too, had bought into the narrative that we were losing to ISIS. He also seemed to understand that most of the folks in the neighborhood feared Iran more than they did ISIS.

Then he took a shot at my boss.

> I will stop Iran from getting nuclear weapons. And we won't
> be using a man like Secretary Kerry that has absolutely
> no concept of negotiation, who's making a horrible and
> laughable deal, who's just being tapped along as they make
> weapons right now, and then goes into a bicycle race at 72

years old, and falls and breaks his leg. I won't be doing that.
And I promise I will never be in a bicycle race.

That did seem like a promise he would be able to keep.

Trump mentioned Putin only in passing.

Our enemies are getting stronger and stronger by the
way, and we as a country are getting weaker. Even our
nuclear arsenal doesn't work. It came out recently they
have equipment that is 30 years old. They don't know
if it worked. And I thought it was horrible when it was
broadcast on television, because boy, does that send signals
to Putin and all of the other people that look at us and they
say, "That is a group of people, and that is a nation that
truly has no clue. They don't know what they're doing."

He mentioned China, Mexico, and Saudi Arabia dozens of times,
and Russia not at all. With Putin, he simply didn't want to look weak.

I had covered many presidential announcements, and I was struck
by how dark a speech it was—very different from the sunny, optimistic
statements that were the traditional opening salvo. He then uttered a
line that I had always thought would spell the end of any presidential
candidate: "The American dream is dead."

Didn't he know that a declinist had never been elected president
before?

He also ventured into my territory: the image of America around
the world. He said we needed a cheerleader for America.

We need somebody that can take the brand of the United
States and make it great again.

On the brand front, he was, at best, a mixed bag. On the one hand, to many people around the world, he seemed to represent the American success story. As Fran Lebowitz had once said, he was "a poor person's idea of a rich person"—and there were a lot more poor people than rich people. (And just in case anyone was in doubt, he said, "I'm really rich.") But to global elites, he seemed to represent every cliché of American gaucheness—the gold-plated bragging, the boorishness, the bad taste. He talked incessantly about "winning," as though winning—whatever that meant—was America's mission. In short, to many of the people we were trying to appeal to, he *was* the Ugly American.

He was also tapping into something we were seeing across the world: fear and anxiety about immigration. Not only was Mexico exporting "rapists," he said, but other countries were "not sending their best." It was immigration that was killing the American dream, he suggested— it was immigration that was undermining what was good and true about America. Never mind that his mother had been an immigrant. That two of his three wives were immigrants. This targeting of immigrants and immigration was something we were seeing all over—especially in Europe. Anxiety about immigration was the fuel behind the rise of white nationalism and right-wing parties in Europe. Parties that were funded and supported by Putin. In Europe, the anti-immigration sentiment stemmed in large part from the millions of Syrian refugees who were making their way west and north. The hemorrhaging of refugees from Syria had been exacerbated by Russia's entry into the crisis, and it was beginning to disrupt politics all across Europe.

I felt like I had known Donald Trump all my life. To people in the national media like myself, he was a local character, the Damon Runyon hustler as showy real estate developer, a guy who plastered everything with gold, including his name—especially his name—which he would always put in the largest letters possible. He was the rich kid from

Queens who used to call Page Six of the *New York Post* pretending to be his own publicist to say how all the pretty girls in Manhattan wanted the Donald. To me, he was not a presidential candidate; he was a punch line.

I'd had dinner with him years before at the Plaza Hotel, which he then owned, and all I can remember about it was that he used the Yiddish word *shtup*—as in, "fuck"—more than I ever heard anyone else use it in a couple of hours. All through dinner he talked about who was "shtupping" whom—and I didn't know any of the names that he mentioned. His conversation was unrelentingly crude.

When I became editor of *Time*, he had been on the cover only once, in 1989. The very '80s cover line was, "This man may turn you green with envy—or just turn you off. Flaunting it is the game, and Trump is the name." It showed a dark-haired Trump in a red tie holding an ace of diamonds. In seven years, I never put him on the cover or even did a feature about him. His office would regularly call about getting him invited to the Time 100 party. We always said no. We never considered him for the actual list of global influencers and he just wasn't the right kind of name to be at a party with scientists and athletes and statesmen and movie stars. Not serious. Too low-rent. Too local.

Back at the State Department, at the Monday afternoon PD meeting, no one even bothered to bring up Trump's announcement, other than to make a joke about it. The Republicans had a large and impressive field. Some of them had considerable foreign policy experience: Marco Rubio, Jeb Bush, Lindsey Graham. No one imagined that Trump's candidacy was going to be a challenge to our public diplomacy or much of anything else.

A Gift Horse

Tension between the White House and the State Department is as old as the republic. From the moment I got involved with CSCC, I realized that it was an irritant for the White House. People at State, who were always suspicious of the White House, thought the NSC wanted to own CSCC. In fact, I think the White House just wanted CSCC to change faster. Some of the friction with the White House stemmed from poor communication, though people at State always suspected the White House of malign intent. But, as a political appointee, I was much more open to White House guidance than foreign service officers were.

In Washington, the Obama White House was the cool kid's table and the coolest of the cool kids were in the White House digital office. I'd had a couple of meetings with Megan Smith and Todd Park, who ran it. Megan had come from Google and was the government's chief technology officer; Todd was her predecessor. They were both supersmart and had the private-sector metabolism that I was used to. Megan's brain seemed to move at hyper-speed; she spoke fast, thought fast, flipping analogies back and forth like a pinball machine. Todd was low-key, driven, and entrepreneurial. I had occasionally consulted with them about CSCC and how best to push back on ISIS content. One day when I was over there they mentioned that they had a tool available called "sprint teams." They could bring in a group of outside experts for three weeks to take an intensive look at a bureau or an agency. They had recently done it for the Labor Department, and it had been a success. Would I be interested in having a sprint team look at CSCC? I had worked before with consultants and it sounded like a hyper-accelerated McKinsey analysis. They said the team would do recommendations at the end of three weeks, and it would be up to me whether to take them. How much does it cost? I asked. That's the best thing of all, said Megan. It doesn't cost you a thing.

I thought about the offer as if I were in the private sector. I would be getting some smart minds to look at a problem and think it through. I would be getting something potentially valuable for nothing. We needed new thinking. And if I didn't like it, I could ignore it.

I'm in, I said.

When I got back to my office and proudly told Jen and some of my senior staff, I got grim looks. While they didn't say so directly, they saw the sprint team as an elaborate Trojan horse for the White House to take over CSCC. C'mon, I said. We can manage it the way we want to. I could see Jen trying not to clobber me in front of the whole office.

Todd was in charge of finding the members of the sprint team and bringing them on board. He was looking for marketing people and digital people and branding people from New York and Los Angeles and Silicon Valley. As if it wasn't hard enough to get good people to interrupt their lives to come to Washington for three weeks, they also needed to apply for security clearances. We thought it was important that they be able to see classified information and be briefed by the intelligence community.

After several months of recruiting and working with diplomatic security for clearances, Todd put together the team. When they finally assembled in my office, it was a little like that classic opening scene of a *Mission Impossible* movie when you meet the cast: there was the rebellious, spiky-haired marketing woman; the nerdy computer whiz; the laconic advertising guy; the earnest, dark-haired journalist. You get the idea. They were young, smart, and stylish, with hipster haircuts—exactly what you never saw in government.

I gave them my now usual riff on the myths of ISIS messaging—that ISIS was not converting nice Muslim boys into terrorists but tapping into a vast well of Sunni grievance; that only a tiny minority of the world's Muslims went to fight for them; that the lion's share of their messaging was positive and in Arabic and not meant for us; that there was really no such thing as "countering" a message; and that, of course, government was the worst messenger because *we* were the grievance! The sprint team members were smart and knew a lot about media and metrics and marketing, but none of them spoke Arabic, none were Muslim. And because we hadn't been able to get some of the security clearances, we couldn't show them any classified material.

During their first week, they met with some of the CSCC folks and representatives from the Defense Department, General Allen's office, and the National Counterterrorism Center. They kept in touch, flying some ideas by us. By the middle of their second week, they were ready to present. We arranged for the big meeting room adjacent to my office.

The presentation began with the stoic advertising fellow laying out the argument.

We're fighting a 21st-century information war with a 20th-century strategy, he said. ISIS has created a tech start-up within a terrorist organization. They're entrepreneurial and innovative.

We need to move to a new messaging paradigm: from tweeting at terrorists to a partnership model; from individual tweets to messaging campaigns. We need our own tech start-up model.

Then they took turns talking.

The marketing woman described ISIS as charismatic, and said that charismatic brands were a mixture of strength and warmth. We needed to "break their brand," she said.

The tech guy asked, What are the drivers of radicalization? We need to try to measure them. We need to create a "radicalization index."

They had the zeal of the newly converted. Their tone was urgent and a little breathless.

But they were looking at it with fresh eyes and with none of the intellectual baggage of experts. I loved some of the language and the ideas. The radicalization index. Breaking a brand. Asymmetry of passion.

Many of their ideas were gussied-up versions of what we'd been saying for a while. They had ratified our evolving notion of creating messaging campaigns rather than doing one-off tweets. Scaling up data science and analytics—great. And they had one genuinely fresh idea: starting a nonprofit foundation to support third-party voices and messages. It could live on after we'd all left office.

Very quickly thereafter, the NSC scheduled a meeting in the Situation Room with the sprint team to hear their findings. Lisa Monaco was running it, and asked me to start off. I simply said that this was the sprint team's show and we were excited about the ideas they had come up with. The presentation was the same, but they had gotten even slicker. They were also much more adamant about "deliverables"—a word that I'd never heard them use before, and which I assumed must have come from White House coaching. One was the idea of turning CSCC into what they called a "global engagement hub." Whether this was an expansion of CSCC or a totally new organization wasn't clear. It made sense, especially if it would help the organization move to the next level. Why not have an entity that combated disinformation wherever it came from? In either case, it would also require changing the original executive order creating CSCC or crafting a new one.

Ben arrived late—as usual—and missed the beginning of the sprint team's presentation. Chief of Staff Denis McDonough arrived even later. When the team finished its presentation, about two minutes after Denis arrived, he looked around the room and said, "Okay, let's go ahead." Hmm. But with what exactly? There wasn't a plan for any of those things.

I supported most of the recommendations—many of which we had already come up with—and was amazed at how quickly it had all been ratified. When the White House wants something, it can move quickly. I was leaving the next day for Malaysia—where I was going to sign a memorandum of understanding with the Malaysians to create an anti-ISIS messaging center like Sawab—and I sent a memo to Lisa and Ben that night. I told them we were eager to move ahead, but I pointed out that the degree of difficulty for the global engagement hub was high, given that we'd have to get a new executive order.

A few weeks later, when the White House was getting ready to make an announcement about the changes, Jen called and said, I have good news and bad news. What's the good news? I asked. She said, You got everything you wanted about how it's going to be done. What's the bad news? She said, They want to stick with the name Global Engagement Center. I think I'd been advocating some nonmaterial difference like Center for Global Engagement; I couldn't even remember. I told her that was good news *and* good news. The whole idea would potentially turbocharge what CSCC was doing and set it up for expansion, and, perhaps, a larger mission.

The Meeting Is All

Government runs on meetings. Meetings are the means and the end, the process and the result, the preparation and the deliverable. The briefing of principals before important meetings is how pretty much everyone gets up to speed on whatever topic the meeting is about. My chief of staff would brief me for a meeting where I would brief the Secretary for his meeting to brief the President. There was a chain of briefings going upward that stopped with the President. And, then, of course, there was a reverse chain going downward to brief everyone about what had happened at the meetings.

The President had called for a security briefing at the National Counterterrorism Center on terrorist threats. The Thanksgiving and Christmas holidays were coming up, and he wanted to be briefed on what threats were out there and be seen to be preparing for them. It was a few weeks after ISIS-inspired gunmen had killed 130 people in Paris, including 90 at a rock concert at the Bataclan theater. The Secretary would be briefing the President at the meeting, and I was called in to brief the Secretary that morning. I had seen the pre-brief for the NCTC meeting the night before, and there was only a small section on CSCC and counterterrorist messaging at the end. I'd fill in the Secretary on the changes under way. I thought they probably wouldn't even get to it, and I had everything in my head anyway.

We gathered in the Secretary's outer office after the 8:30 meeting. As usual, people arrived in a haphazard way. Claire, the Secretary's longtime assistant, came in and started a fire in the fireplace. Then the Secretary ambled in, in shirtsleeves, holding a sheaf of papers. He sat down and looked around. One of the things that being a principal in government does to you is that it makes you a little passive about seeking information. It's a kind of learned helplessness. Sometimes I would walk into a meeting where I was to be briefed on something without knowing the exact topic and wait for it to be revealed. I could see the Secretary was discreetly waiting to hear what the meeting was about.

Jon Finer had become the Secretary's chief of staff, and only confirmed the wisdom of that appointment by swiping Jen Stout for the Secretary's deputy chief of staff. I consoled myself because I suspected Jen could be even more helpful on the 7th floor. Jon explained this was a pre-brief before the national security meeting for the President at NCTC. Kerry nodded. He got a quick rundown on the coalition and what was happening on the ground, and then Jon turned to me to talk about the changes in the messaging space. I quickly mentioned the sprint team and the four principles guiding CSCC's evolution: data, partnerships, campaigns, and hubs. I said we would need an executive order to make the envisaged changes. I noted that ISIS messaging was on the wane, while anti-ISIS messaging was growing.

My general strategy in these kinds of meetings is not to speak too long. Some folks drone on and on, and I never wanted to be one of them. Sometimes Kerry would get a little testy when people spoke too long. But this morning, I had perhaps been too short. He didn't quite seem to be processing what I was saying. From the corner of my eye, I saw Finer lean over to Jen and whisper something in her ear. A few minutes later, the Secretary cut short the meeting by saying he had a call with the Russian foreign minister about Ukraine. He muttered something about the Russians not adhering to the Minsk agreement. When the Secretary went back into his private office, Jen made a beeline over to me and said, "You're going to be the Secretary's plus-one at the NCTC briefing."

Sure, I said, without quite understanding what that meant. And then she lit into me. "You have to give fuller explanations. You can't assume that he knows all of this or the backstory or all the acronyms. Be very simple and straightforward. And when you speak at the NCTC meeting, don't use all those phony jargony phrases the sprint team loves. POTUS hates that stuff. And make sure you say everything you want to say the first time you're called on, because you won't get a second chance!" And then she dashed off.

I hustled back to my office to make a few notes, but Kathy informed me I needed to be back on the seventh floor to meet the Secretary. I ran back up, and as I arrived, the Secretary was walking into his private elevator to go down to the garage. I jumped in. When we got downstairs, I looked around to see who else was coming. But there was no one else. The driver motioned for me to get in. The first thing the Secretary did was pull out his briefing books and start reading. Good. That gave me time to collect my thoughts.

It's about a 20-minute drive from State to NCTC in Tysons Corner. The Secretary read as we cruised along the George Washington Memorial Parkway, but as we got into the Potomac Hills, he put the books down, gazed out the window, and started reminiscing a bit about his early days in Washington. As we passed through McLean, he gestured out the window to the right and said, That's where Hickory Hill is, Bobby's house. He talked about visiting the Kennedy house when he was a young man. He said there were so many kids running around you couldn't even count them.

Then he asked me about messaging. I had Jen's advice still ringing in my ears. I said that most Americans and even most people in government didn't really understand this messaging battle. It wasn't ISIS versus America; it was ISIS versus the world. Less than 10 percent of their messaging was in English; most of it was in Arabic. They did more in Russian and French than in English. Russian was their second-biggest language. It wasn't what we were doing against ISIS; it was what mainstream Islam was doing against ISIS. He was listening.

We pulled up to the NCTC entrance quite a bit before the President's motorcade. It was raining. A military aide rushed over with an umbrella for the Secretary. I realized that as the only one there, I was also *staffing* the Secretary. I grabbed his notebooks, and tried to shield them from the rain. When we got into the building, lots of folks were milling around, but no one told us where to go. The Secretary just charged off in one direction, with me tailing behind. *Bad staffing.* Eventually, some people noticed a six-foot-four Secretary of State wandering the halls of NCTC with a perplexed staffer and guided us up to the meeting room.

It was a secure, modern triangular room. In the middle was an enormous V-shaped table, with three seats at the front for the President, National Security Advisor Susan Rice, and Lisa Monaco. The other chairs were for Director of National Intelligence James Clapper, Attorney General Eric Holder, FBI Director James Comey, NCTC head Nick Rasmussen, and a few others. I took a seat against the wall. Secretary Kerry was talking intently to the Attorney General about something, and then waved me over. He asked if I was prepared to give the President an overview of counterterrorism messaging (Jen had not told me that!), and I said, Absolutely. I'm not sure whether he and the Attorney General saw me gulp.

The President, Susan, and Lisa arrived through the back door, said a few hellos, and then found their seats. Obama seemed relaxed and began in a low-key way by saying he wanted to do this meeting here at NCTC rather than in the Situation Room at the White House as a way of thanking the men and women of the operations center who were working 24/7 through the holidays. He wanted to hear about threats to the homeland and make sure we were prepared for any eventuality. Lisa took over and ran the meeting crisply. Nick Rasmussen went through an extensive list of homeland threats. They were mostly, as the intelligence community would say, "aspirational." James Comey was up next. He's an impossibly tall guy—six feet eight—and his voice seems as big as he is. He began to talk about the follow-up to the San Bernardino, California, shooting. He made it clear that he wasn't at all happy with Apple's refusal to break the encryption on the shooter's phone, but he said that the FBI was exploring some work-arounds he thought would be successful. The President nodded.

Next up was Secretary Kerry. When Lisa introduced him, she mentioned that I was there as well to talk about counter-messaging. The Secretary began by saying that the department had contacted all posts and embassies about security as well as threats internationally and domestically. And then he swung into counter-messaging and basically repeated word for word what I had briefed him on in the car, including the actual proportions of what ISIS did in Arabic (82 percent) versus English (8 percent).

When he finished, he turned toward me, and Lisa said, Rick, go ahead. I was sitting against the wall, while all the main speakers were at the table. I looked down at my notes for a second and then heard, "Stand up, Rick." It was the President. I stood. I swung into my overview of the changes we were making at CSCC and said that we had been informed by the good insights of the sprint team and that we were remaking CSCC along the four lines of data, partnerships, campaigns, and hubs. But then I paused and said my hope was that it would basically become a kind of media company, either creating content for us or helping others do the same for themselves. I wheeled out the slogan I sometimes used at State: Let's do what we do best and outsource the rest. I saw the President smile at that. It's a very Obamaesque notion. I mentioned the Sawab Center and how I'd just returned from Malaysia with a memorandum of understanding for another counter-ISIS messaging center. You always try to get your successes out in a drumroll.

When I paused for a moment, the President jumped in.

"Rick, I like what I'm hearing, but I have a question, and it's not a facetious one."

He asked me what I, as a longtime journalist, thought of the idea that Western media had contributed to ISIS's success in the information war. He finished by saying, If you agree, what would you do about it? I told him that I didn't think it was a facetious question at all and then explained that I thought media turned ISIS from a niche brand into a global one by playing up their wanton violence and their victory narrative. Which was ISIS's marketing plan. I mentioned the old local news slogan "If it bleeds, it leads." The problem with TV news was that there was never any sense of scale, of proportionality.

I added that I thought it would be useful for media organizations to know some of the things that we did about ISIS messaging, Russian disinformation, and the weaponization of information in general. I thought, in fact, it was our obligation to tell them. Why not have the heads of the networks and news divisions come to the White House and the State Department to be briefed on what the reality was? There was much more ignorance in the media than I would have imagined about what was happening in the global information war.

Well, I could see pretty quickly that the President didn't care for the idea of bringing in media and news leaders. He shook his head and said he didn't think he could do that, but that it wasn't a bad idea. He let me down easy.

The President then pivoted the discussion back to the domestic space, and I let my mind wander back to what had happened in our interaction. One thing I did wish was that the President and the whole White House would push back against the stuff they didn't like. I sometimes felt that the President had so willed himself to ride above negative coverage that it gave media too free a rein to criticize him. It felt like there were no consequences. Having the White House and the President privately criticize news executives would definitely have an effect on them. I know—I used to be one of them. Even though the NSC felt that it was responding to mistaken or unfair media coverage, we usually did so in a kind of passive-aggressive way, rather than just calling it out directly. The pollution of our own news ecosystem with disinformation was in fact a national security issue—and media leaders needed to understand that. They were part of the problem.

When the meeting was finished, the Secretary headed over to talk to Susan, and I made a beeline for Lisa. Lisa said that we would definitely need a new executive order for the changes at CSCC and that we should take the first crack at it.

When Kerry finished talking to Susan, he handed me his notebook and we headed downstairs. Again, there were no signs and no one was pointing the way. All the White House folks had vanished; they had been escorted out and led to their motorcade. When we finally made it to our car—in the rain, again—we were stuck behind the President's endless column of black SUVs. Kerry tapped his knee in irritation.

Shutdown

Donald Trump had a rally scheduled on the USS *Yorktown*, a World War II aircraft carrier that had fought in the Pacific and was now berthed in the harbor at Mount Pleasant, South Carolina. It was December 7, 2015. Pearl Harbor Day. The Yorktown was a museum ("Walk in the steps of heroes"), which cost $22 for adults and $14 for children. It was also a popular place for corporate events ("Keep your company afloat," said its events brochure) and weddings ("Love sets sail"). The Trump campaign had reserved space inside the 42,000-ton boat, and like most of Trump's rallies in South Carolina, this one was overbooked.

The day before, President Obama had given a televised address to the nation about the terrorist attack in San Bernardino, where 14 people were killed by an ISIS-supporting Muslim American man and his Pakistani-born wife using semiautomatic weapons. It was the worst mass shooting in the U.S. since the 2012 Sandy Hook Elementary School shooting. It also came a little less than a month after the Paris attacks in which three ISIS-pledged terrorists killed 130 people.[2]

On a podium in front of a boisterous crowd, Trump began by saying, "We start by paying our great respects to Pearl Harbor!"— as though Ms. Harbor were some venerable local politician who was unable to be at the rally. The crowd roared. Then he spent a few minutes reading polls showing him leading in Iowa and across the country and criticizing his rivals before referencing the San Bernardino shooting. He said he heard President Obama last night. "He refused to use the term 'radical Islamic terrorism.'"

Trump then held up a sheet of paper to show to the crowd and read from it:

"Donald J. Trump," he said, "is calling for a total and complete shutdown of Muslims entering the United States until our country's representatives can figure out *what the hell* is going on." Lots of cheering and clapping.[3]

To back up his call for a "shutdown," he cited dubious polling data from Frank Gaffney Jr., a man the Southern Poverty Law Center called "one of America's most notorious Islamophobes." Trump quoted from an online poll conducted by Gaffney's organization that said that "a majority—51 percent" of Muslims living in the U.S. believe they "should have the choice of being governed according to Sharia."[4]

Trump's proposed Muslim ban created a firestorm. The idea that the U.S. would impose a religious test for immigrants, and that Trump wanted to bar everyone from one particular religion, caused almost universal criticism. To cite just one reaction: former Vice President Dick Cheney said, "It goes against everything we stand for and believe in."[5] A joint statement from the Defense Department and State said that anything that suggests the U.S. "is at odds with the Muslim faith would be counter-productive to our efforts" to defeat ISIS.[6] In defending his policy the next day, Trump doubled down and likened his Muslim ban to Franklin Roosevelt's internment of Japanese Americans during World War II, one of the darkest moments in American history. "Take a look at what FDR did many years ago," he told George Stephanopoulos on ABC's *Good Morning America*, "and he's one of the most highly respected presidents."

I asked CSCC to monitor what was going on in social media in the Middle East and among ISIS fanboys. The reaction was predictable: Trump became Exhibit A in ISIS's narrative that America was at war against Islam. ISIS's media hub followed Trump closely and highlighted everything he did that was considered anti-Muslim. But it wasn't just the usual ISIS fanboys; we saw a spike in regular people in the Middle East talking about Trump. On my Twitter feed, a young Muslim woman from the Gulf had posted: "How can someone like Trump govern the most powerful country on earth? I swear to God, this man will be the end of America."

From the moment Donald Trump declared his candidacy, embassies around the world had flooded us with questions as to how to talk about him. What was our response to his remarks about Mexicans and Muslims and Russia? After the Muslim-ban speech, we were bombarded with questions. I was much more inclined to lean forward and say that we were a country founded on religious freedom and Trump's comments on barring Muslim visitors and immigrants went against what we stand for as a nation. We even sent out guidance like this, including pointed language from the President and the Secretary. Can't say it was really used. Most embassies, including those in the Middle East, were chary of commenting on anything that involved the presidential election. In the case of our own counter-ISIS messaging efforts, we played it straight. Both CSCC and the Sawab Center in Abu Dhabi tweeted out stories about the proposal and the negative reaction that it had caused.

After Trump's comments, I reached out to some of my close Arab partners. I spoke to a number of Middle Eastern ambassadors in D.C. as well. No one was happy about it, but the main question was, Should we speed up visa applications for visitors from their countries? And then, Isn't Secretary Clinton going to win and then all this will be water under the bridge? Well, it seemed that way, was all I could say. Inshallah.

The Trump Muslim ban and the hysteria around it did affect one of my initiatives for countering violent extremism. According to the U.N., there were more than 20 million refugees in the world, the highest number since World War II. Some 5 million of them were Syrian refugees. The image of the tiny drowned body of Alan Kurdi in the summer of 2015 had brought the issue home to the American public. President Obama had doubled the number of Syrian refugees the United States would accept, from 10,000 to 20,000—still an absurdly small number. Canada had already accepted 100,000.[7] Germany, over a million.

Along with the Institute of International Education, which implemented the Fulbright Scholarships, we had put together a scholarship program for 1,000 displaced Syrian university students to study in the U.S. Why not use our soft-power programs to help victims of hard power? The idea was we could use funding for educational exchanges, which Congress liked, to help deal with the refugee crisis.

We had gotten pledges from 750 universities to accept at least one Syrian student. Many told us they would be willing to accept more. But then Paris happened. And San Bernardino. And now the Muslim ban. On the advice of our legislative affairs office, we started to trim the plan. Any plan, of whatever size, required approval by Congress. We pushed it down to 500. Then, finally, to 100 students. Even a program this small still required congressional notification, or a CN, as it was called. What this meant was that the proposal had to be sent through the appropriations committees in the House and Senate, and they had 15 days to let us know whether it was approved or not. During that period, any member of the House or Senate—any one of 535—could place a "hold" on the program for any reason at all. Even with the reduction in the number of scholarships to 100, State's congressional affairs office advised us that it was a bad idea to move forward. The atmosphere was just too poisonous toward Muslims and refugees.

But I wanted to try, and we pushed ahead. Within 24 hours of the CN letters being delivered, we were notified that Representative Kay Granger of Texas had put a hold on the program. But Kay Granger was not just any representative. She was chair of the House Subcommittee on State, Foreign Operations, and Related Programs, which meant that she oversaw funding for all State Department foreign assistance programs. Not a small thing. The 7th floor was adamant that I not violate her hold and thereby jeopardize funding for the whole department. We talked about what to do. There weren't a lot of good options. I thought, Why don't I just call Congresswoman Granger? People were skeptical, but a call was duly set up. She was down in Texas. Granger was the first Republican woman to represent Texas in the House. She had been an English teacher, and then became the first woman mayor of Fort Worth. On the phone she was friendly but cautious. I walked her through the program. I explained that the Syrians were all graduate students whose studies had been interrupted. They weren't terrorists. In fact, they were fleeing terrorism.

She listened patiently and then said, "Well, Mr. Stengel, where I come from in North Texas, people down here just don't want to take a risk like this." She didn't mention terrorism or Syria or Islam or Donald Trump or Russia, but then she didn't have to. "I'm sorry," she said.

"Lisa"

A few weeks later, Russia's main state-run news channel led its 9 p.m. news broadcast with an explosive report from Berlin. "Evidence has emerged," said the female presenter, "that migrants in Germany have started raping children." And not just any child, but a 13-year-old girl of Russian heritage named Lisa whose aunt said she had been kidnapped on the way to school and held for 30 hours by Syrian migrants who had repeatedly gang-raped her. Lisa was said to hold both Russian and German citizenship. The broadcast then aired a blurry video that allegedly showed a Syrian immigrant bragging about raping a "virgin."

The next morning, German police confirmed that the girl had indeed been reported as "missing." Russian Foreign Minister Sergei Lavrov called a press conference in Moscow and raised the issue of "our girl Lisa," saying, "I really hope that the migration problems won't lead to an attempt to whitewash reality with political correctness for domestic political reasons."

Russian media went to town on the story. RT ran several pieces on the fear Germany's Russian-speakers—almost three million people—had about refugees. "They are all parasites," said one Russian-speaking woman. RIA Novosti reported that 500,000 of these "Russian Germans" were keen to move back to Russia because of their anxiety about Syrian refugees. Germany, the stories suggested, was disintegrating because of the refugee crisis, and Western countries were unraveling because of a foolish multiculturalism. In Berlin, more than 500 protesters, supported by the German anti-Islam movement PEGIDA (the German acronym standing for Patriotic Europeans Against the Islamization of the West), gathered in front of the Federal Chancellery holding signs that said, "Our Children Are in Danger." The German-language version of RT televised the rally live.[8]

I was in Berlin at the time on a trip designed to advise our German allies on how to help Syrian immigrants assimilate. I was scheduled to confer with German public affairs people and nonprofits about the best way to talk about immigration and assimilation. But I was mindful of the fact that the United States, despite our long history of welcoming immigrants and refugees, had accepted only a tiny fraction of the number of Syrian refugees taken in by Germany.

On my first evening in Berlin, in an elegant restaurant filled with striking modern art, I moderated a panel of young Germans who were called *Migrationshintergrund*, a term that means "people of immigrant background." They were bright, appealing, and articulate. Each of them talked movingly about their desire to be fully German and be accepted by German society. There was a tall, polished young woman in uniform whose parents had emigrated from Egypt. She was a sergeant in the German army, and proud of it, but felt that ordinary Germans did not accept her as German. "And I am fighting for them," she said.

The next morning, I visited a school on the outskirts of Berlin that was hosting dozens of Syrian refugees who were learning German. They were all in their late teens or early twenties. I chatted with a number of them who seemed grateful to Germany for opening its arms to them. They wanted to reciprocate. They wanted to learn German. They all had individual German tutors, courtesy of the local community and government. I got into a longer conversation with a slight, blue-eyed

Syrian refugee with a scraggly beard who spoke pretty good English. He told me he had left Syria because of ISIS and Assad, and said he wasn't sure which was worse. He related how he had spent the last four years traveling from Syria to Lebanon to Turkey to Greece and finally to Germany. I mentioned that German Chancellor Angela Merkel had said the other day that if there were no war in Syria, the immigrants would return home. I asked him if he would go back to Syria if there were peace. He smiled ruefully and said, "Maybe in 100 years." There was nothing to go back to, he said. "My country has been destroyed."

Within days, the Lisa story changed dramatically. A spokesperson for the Berlin police told reporters that a medical examination showed that Lisa had not been raped or assaulted. "There was neither an abduction nor a rape," the spokesperson said. What emerged was that the girl had been hiding from her parents at the apartment of a 19-year-old German friend because of difficulties at school.

Not only did the whole story unravel, but the role of Russian disinformation was clearly exposed. Germany's newspaper *Bild* reported that the video aired by Russian Channel One that first evening of an immigrant boasting about raping a virgin had appeared on YouTube some six years earlier. The German broadcaster Deutsche Welle revealed that a woman who had been filmed for Russian TV saying she planned on moving to Russia was one of a number of regular paid actors for Russian TV.[9]

Russian media, Russian trolls, and the Russian government had used the disappearance of the girl to create a wave of disinformation around the integration of refugees into Germany. The Russians clearly saw that immigration was a wedge issue in Germany. It was part of a larger Russian strategy to create discord in Germany and undermine Mrs. Merkel by weaponizing immigration. At the same time, the Russian military's bombing in support for Bashar al-Assad was displacing hundreds of thousands and increasing the flow of immigration.

The Lisa story followed a trajectory common in Russia's information war with the West:

1. A state-sponsored Russian media outlet airs a piece of fraudulent news, which is then amplified by other Russian media and Russian trolls.
2. A Russian state official cites the bogus report at a press conference or news event.
3. Western media then report on the official citing the story, and the initial false information becomes part of the mainstream debate.
4. Demonstrations are organized via Facebook and other social media.
5. Finally, if and when the story is debunked, the same Russian officials decry the criticism as anti-Russian propaganda.

Russian active measures in Germany have a double edge: they seek to sow discord in German society and to boost support for Russia. Putin, who served as a KGB officer in Dresden during the Cold War, sees Germany as a critical target in the Russian information war. After Mrs. Merkel had led the drive for European sanctions against Russia following its annexation of Crimea, Putin ramped up Russian disinformation in Germany. RT opened a German-language channel called RT Deutsch, which parroted the Kremlin's line on Ukraine and published reams of anti-U.S. and anti-NATO stories. Kremlin disinformation sought to exacerbate Germans' distrust toward the mainstream media by calling it "fake news." A poll in late 2014 showed that 44 percent of Germans believed that mainstream media distorted the news.

Russia's weaponization of immigration was also a way of increasing support for right-wing anti-immigrant movements and white nationalism across Europe. In Germany, Russia supported anti-Islamic organizations like PEGIDA. Putin was positioning Russia as the beacon of traditional white Christian values.[10]

After Mrs. Merkel's leadership on Russian sanctions, German intelligence warned that Russia was increasing its espionage activity in Europe with the idea of destabilizing European unity and support for NATO. One piece of evidence they cited was a cyberattack on the main servers of the German parliament earlier in the year, which was traced back to Russian military intelligence, the same shadowy group that would later attack the servers of the Democratic National Committee in the U.S.[11]

Putin pivoted off the Lisa story to make a larger propaganda point. In a speech to the state Duma a few weeks after the incident, he said that Germans understood Russia's ethnic nationalism and its annexing of Crimea. He likened Russia's quest for ethnic unity to Germany's desire for unification. Let me remind you, he said, that Russia had supported German reunification. "Our nation," he said, "unequivocally supported the sincere, unstoppable desire of the Germans for national unity. I am confident that you have not forgotten this, and I expect that the citizens of Germany will also support the aspirations of the Russians, of historical Russia, to restore its unity.[12]

Perfectly played.

They Always Accuse You of What They're Doing

Want to hear a joke making the rounds in Moscow? Will Stevens asked me. It was the spring of 2015, and he had been the spokesperson at the embassy there for a few months.

Sure.

An American and a Russian are arguing about which country has more freedom. The American says, "I can go stand in front of the

White House and shout, 'Down with Barack Obama,' and nothing will happen to me."

The Russian replies, "I can go stand in front of the Kremlin and shout, 'Down with Barack Obama,' and nothing will happen to me either."

I laughed. Things were pretty grim in Moscow, Will said. After leaving the Ukraine Task Force and helping start the Russian Information Group, Will was now in the belly of the beast. It had changed his views on some things.

In Washington, he had been an advocate of trying to direct some messaging toward an audience in Russia itself. I'd always been skeptical. I used to joke that we didn't have any subscribers there. Will had wanted to give it a try, but now he had concluded that it wasn't worth it. Not because the government would censor us, but because Russians wouldn't listen. State propaganda in Russia was so relentless and comprehensive that there just wasn't an audience for an alternative view. He said 90 percent of Russians got their news from state newspapers and broadcasters. The Russian Information Group had continued to put out content that was attempting to rebut Russia's false narratives. Will was candid. It's certainly not having an effect in Russia, he said, and I'm not sure it's having an effect anywhere.

I was curious about how Donald Trump was being portrayed in Russia. Will said there wasn't all that much on him. Russian media liked the idea that Trump thought the U.S. should be friends with Russia. But, he said, no one in Russian media seemed to think that Trump had a chance.

Will had started sending back a smart weekly memo summarizing how the Kremlin had handled the main stories of the week. I found it useful because what they did at home was usually a model for what they eventually did elsewhere. Here's an excerpt from one of Will's memos summarizing the themes of domestic Russian media.

The West is preparing for war—the conflict in Ukraine is the beginning. TV outlets warned that NATO is building up its forces along Russia's borders under the guise of exercises, which are capable of delivering "free-fall nuclear bombs" with little warning to Russia.

Distract them with threats of Western mercenaries. TV outlets ran countless stories of newly discovered Western-supplied weapons and the dead bodies of pro-Kyiv fighters "in NATO uniforms." New footage appeared of "uniformed armed men speaking fluent English" around the scene of recent artillery explosions in Mariupol.

Europe is divided under the consequences of sanctions and American pressure. Russian state media—especially online and print media—continued to portray Russia as fully in charge of its economic situation, and Europe in disarray. Pro-Kremlin *Vzglyad* reported that the seven countries forming "the important part of Europe" opposed new Russian sanctions: Austria, Hungary, Italy, Slovakia, France, Greece, and the Czech Republic.

Will told me about one of the most popular talk shows on Russian TV, which was hosted by Dmitry Kiselyov, whom Putin had personally appointed to head the state-owned news agency Rossiya Segodnya. His signature catchphrase on the program was "A coincidence? I don't think so!" For Kiselyov, no conspiracy theory involving American power was too far-fetched. He was famous for saying that Russia was the one country that could turn America into "radioactive ashes."[13]

Will said the Russian media environment was so relentless that even the traditional effort by our public affairs people to pitch pro-American stories was useless. Putin had gotten rid of most of Russia's independent media, and state media weren't interested. Putin's discovery that the protesters in 2011 had used Facebook to organize had stimulated a number of countermeasures: the rise of state-sponsored trolls, the creation of VKontakte, and the passage of the Russian data-localization law in 2014. This law states that tech companies must store Russian citizens' personal data on Russian servers on Russian soil. Facebook and Google were upset about the law, which they saw as a threat to their businesses. Putin described the law as protecting the Russian people's personal information from spying by the American NSA. In fact, the law gave the Russian security services unrestricted access to Russian citizens' data.

Russian propaganda tapped into all the modern cognitive biases that social scientists write about: projection, mirroring, anchoring, confirmation bias. We put together our own guide to Russian propaganda and disinformation, with examples.

- **Accuse your adversary of exactly what you're doing.**
- **Plant false flags.**
- **Use your adversary's accusations against him.**
- **Blame America for everything!**
- **America blames Russia for everything!**
- **Repeat, repeat, repeat.**

What was interesting about this list is that it also seemed to describe Donald Trump's messaging tactics. Was this a coincidence (with apologies to Mr. Kisleyov), or some kind of mirroring? I took a look at how Russian state media had portrayed Trump during the first few weeks and months of his candidacy. When Trump announced his candidacy, RT wasn't very bullish on him. That first day, they led with a story titled "Trump Trumped by Twitter Trolls," and the first one they cited was someone who said, "I demand to see Donald Trump's hair's birth certificate." The story recounted tweets that mocked not only his hair but also his "I'm really rich" statement and the fact that he kept talking long after he'd made his actual announcement.[14]

Though RT wasn't too favorable on Trump's candidacy at the outset, within a couple of months they had changed their tune. A month after he entered the race, hundreds of Russian-backed trolls were tweeting positively about him. A story by the *Wall Street Journal* later showed that of the more than 100,000 tweets from accounts orchestrated by the Internet Research Agency in St. Petersberg during the first three months of Trump's candidacy, pro-Trump tweets outnumbered anti-Trump tweets by a 10-to-1 margin. Many of these accounts, as per the guidance from the IRA, pretended to be Americans.[15]

Even though we monitored Russian media coverage of Trump and saw the occasional pro-Trump tweet, the truth was that we were not at all focused on Russian messaging within the U.S. And, frankly, even if we were more aware of it, there wasn't much we could have done. By law, State Department communications had to direct its messaging toward foreign audiences. Putin didn't have the same legal restrictions.

A week after Trump's speech in South Carolina on Pearl Harbor Day, Putin had his annual press conference with Russian journalists. Putin was asked about Trump. He was diplomatic. "He is a very flamboyant man, very talented, no doubt about that," Putin was quoted as saying. "He is the absolute leader of the presidential race, as we see it today. He says that he wants to move to another level of relations, to a deeper level of relations with Russia. How can we not welcome that? Of course we welcome it."[16]

The Brexit Predicate

Brexit rattled the State Department. Not only was it disastrous on its own—a blow to the Atlantic alliance, the EU, the special relationship!—but it seemed a terrible augury for America. It was not that we hadn't considered the prospect that Leave might win. I'd convened a PD meeting to plan for that possibility. It's just that no one deep down thought it would happen. The calm and levelheaded British people would put the brakes on this global gallop toward nationalism. No one could believe that England—that green and pleasant land!—would reject what our two countries had advocated for 75 years. Was this the beginning of the end of the post-1955 world order that we had created and managed? In a million different ways, the State Department had been the backer and promoter of this postwar order of globalization and free trade, indeed, the very idea of Europe itself.

The Brexit vote confirmed the rise of a kind of insular nationalism that spurned immigration and demonized "foreigners," a nationalism that chose walls over bridges. The EU itself was conceived as an antidote to the toxic nationalism that caused two world wars and the deaths of more than 100 million people in the 20th century. The vote was also a triumph for Vladimir Putin, who had sought to undermine European unity at every opportunity. We seemed to be entering a world that was no longer divided between left and right, but between open and closed. A world of blood and borders. It felt like the beginning of the end of the post-1945 world order.

I held an all-hands PD meeting a couple of days after the vote. There was a lot of dismay, a lot of frustration with the British media and with voters who were susceptible to sensationalist news coverage. Secretary Kerry was already headed to Brussels and London and said the U.S. would work with the U.K. and the EU for a "sensible, thoughtful transition." We uttered all the usual platitudes. The people had voted.

It doesn't alter the special relationship. The European Union will go on. But of course, one couldn't really know any of that.

Even though the vote was about whether to leave the European Union, polls showed that Leave voters were motivated mainly by anti-immigration sentiments. While young Britons voted to remain, older white Britons and those living in rural areas where there were few if any immigrants voted to leave. These Leave voters believed that immigration was destroying traditional British life and that being a member of the EU opened the U.K. to swarms of immigrants. But the fact that almost all studies showed that immigration had actually boosted Britain's economy and lowered the cost of government services did not seem to affect those voters. Their doubts—their *prejudices*—were inflamed by a British tabloid press that splashed on its front pages lurid stories about refugees committing crimes. The British press did its own versions of the Lisa story. Tabloids featured stories about two 14-year-old girls from Newcastle who were allegedly sexually assaulted by four Syrian refugees.[17]

We had seen some worrisome signs in the run-up to the vote. Even though Putin had said he was officially neutral on the vote, he talked about how immigration was undermining traditional Europe. As did Donald Trump, who called himself "Mr. Brexit." Trump said immigration was changing the fabric of Europe, and talked about how his friend "Jim" did not go to France anymore because "Paris was no longer Paris."[18]

I had the Russian Information Group go back and look at what Russia had done in the months before the vote. It was disturbing. Although the Russian government said it was officially neutral on Brexit, Russian state media was not: in the six months before the vote, RT and Sputnik ran more than 250 stories tilted in favor of Brexit and against immigration. In addition, hundreds of Russian bots and trolls from the Internet Research Agency in St. Petersburg were posting about Brexit on thousands of Twitter accounts. And then there was Nigel Farage, the Trump-like British politician who became a star of Russian state media.

Farage was a member of the European Parliament who became the leader of the U.K. Independence Party (UKIP), which campaigned to leave the European Union. He was theatrical and alarmist, and never let a fact get in the way of an embroidered story. His two refrains, which he tweeted regularly, were "We must break free of the EU and take back control of our borders" and "We must put the British people first." His campaign was "Britain First" in everything but name. Farage was featured in dozens of stories from RT, like this one:

> UKIP leader Nigel Farage said women could be at risk of "mass sex attacks" by gangs of migrants due to "big cultural issues" should Britain choose to remain in the EU . . . In a scathing attack against David Cameron, Farage called the prime minister "Dishonest Dave," and accused him of lying to keep Britain in the 28-member EU bloc . . . The UKIP leader also said "migrant-related crime" has risen and that "41% of crimes last year were committed by people who don't have British passports."[19]

There it is in one story: racist accusations against immigrants of color; a belittling nickname for his opponent; and statistics that are made up or wildly off. It is the Trump formula to a T. Who was mirroring whom is hard to say. Farage is quoted extensively and approvingly in an RT story with this headline: "Trump Backs Brexit, Brands Migration Crisis a 'Horrible Thing for Europe.'" In September 2016, it was widely reported that RT had offered Farage his own show.[20]

For months, Farage had also been a regular writer and presence on another dubious platform: Breitbart News. Farage says he was recruited by Brietbart's editor, Steve Bannon. On Breitbart, he wrote pieces titled

"TTIP Is About Giant Corporates Dominating Our Economies" and "UK Migration Cover Up: The Government Must Release the REAL Figures Immediately." He gave an "exclusive" interview to Breitbart in which he said that President Obama's visit to the U.K. before the vote backfired and caused a "Brexit bounce."[21]

Later, Farage crossed the Atlantic to actually campaign for Donald Trump, speaking at a Trump rally in Jackson, Mississippi. He came over for two of the presidential debates—St. Louis and Las Vegas—and was an enthusiastic surrogate for Trump in the spin rooms afterward.[22]

The Brexit vote was a setback for both counter-Russian and counter-ISIS messaging. Digital jihadis saw it as further evidence that the West was anti-Islam.[23] Russian trolls crowed about the Brexit victory, saying it was a blow against the immigration crisis that was destroying Europe. But to focus exclusively on what Russia—or ISIS—did in the messaging space misses the larger issue of mainstream media coverage. The problem, frankly, was not that Russia Today overcovered the Leave campaign, but that the liberal mainstream British press, from the *Guardian* to the BBC, undercovered it. RT had a tiny fraction of the market share that the BBC had. But the BBC seemed to have underestimated the power of the Leave campaign. They missed the intensity of anti-immigrant sentiment. Polls did not reflect public opinion, in part because mainstream U.K. media had made being pro-Brexit socially unacceptable. That was a dangerous predicate. I wondered whether the liberal mainstream papers we so carefully analyzed every day at State—the *New York Times*, the *Washington Post*—were underreporting anti-immigrant sentiment in the U.S. and underestimating support for its champion, Donald Trump.

The Prince of Darkness

After almost two years of counter-ISIS messaging, the bright spot of our strategy was the growing partnerships on international hubs. In addition to forming the Sawab Center, we had signed a memorandum of understanding with the Malaysians and had been in talks with the Jordanians and the Nigerians.

Kerry liked this strategy, and one day, in February 2016, when we were seated next to each other at an anti-ISIS coalition meeting in Rome, he asked me if I'd thought about the Saudis as a partner. I said I hadn't. Well, he said, they had the religious credibility—the two holiest sites in Islam—and the money to do it. At which point he grabbed my arm and guided me over to Adel al-Jubeir, the Saudi foreign minister. In a loud whisper, he said, Rick wants to talk to you about a joint messaging center.

If I was a little less than enthusiastic about the idea, it was because I knew it would be an uphill struggle. The reason was pretty simple: the White House and many people at State were allergic to doing almost anything with the Saudis. They saw Saudi Arabia as an authoritarian monarchy that promoted and financed Islamic terrorism through its sponsorship of Wahhabi Islam and sharia schools around the world. Their attitude was, Why should we publicly partner with them in fighting ISIS messaging when they were privately helping ISIS—or, at the very least, turning a blind eye? It was a good question.

But even if I was skeptical—and I was—my job was to see what might be possible. It would be up to the White House to move forward or not.

The trip was duly arranged, and the day before I was to arrive in Riyadh, on March 10, the *Atlantic* magazine published a cover story by Jeffrey Goldberg on President Obama's foreign policy, in which it was widely reported that Obama had called the Saudis "free riders" of the United States and had said Saudi Arabia must "share" the Middle East with Iran.[24] The Saudis weren't happy. I was the first U.S. official to visit the country after the piece, and I was given language to try to mollify them. No one suggested I should apologize, but the idea was to be positive about the U.S.-Saudi relationship.

On the morning I arrived in Riyadh, I was presented with my schedule. There were a half-dozen appointments listed, but every single one was flagged "TBD"—To Be Determined. Except for one, the one I didn't really want to do: a speech that evening at the U.S.-Saudi Business Forum. The Saudis never confirm any meeting until the last minute, or they just continually push back appointments later and later in the day. When meetings do happen, they never start on time, and then go way longer than scheduled. In Saudi Arabia, there is always the presumption that you have endless amounts of time.

I sat in the lobby of the Four Seasons that first day. Most of the TBD meetings were determined not to be happening. That night, though, I did give my speech, talking about the history of the American-Saudi relationship. Afterward, a young Saudi man came by to say he ran Mohammed bin Salman's media company. He told me that the prince had started his own ISIS counter-messaging center. I did not know about it and neither, it seemed, did our own intelligence. We had an animated conversation about counter-ISIS messaging for half an hour, at which point he stood up, bowed, and was gone. When I got back to my room that night, I learned that our schedule had firmed up for the following day. We were now set to visit bin Salman's messaging center and to see the prince himself at the end of the day.

Mohammed bin Salman—MBS, as he was invariably called—was then the great unknown in Saudi Arabia. Just 30 years old, he was a favorite son of the king, and seemed to be gunning to displace his older, more cautious cousin, Mohammed bin Nayef, as the crown prince. MBS was colossally ambitious. He had pioneered something called Vision 2030 for Saudi Arabia, a road map to the kingdom's future which included privatizing Saudi Aramco, tripling non-oil revenue by 2030, and reforming the culture. He knew how to appeal to the West: "Our vision for 2030 is a tolerant country with Islam as its constitution and moderation as its method." He saw himself as a progressive. The rap on him was that he was headstrong, even reckless.

The next afternoon, a fleet of black Saudi Suburbans picked us up for a visit to the Mohammed bin Salman messaging center at the royal court. The royal court was the seat of the Saudi government, and the messaging center was in a stunning Moorish-style building that featured acres of white marble and abundant gold leaf. Walking into the vast, high-ceilinged lobby with people scurrying to and fro holding sleek silver laptops was a little like the scene in old James Bond movies where you suddenly glimpse the lair of the Dr. No character—it's meant to dazzle with its modernity and sophistication and industry. I thought about the small, grotty space that CSCC occupied back at the State Department, with its tiny cubicles and Dell desktops.

It was about five o'clock when we finished at the center, and the meeting with MBS was scheduled for seven. We decided to head to the palace and wait. There was tea, and the ever-present bowls of dates. At 6 p.m., we were told the meeting would be at 8. At 7, we were told that it would be at 10. At 10, nothing. Finally, at 11 p.m., there was some movement. The dates and tea service were removed. At five minutes to midnight, an escort led us into an ornate ballroom with 50-foot ceilings and towering mirrors on all sides. Two rows of plush chairs with side tables with more tea and dates. At the front of the room was a tall high-backed chair. Slowly MBS's retinue filed in and occupied the 12 chairs on his side. I had only two other people, but we also had 12 chairs. Finally, MBS sauntered in. He's big and burly, maybe six feet two, with a scraggly black beard and penetrating eyes. He took the seat in the front of the room and then moved his chair over to be closer to me. He launched right into it—no preamble, no courtesies, no apology for being late—a whirlwind.

"We are old friends, the U.S. and Saudi Arabia," he said. "We go back through many U.S. presidents. We share many interests. America is our indispensable partner. Our political, military, and economic systems are all based on America. If the U.S. had not guided Saudi Arabia for the last 70 years, we'd be an Arab version of North Korea." Then he smiled and said, "But if we were allied with China or Russia, they would be the premier power in the Middle East, not you."

He seemed intent on rebutting the *Atlantic* article without actually referring to it. Not only was Saudi Arabia not a free rider, but it was a vital partner in a mutually beneficial relationship. "We listen to you," he said, and then with another smile, "and we buy a lot of hardware." And then he paused. "But you cannot expect us to be as modern and democratic as America," he said. "When you were putting men on the moon, we were riding camels in the desert! It's taken the U.S. 300 years to get where it is today. Only 50 years ago in America, blacks and women barely had any rights. My country, as a country, is not even 100 years old. Women cannot drive, but they are lawyers and doctors and journalists and executives. We are making progress."

Then he offered his grand unified theory of the Middle East. "Before the 1979 Iranian revolution, there was no such thing as Islamic terrorism," he said. "There was no sectarianism. Before 1979, women could drive in Saudi Arabia. Before 1979, we had movie theaters and concerts. I want to bring them back. Women *should* be able to drive. Why shouldn't we have movie theaters? Our culture needs to be more modern. But everything changed in 1979. The Iranian revolution turned us all backward toward a conservative version of Islam. The Iranians have tried to dominate and take over the Islamic world. Before 1979, no one knew or cared who was Sunni and who was Shia. It was not an issue."

Of course, this view of the Middle East was fundamentally at odds with how President Obama saw things. In that same *Atlantic* article, Obama had said that sectarianism in the Middle East had existed for millennia and that countries were forever trying to draw the U.S. into religious battles that were none of our business.

MBS paused, and I thought that before he caught his breath again, I would raise the idea of a messaging center. I said we now faced a common challenge with ISIS and Islamic extremism. I said that I had been impressed with his royal messaging center and that we'd like to explore a potential partnership like the one we had with the UAE to create the Sawab Center in Abu Dhabi.

"Ah, yes!" he interrupted me—the whirlwind was back. "Yes, yes, I apologize if I'm insulting you, but we don't think much of this Sawab Center. We are much more ambitious than that, and we envision something much, much bigger. And, of course, the Emiratis do not have the credibility in the Muslim world that we do. We want to create a joint Saudi-American messaging center that would work with the Western coalition, the Islamic coalition, and our religious leaders in Mecca and Medina. And," he said dramatically, "we want to have it all done in time for President Obama's visit!"

President Obama's visit was one month away.

That *was* ambitious. MBS was a powerful salesman, but I knew how difficult this would be, even from just a logistical standpoint, not to mention the political opposition to it. I was diplomatic—too diplomatic for him, as it turned out. It was a worthy goal, I said; let me take it back to Washington to consider. He looked at me blankly. He was disappointed, more than disappointed. He had obviously been hoping for an immediate yes. Instead, he pivoted in his chair abruptly, looked out at the queue of people waiting outside, and summoned the next group. We were done.

As we were leaving, I asked our Saudi staff to work with my office in Washington to put together a potential two- or three-page memorandum of understanding for a joint U.S.-Saudi messaging center along the lines that MBS had suggested. I said it must include two points that were nonnegotiable: the U.S. gets to approve all content the center produces, and the Saudis cannot use any digital information domestically.

I sent a memo to the Secretary about the trip. A day later, we sent the proposed memorandum of understanding to the White House—leaving plenty of time if they wanted to have an agreement to sign during the President's visit. The President never raised the idea during his trip.

The Showdown That Wasn't

On one side of the long rectangular table were Tim Cook, the CEO of Apple; Sheryl Sandberg, the chief operating officer of Facebook; Reid Hoffman, the founder of LinkedIn; and Susan Wojcicki, the CEO of YouTube. On the other side were Denis McDonough, the President's chief of staff; Jeh Johnson, the Secretary of Homeland Security; James Comey, the head of the FBI; and Lisa Monaco, the President's deputy national security advisor.

We were in San Jose, California, at the West Coast branch of the U.S. Patent and Trademark Office, for the much-discussed "summit" between the Obama administration security team and Silicon Valley. The preparations for the meeting had been made in secret, but when word got out that it was happening, the media depicted it as a "showdown." Ever since the San Bernardino terrorist attack, when Apple was either unable or unwilling to open up the shooter's phone to law enforcement, the tension between Silicon Valley and the White House over encryption had escalated. The White House was anxious to protect

Americans from the threat of domestic terrorism inspired by ISIS, and Silicon Valley was anxious to protect its users' privacy. It was the high-tech version of the age-old security-versus-privacy debate. Law enforcement wanted a way to get data from encrypted phones, while Apple and others said their users' privacy trumped concerns about security. The media kept asking, Would Obama's team confront the mandarins of Silicon Valley over encryption?

I wasn't sure of the answer.

For some months, there had been internal talk of a summit meeting between the White House and Silicon Valley on issues of domestic terrorism and privacy. Ever since the rise of ISIS, the NSC had thought the big tech companies were not doing enough to take violent extremist content off their platforms. During the preparation for the meeting, I realized that the White House's push on the sprint team and the new name, Global Engagement Center, were "deliverables" for the summit. Denis McDonough was the summit's impresario, and he wanted to show the tech folks that we were making some progress.

A couple of weeks before the meeting, I was informed that I was going to be backbenching deputy secretary Tony Blinken, who was our lead. My role was to talk about our counter-ISIS messaging efforts. In the first of the NSC's memos I received on the summit, encryption wasn't even on the agenda. I then participated in a number of video calls to get ready for the meeting. One of them surprised me. Two days before the meeting, I'd joined on a call between the White House, the FBI, the Justice Department, and the CIA. It was testy. The representatives of those agencies were close to open revolt. Their bosses had all been outspoken in their belief that the tech companies needed to provide a "back door" to law enforcement in order to fight terrorism. We do not want our principal to fly all the way out to San Jose unless encryption is on the agenda, they said. The NSC said, We hear you.

The debate on encryption had become a public one. But to me, encryption was a side issue. The larger question was what do we do about the extremist material and disinformation that were seeping onto social media platforms? What could the tech companies do to purge their platforms of this poison? What could government do within the constraints of the First Amendment? What could be done about content that was false and designed to deceive people?

The platform companies were regularly pilloried in the press for not doing enough. I saw that a few White House folks shared this view. But I had seen what the tech companies were doing about ISIS messaging. Just that week, Twitter had announced that they had taken down some 250,000 handles of what they considered to be violent extremists who had violated their terms of service. We knew that they had removed significantly more than that. We had worked with Facebook and saw them ramping up their hiring of people who could vet and delete violent Islamist content. They now had hundreds of them and dozens of Arabic-speakers. There was a great deal more going on behind the scenes than most folks knew. More than the public or the White House knew.

I flew out the night before and got an urgent message from White House security saying the entrance had changed. Apparently, some press photographers were lurking around the main entrance to the building, and the digerati royalty didn't want their pictures taken. I went in the back way, as instructed. Most of the tech heads were there already. I knew a number of them from my years at *Time* and said quick hellos.

The White House crew arrived last. The greetings were friendly. Denis opened by saying how appreciative he was—and the President was—of everyone coming to the meeting. He was folksy and humble. He said, All of you are the symbols and the reality of the technical innovation that has made America the wonder of the world. And yet, we are being challenged by one of the most backward and barbaric groups the world has ever seen in the very space that we invented. How can that be? We have to figure out a way to fight them on these platforms, and we have to do it together. And then, he went at encryption head-on: we have a significant difference of opinion on this, he said, but that shouldn't stop us from talking about it. Nods of agreement around the table.

He introduced Lisa Monaco by saying she briefed the President every morning about every threat that was out there. Lisa began by saying that we were living in the most complex threat environment since 9/11. She said ISIS was an insurgency that was using the internet to tap into the disaffected and recruit new adherents. Now, they are looking outward from the so-called Caliphate and telling people to attack the West wherever they are. Yes, it's a war of ideas, but it's also a war. And it's here at home.

Next up was Comey. He began by earnestly thanking all those on the other side of the table. Because of the help you have given to law enforcement, he said, many people are alive who wouldn't otherwise be. Some murmurs of approval on the other side of the table. And then he told a story. It was about a potential domestic terrorist. He couldn't reveal any names or locations. He said the FBI had very little information to go on. He talked about the different tactics and tricks they used to try to locate the terrorist: wiretaps, cutouts, honeypots. He said they used hundreds of agents all across the country. It could have been a movie pitch.

At first, I think everyone was a little confused—though fascinated— by the story. But then the moral became clear. He said they eventually got a tip that led them to their man, averting a potential mass terrorist attack on American soil. The tip, he said, was a phone number. Comey then paused and said that if they'd had a back door into the suspects' phones, they would have gotten that number in the first few days of the investigation. The tech heads sat very still. Very few people will ever know that story, Comey said, and I've entrusted it to you. But just to be clear, he said, what is a business decision for you is a life-and-death matter for law enforcement and the American people. No one was nodding on the other side of the table now.

Jeh Johnson was next after Comey. He began in a self-deprecating way by saying he was really just a patent lawyer who had argued that Gillette's three-blade razor was incomparably better than Schick's four-blade razor. But then he got serious. The number one threat that keeps me up at night, he said, was a one-off event like San Bernardino. From his perspective, he said, he wanted to know how we could make terms-of-service agreements stricter and more effective. He said hate speech is protected in America, but terrorist speech is not. He defined "terrorist speech" as language that leads directly to or encourages violence.

Sheryl Sandberg was the first of the tech leaders to speak. She picked up on what Jeh had talked about and said, How do we get people who are passionately against such violent extremism to form a community? At the same time, she said, Facebook was expanding efforts to police its own community and platform. That will continue, but we're not experts on this. We need your help. We've been successful in looking for fraud, criminality, and child pornography—that can offer a road map for finding terrorists.

Then Tim Cook took the floor. He seemed to be the agreed-upon spokesperson for the group. He began by saying that the rest of the world is waiting for us to take the lead on coming up with standards for technology and speech and encryption. People will follow what we do. All of us here, he said, deal with foreign markets and governments. The irony, he said, is that we have much stricter laws on personal privacy than anyone else, especially the Europeans, who like to criticize us for our lack of privacy. Data in the U.S. has more privacy protection from government than data in any other country. Comey nodded in agreement.

We need a combination of social science and data science to figure out who is being radicalized, Cook said. Radicalization isn't a singular journey. It's not about being able to see what is on people's phones, he said. There were many paths. Then he addressed encryption and looked directly at Comey. "Let's be clear, the horse has left the barn on encryption. It's not going away and will only get more powerful. We need to think about how to protect ourselves in a world where encryption is a given." He said he knew that people in law enforcement and intelligence want a "back door." And then he paused. "If I felt that this was the thing that would protect us all, I'd be for it." Our users, he said, expect their private information to be kept private. He said that there is so much other data outside of encrypted information. "How do you optimize your ability to find a terrorist in a world where there is encryption?" he asked. "That is the question."

It was clear that Cook was speaking for all of them on this. The security folks were not happy. But Cook had not left any daylight on the encryption discussion, and no one seemed inclined to relitigate it. The rest of the meeting devolved to a more practical discussion of how we would all communicate with one another. Some of the tech leaders complained that they got requests from dozens of different government agencies, not to mention foreign governments.

I mentioned that we had started a counter-ISIS messaging center with the Emiratis and hoped to do more. I said our Arab coalition partners all want to be able to communicate directly with you rather than through us. Sheryl said, That's what we want too! We resolved to figure out a better way to communicate. The meeting began to break up because the White House folks had a military plane to catch back to D.C. There was definitely a spirit of cooperation in the air. There just wasn't a practical path to make anything happen. And not much did.

*   *   *

The meeting in San Jose wasn't my only foray into Silicon Valley. A couple of months later, in the summer of 2016, I saw that Secretary Kerry was going to the Global Entrepreneurship Summit at Stanford University—a public diplomacy effort started by President Obama. I set up a meeting between the Secretary and Mark Zuckerberg. We were running a terrific program with Facebook called P2P, short for People to People, that supported college students around the world who were creating anti-violent-extremist content. It was up and running at 100 colleges, and our plan was to expand it to 1,000. That was the ostensible subject of the meeting.

After Kerry's opening remarks at the summit, we piled into a couple of Suburbans to go to Facebook. The meeting was at the company's new Frank Gehry–designed headquarters, which had opened only the month before. As we walked in, the receptionist handed us badges that already had our names and pictures on them. It was the polar opposite of trying to get into the State Department.

The building featured what Facebook said was the largest open floor plan in the world. In the center of it was a giant glass box—they referred to it as "the aquarium"—where Zuckerberg had meetings. Zuckerberg was already there in his signature uniform: heather gray T-shirt, jeans, sneakers. He was wanly friendly, his demeanor even—not warm, not cool. He chatted with the Secretary as we were settling in, and then turned to me and said, When was the last time you were at Facebook? I knew he was referring to the time I had come there when we made him *Time*'s Person of the Year, but for the life of me, I was blanking on what year that was. I said, not very confidently, "2008?" He replied, "No, 2010." He was better prepped than I was. In fact, our team hadn't prepared at all.

Zuckerberg had one of Facebook's top lawyers there as well as their head of product policy and counterterrorism, Monika Bickert. We had been working closely with her for almost two years on removing ISIS content from their platform, as well as P2P. I had briefed the Secretary on the way over about the P2P program, and he launched right into how great and effective it was and how we'd like to ramp it up. As ever, he had processed his talking points perfectly, but the problem was that I had neglected to tell him Facebook was paying for everything! I quickly jumped in and thanked them for underwriting it.

Bickert, who knew more about the program than anyone else, then turned to Zuckerberg and said she'd love to scale it up to 1,000 universities. She mentioned how in her work with the State Department, we had both come to the conclusion that third-party voices were more effective than either of ours. That was the principle behind P2P. She then went into a presentation on what Facebook was doing about extremist content. She said they flagged about a million pieces of content a day. Then teams of content moderators—they have hundreds of them—decide what violates Facebook policies and should be referred to their legal team. When users are flagged for advocating violent extremism, Facebook also looks at their friends and "likes" to find others who might be similarly inclined. Let's say someone posts "Isis is cool," she said. Facebook will then look at posts that person has shared and see if any of the person's friends have expressed similar sentiments.

When she finished, Zuckerberg launched into a discussion about the potential of artificial intelligence to spot violent-extremist content and disinformation. He actually got excited. It was clear that Zuckerberg thought AI was *the* critical tool in combating extremist messaging or any undesirable content. He said it was still years away, but he thought that artificial intelligence would eventually be able to flag about 80 percent of the dangerous content that's out there, and humans would find the remaining 20 percent. This would be much more efficient than methods today, he said. He was confident that this was a solvable problem and added that we need to use computers for what computers are good at, and people for what people are good at. This seemed to be his mantra, and it wasn't a bad one.

Then he pivoted. He turned to the Secretary and said that there was something he'd like our help on. He then mentioned data localization, and specifically cited Russia's law. This was the law mandating that information on Russian citizens be stored in Russia. Will Stevens and I had talked about it a few months before. Zuckerberg was concerned that the law was now being copied in places like Turkey, Brazil, and Mexico. He explained that while Putin claimed it was a response to the Snowden revelations, it had more to do with a kind of digital nationalism and the Kremlin's desire to censor dissent. It was also meant as a slap at American tech companies. The law, he said, made it less appealing for anyone to do business in Russia or anywhere else that passed a similar statute. Ultimately, these countries were trying to impose state sovereignty on the digital sphere, he said, and that's not good for anybody. He wanted to see if the Secretary could take this up with the Russians and explain to them how it was not in their self-interest.

I hadn't briefed Secretary Kerry on the data localization law, and hadn't known that it would come up. But the Secretary's answer was diplomatic, in the best sense. He said talking to the Russians about anything involving their sovereignty was a pretty hopeless proposition. He said they were particularly sensitive about such things and looked at the American tech companies as tools of American soft power. Putin saw these American platforms as impinging on Russian sovereignty, and the law was his way of hitting back. Zuckerberg listened stoically and nodded. After that, the meeting petered out, and folks said goodbye and wandered off. Bickert found me as we were walking out, and told me that Zuckerberg had approved the funding for P2P to go up to 1,000 universities.

Before You Leap

I had always thought of myself as an accidental manager. I had started as a writer at *Time* and never had any desire to be an editor. That is, until I got frustrated by the management above me. I tended to be more motivated by negative examples than positive ones: if I saw poor leadership and thought I could do better, I jumped in. One of the things I had found frustrating in journalism is that so often the heads of news organizations were cerebral and reserved, and not the kind of leader who would jump out of the trenches and yell, Charge! Government was the same way.

Rashad Hussein was an absolutely brilliant guy, but he inherited an unhappy place that still had not found its footing. I knew he was not happy himself. With the guidance and direction of the sprint team report, I began to look for a new leader. The new head would need to transform the organization into one using data and campaigns, and supporting other credible voices. It was a turnaround.

I went back and looked at the list of potential heads of CSCC. I encountered the same problem I'd experienced before: the people I wanted weren't interested, and the people who were interested weren't people I wanted.

Over the past year, I'd gotten to know Joe Votel, a four-star general who had recently become head of U.S. Central Command and was in charge of the fight against ISIS in Iraq and Syria. Votel was bright and thoughtful and knew a lot about information operations. One day he said to me, Have you thought about an ex-military person or a retired general to run CSCC? There were several appealing aspects to this idea. One was that an ex-military person would not only understand the interagency process but also be able to get buy-in from the Defense Department and the intelligence community. Plus, I assumed that navigating the State Department bureaucracy would seem like child's play to someone from DOD. Through the State Department grapevine, I'd heard that Michael Lumpkin, the assistant secretary of defense for special operations/low-intensity conflict (SOLIC was the usual acronym) and a former Navy SEAL, was interested in CSCC. SOLIC was a serious job that encompassed counterterrorism, unconventional warfare, and information operations. I had met Lumpkin and seen him at meetings. He was impressive: intense, buttoned-up, well spoken.

A few days later, at a meeting at the State Department, Lumpkin wandered over and started talking to me about CSCC, how important its mission was, how vital the information war was, and how much he cared about it. It was music to my ears—which I suspect he knew. It was obvious that he was a salesman—not a bad thing in my book. CSCC could use one. I saw him again a few weeks later when we were both on General Votel's plane flying down to Tampa for a senior leaders' retreat on ISIS. He made an impassioned pitch for the job. There was nothing more vital right now than the battle against ISIS, he said. As for CSCC, he said, I know how to fix it

Lumpkin felt right. He satisfied my conditions: He knew the region, knew a fair amount about the digital space and messaging, and was a leader. I also wanted someone who would garner a little pop when it was announced, and bringing in a sitting assistant secretary at DOD would get people's attention. Plus, I didn't have a whole lot of alternatives. Or time.

The administration was winding down and we wanted to execute on creating the Global Engagement Center. I shared with him the sprint team's plan, and he not only agreed with it but was even more ambitious for the future of the GEC. He was talking about getting tens of millions of dollars to take it to the next level.

I told Lumpkin that if he was game, I wanted him to do the job. He said he was. I vetted the idea with Ben Rhodes and Jon Finer. We let State's office of personnel know, and they began their bureaucratic process. I talked regularly to Lumpkin, who told me that it was not going to be a problem with DOD.

But it turned out that it was a problem in an even more important place. I heard that National Security Advisor Susan Rice was concerned about the difficulty of replacing him at DOD with so little time remaining in the administration. It was a Senate-confirmed position. I went to see Ben, who told me that it was a messy situation but that he would be able to push it through. He did.

Who Has the Pen?

After the announcement of the creation of the GEC and its new leader, we all thought it was a good idea for Lumpkin to have a town hall with his new staff. I introduced him and said he was the right man at the right time for the right fight. Lumpkin stood up and said this was the most significant battle of our time. That it was a new kind of warfare. All modern warfare, he said, is hybrid warfare—a mixture of traditional kinetic fighting, information operations, cyberwar, and psychology. He compared the start of the GEC to the beginning of the Office of Strategic Services during World War II, the predecessor to the CIA. He said that the GEC could be something new in government.

Lumpkin had a lot to do. He needed to reshape the organization according to our new guidelines for the GEC and hire a number of new people, but the first order of business was writing the executive order that would create the center. This was not a simple thing. The technical definition of an "executive order" is a directive with the force of law issued by the President to manage the federal government. "Executive orders" don't appear in the Constitution and they don't require the assent of Congress, but they are the modern means by which presidents run the government. The most famous—and momentous—executive order in American history was Abraham Lincoln's Emancipation Proclamation. Since that time, presidents have used them a lot more frequently. Abraham Lincoln issued 48. Barack Obama, 276.

EOs, as they are often called, are one of the most fought-over pieces of business in the executive branch. They will sometimes take years to execute because lots of different agencies get to weigh in on them, and they basically decide how power and authority are distributed, which is what people in government care about.

In government, people often ask, Who has the "pen"? In other words, Who is really writing the law or the order or the memo? In this case, Lumpkin had the pen on behalf of the State Department. The person or entity that writes the order or legislation has a certain primacy—but in the end, it's not the person who writes the first word that matters, but the one who signs off on the final word. That's the White House.

Lumpkin focused a lot of attention and energy on the executive order. I suspect he saw it as a way to mold the organization according to his vision. Different variations of the EO had the GEC not as part of the State Department. One version of it had the head as a Senate-confirmed job. But just because you had the pen didn't mean that others weren't working on it. There were folks from my office and the NSC; the Middle Eastern bureau was weighing in, as was the Bureau of Counterterrorism. There were more than enough cooks.

In the end, Jen Stout along with NSC staff put the EO through the way we originally envisaged it, and the President signed it. To someone outside government, the issues people were fighting about in an executive order would seem microscopic. But they are the blueprint for how an organization is constructed. The EO for CSCC had taken a year to sort out, and this one, by comparison, was done in record time—ten weeks. Here's the top of it:

> *Executive Order 13721*
>
> **Section 1.** *Establishment of the Global Engagement Center.* The Secretary of State shall establish the Global Engagement Center which shall lead the coordination, integration, and synchronization of Government-wide communications directed at foreign audiences abroad in order to counter the messaging and diminish the influence of international terrorist organizations, including the Islamic State of Iraq and the Levant, al Qaida, and other violent extremists abroad.[25]

But, as it turns out, this was just the beginning.

Going For It

Senator Chris Murphy of Connecticut looked even younger in person than he did on television. He was warm, easy to talk to, knowledgeable. Our staffs had gotten us together, and we had that superficial friendliness that comes from having been on cable television together—even if we were never in the same studio. I wanted to brief him on our counter-ISIS efforts and get his support for the new Global Engagement Center. I had belatedly realized that I hadn't spent enough time talking to members of Congress.

I started telling Murphy what CSCC was up to, what we had learned about countering ISIS's messaging. I told him about the journey from CSCC to the new Global Engagement Center. I told him about the Sawab Center and the idea of creating other hubs with our allies.

He was listening, but I could see he wasn't really *listening*. He was being polite. He didn't have many questions. Then, I mentioned that I had also started a counter-Russian messaging group at the State Department, which, as far as I could tell, seemed to be the only one that existed in government. It was as though I'd told him he'd won the Connecticut Powerball lottery—he lit up and started shooting questions at me.

How big is it?

What does it do?

Where does it live at State?

Do you work with EUR?

Does Voice of America or Radio Free Europe have any role in it?

How many Russian-speakers do you have?

Murphy clearly knew a lot about Russian disinformation, and it was obvious that he saw it as a serious problem that wasn't being addressed.

In 2012, Murphy had run for and won Joe Lieberman's old Senate seat, and he shared Lieberman's interest in foreign policy. He was then 39, the youngest member of the Senate, and went on Foreign Relations, where he became chairman of the Subcommittee on European Affairs. That's where he got interested in Ukraine, first learned about Russian disinformation, and became friends with a more senior senator who had long been alarmed by Russian influence, John McCain. He traveled to Kiev at the end of 2013 with McCain and stood on the barricades of the Maidan and proclaimed, "Ukraine's future stands with Europe, and the U.S. stands with Ukraine."[26] Hard to say it better than that. Russia's annexation of Crimea, Murphy told me, was a crucible moment for him. Shortly after his trip to Kiev, he held a town hall in Hartford for Connecticut's robust Ukrainian community. "Today, Putin is marching on Ukraine," he told them. "But tomorrow he could be marching on a NATO ally that the United States has a treaty obligation to defend."[27]

Murphy's first reaction to the epidemic of Russian disinformation, like almost everyone's in Washington, was "How do we counter it?"

But he was more sophisticated than most and understood that simply "countering" it—whatever that meant—was not the answer. He was frank in his assessment that we were behind the curve when it came to confronting disinformation. The Russians, he knew, had been at it for longer than we had.

He wanted to know whether I thought boosting the budget of Voice of America or Radio Free Europe would help. I told him how we had started *Current Time*, the nightly half-hour Russian language broadcast. He hadn't known of that and was interested in how it started. I said that we had pitched the idea after realizing that there was no Russian-language news broadcast that wasn't done by Russian state media. Now it was expanding from a single half-hour nightly broadcast to a 24/7 network.

I said that the Russian Information Group was trying to incorporate what we had learned from countering ISIS. I explained that working with credible third parties and NGOs and investigative journalists produced better material than anything we could do ourselves. I mentioned that we were also doing tech camps in the periphery, to help local content makers with Russian disinformation, and training investigative journalists.

I returned to the Global Engagement Center, and I mentioned that we would be using metrics and analytics more heavily, as well as third parties and campaigns, to counter violent, extremist messaging. Murphy began thinking out loud. That all made sense, he said. It was a good general strategy for countering any kind of disinformation. Maybe we could take this new Global Engagement Center and expand the mission to countering all kinds of disinformation, from both state actors and non-state actors? It was a lightbulb moment. We had reached that point in a conversation—rare in Washington—when there was an actual idea in the air. What about creating a larger counter-disinformation hub that would do not only counter-ISIS but counter-Russia and, well, counter-China and counter-Iran and everybody else playing the game? It was a big idea, and what often happens in Washington is that you admire it for a second, and then retreat. But Murphy did not retreat.

Murphy continued to talk about this idea of a government-wide counter-disinformation center, not an information ministry, but a place that could help partners and credible third parties combat Russian disinformation. He looked around and saw State and DOD and the intelligence community doing stuff—how can we put this all together? How do we make a whole-of-government effort? This was all going on in parallel with the evolution of CSCC into the Global Engagement Center, but that was separate from any legislative process.

One person Murphy was talking to was Senator Rob Portman, a Republican from Ohio, who had been thinking along the same lines. They began to work on a bill together. We sent them a draft of the GEC executive order and our plans. The question for Murphy and Portman was do we create a separate entity to run the broader messaging effort, or do we build on the new GEC to do it? They decided on the latter. The idea was to give the new GEC a wider mandate and more money, a lot more money. They had an ambitious vision, but they were two junior senators without a lot of legislative clout. As often happens in the Senate, a bill is sometimes put forward not so much to pass but to spur discussion, to focus Senators on a problem that they might not have been aware of. That's how they saw their bill. They announced S.2692, the Countering Information Warfare Act in March, in the middle of the presidential campaign. At first, it didn't get much attention. But sometimes a bill meant for discussion catches fire, and that's what happened. In November, the Senate leadership attached it to the Defense Authorization Act of 2017. Sometimes— most of the time—bills are mushy-headed, legalistic, and hard to read. Not so S. 2692.

Here is the beginning of it:

S. 2692

A BILL

To counter foreign disinformation and propaganda, and for other purposes.

Be it enacted by the Senate and House of Representatives of the United States of American in Congress assembled . . .

SENSE OF CONGRESS.

It is the sense of Congress that —

(1) foreign governments, including the Governments of the Russian Federation and the People's Republic of China, use disinformation and other propaganda tools to undermine the national security objectives of the United States . . .

(2) the Russian Federation, in particular, has conducted sophisticated and large-scale disinformation campaigns that have sought to have a destabilizing effect on the United States' allies and interests;

(3) in the last decade, disinformation has increasingly become a key feature of the Government of the Russian Federation's pursuit of political, economic, and military objectives in Ukraine, Moldova, Georgia, the Balkans, and throughout Central and Eastern Europe;

(4) the challenge of countering disinformation extends beyond effective strategic communications and public diplomacy, requiring a whole-of-government approach leveraging all elements of national power.[28]

They had gone for it. The bill openly accuses Russia of using disinformation and other propaganda tools to undermine the national security of the United States. You can't get more direct than that. It talks about the promotion of a free and independent press; of using data analytics to expose disinformation; of supporting third parties like think tanks to combat disinformation; of coordinating with our allies and such entities as the NATO Center of Excellence in Latvia; and of choosing exchange students from countries that are vulnerable to Russian propaganda. It connected the dots of so many of the things I had been trying to do over the past three years. And most important of all, it appropriated $20 million to the Secretary of State to expand the Global Engagement Center and directed the Defense Department to give it another $60 million to coordinate government-wide counter-disinformation efforts

As Jen would say, it was a big f------ deal. If in fact it was the real deal. Like so much legislation, it doesn't always compel agencies to comply with it. Even before the bill passed, Lumpkin was getting the GEC to align with the bill's new directive. It would be all that we could do to get it off the ground before the election, and so it would be for the next administration—the Clinton administration—to get it running. I felt confident about that because I knew that Hillary Clinton understood the Russian threat better than anyone else.

When the bill was published, Sputnik, the Russian state news outlet, likened the Global Engagement Center to the Ministry of Truth in George Orwell's *1984.*

President Obama would eventually sign the bill into law on December 23, 2016.

The Bar Scene in *Star Wars*

The House Foreign Affairs Committee hearing was called "Countering the Virtual Caliphate: The State Department's Performance." Over the last two years, I wouldn't say that I'd avoided testifying before Congress—but I hadn't solicited it either. I'd politely dodged a couple of requests to be part of long panels. But here I was asked to be the sole witness. The request had come from Ed Royce, the committee's chair. I saw it as an opportunity to push back on the narrative that we were "losing" in the information space and talk about the larger disinformation war and the role that the new Global Engagement Center might play in it. I knew that Royce was a skeptic about the Global Engagement Center, and I thought the hearing might give me a chance to win him over.

Within State, Legislative Affairs, a hearing of the House Foreign Affairs Committee, was often compared to the famous cantina scene in *Star Wars*, in which a hodgepodge of eccentric and unpredictable characters (46 of them in the committee's case) could sabotage anything you were trying to do. The people at Legislative Affairs said not only was it likely that I would get hit with some esoteric question about the Koran, but it was also possible they would ask me about Hillary's emails, the Iran deal, Vladimir Putin, Donald Trump, or any other topic that happened to wander into a member's mind.

Along with a couple of aides, I arrived at the hearing early, and was parked in a holding room off the main committee room. A couple of committee members wandered through and said hello. About 15 minutes before the hearing was to start, I was handed Royce's opening statement. By the time I finished reading the first paragraph, I was furious. "The internet is awash with terrorist propaganda . . . Horrific videos of beheadings . . . ISIS operates a vast network of online recruiters." The same outworn clichés; the same obsolete paradigm of us "losing the information war." Fairly or not, I felt I was being set up—and I resolved, without telling my folks, that I would rebut it.

Room 2170 of the Rayburn House Office Building is impressive. It holds a few hundred people, with a long, rectangular witness table facing the committee, whose seats are sloped up like the rows in a high-school gym. Chairman Royce gaveled the hearing to order. There was a pretty big crowd, and Royce began to read his statement. When Royce finished, he called on me, and I began reading mine. But when I got to the section on ISIS's use of social media, I took off my glasses and put the paper down. "Now, " I said, "I am just going to take exception to something the Chairman said in the beginning of the hearing." I could see committee members' heads pop up from their papers and phones.

> This idea that the Internet is "awash" with ISIS or pro-ISIS content. There is a RAND study that came out recently, and it is confirmed by our own GEC study that there is now six times as much anti-ISIS content on the Internet as pro-ISIS content. When I started in this job, it was one-to-one. The tide is shifting. We did an analysis recently: 0.0124 percent of Twitter's content is pro-ISIS. And these beheading videos that people talk about—every week I have a briefing about ISIS's top 10 videos and I had one yesterday. And the problem is that the videos are being taken down so quickly that we don't even get to monitor them. So I think this narrative that we are losing the information war with ISIS is wrong. In fact, mainstream Muslims are winning the information war with ISIS. And there is a larger issue facing public diplomacy all around the world. There is a digital iron curtain going up around the world. There is a gigantic increase in disinformation

coupled with countries that are decreasing their free
speech. This is a gigantic challenge for democracies, and I
am happy to talk about that as well.[29]

The room had gone quiet. Almost all the members were looking up. When I finished, Chairman Royce paused for a moment, and
then said, "Well, I think you make a good point, Mr. Stengel." He was
generous and gracious, and then added that he and the committee had
seen a "quantum increase in the effort to push back."

And then we began to go down the line.

Congressman Dana Rohrabacher of California—who had historically been a Russophile and was sometimes jokingly referred to as
"Putin's congressman," asked if we were providing any messaging help
to the Muslim Brotherhood. We are not, I said.

Congressman Mo Brooks of Alabama asked me, "Have you ever
read the Koran?"

I replied that I hadn't read the entire Koran, but I had certainly
read parts of it, though I was far from being an Islamic scholar.

He then read two lengthy passages from the Koran, one telling Muslims to "smite the necks" of unbelievers and the other urging
believers to "slay the idolaters where you find you find them"—all to
suggest that Islam was a religion of violence.

Representative Ted Deutch of Florida questioned whether Hamas
and other foreign terrorist organization should be allowed to use American social media platforms.

Once it got going, I realized that it was best to let the members
talk for as long as possible—they had only five minutes each—so they
would eat up their time without a question.

When his time came, Royce began by saying that the announcement of the Global Engagement Center "kind of caught me by surprise." He said the current task of fighting violent extremist messaging

seemed difficult enough without adding to it the expanded mission of state propaganda "such as the disinformation coming out of Russia."

I agreed with him that as it was presently constituted, the GEC was too small to take on the Goliath of Russian disinformation. But I thought it was a start. I said not all disinformation was created equal, but that there were economies of scale that could be derived from a centralized data bank and a place to analyze metrics. Having a centralized entity with which the tech companies could cooperate would also be useful. I said I thought it was a promising idea that could be executed by the next administration, which everyone in that room assumed would be the Clinton administration.

Interference

In the summer of the presidential campaign, Alexander Dugin, the bizarre Russian philosopher we had discussed at the Gray Zone senior leaders' seminar, loaded onto YouTube a video of himself in which he said, staring directly at the camera, "In Trump we trust."

"I really like Donald Trump," he said, with his heavy Russian accent. "Trump is the voice of the real right wing in America, which doesn't care about foreign policy and America's hegemony."

He expressed disdain for American democracy. "There is nothing more stupid and fake than the American vote-counting system," he said. He mocked America's support for democracy around the world: "How dare they lecture us about human rights and the fight against corruption?"

He castigated Hillary Clinton's campaign as a bunch of "storm troopers."

He lambasted what he called the American "obsession with the fake Russian threat." He said it was an excuse for losers.[30]

The production values were poor, the audience was small, but the video revealed an extraordinary mirroring of language and ideas between Dugin and other Russian voices and candidate Trump. I had no idea what to make of it. The notion that there was some kind of shared rhetorical playbook just seemed too fanciful to believe. While the messages did not exactly repeat each other, they certainly rhymed.

At the same time as Dugin was uploading his video, according to public U.S. intelligence, the GRU—the Russian military intelligence service—began going through the email accounts of DNC officials.[31] According to the FBI, Russian hackers had roamed through the DNC's network for seven months. They said the hackers had financial ties to the Internet Research Agency at 55 Savushkina Street in St. Petersburg.[32]

In June, with the first release of the hacked DNC documents, including a file of opposition research on himself, Trump did a very Putinesque thing: he accused the victim. "We believe it was the DNC that did the 'hacking' as a way to distract from the many issues facing their deeply flawed candidate," Trump said in a statement.[33] His response used all the tenets of Russian active measures: distraction, deflection, projection.

A declassified U.S. intelligence assessment[34] said that Guccifer 2.0 was a front for Russian military intelligence, which delivered to WikiLeaks thousands of DNC emails, as well as hundreds more from Clinton's campaign chairman John Podesta. On July 22, three days before the Democratic convention, WikiLeaks released 19,252 emails from the DNC.[35]

That same month, the FBI began investigating possible ties between the Trump campaign and Russia. This was not something I was privy to at State—what I knew about it, I learned from the *New York Times* and the *Washington Post*. But I was monitoring how it played on Russian state media. On RT, reporter Gayane Chichakyan, who had done a number of stories on me, said the accusations of Russian hacking were fanciful and that people always pointed the finger at Russia.

Chichakyan said: "When, immediately after the leak, the Clinton campaign began to blame Russia instead of addressing the revelations in the
leaks, to many it sounded like a joke, like something you would see in
the Onion fake news. Except it was real news. Donald Trump picked up
on the irony, tweeting that 'the new joke in town is that Russia leaked
the emails because Putin likes me.'"

During the opening of the Republican convention in July, the
Trump campaign weakened language in the party platform that had
urged the U.S. to supply lethal weapons to Ukraine.

On July 27, Trump held a press conference and was asked whether
he would publicly tell Putin not to interfere with our election.

"Why should I tell Putin what to do?" said Trump. In that same
press conference, he famously said, "Russia, if you're listening, I hope
you're able to find the 30,000 emails that are missing."[36]

Four days later, in an interview with ABC News, Trump questioned
the U.S. commitment to defending NATO members from Russian
aggression, adding, "You know, the people of Crimea, from what I've
heard, would rather be with Russia than where they were."[37]

The Far Enemy Is the Near Enemy

Sunday, June 12, 2016, 2:35 a.m.

911 OPERATOR: Emergency 911. This call is being
recorded.

SUSPECT: *Al-ḥamdu lil-lāh, alayhi s-salām.* [Praise be to
God and peace be upon him.] I wanna let you know I'm in
Orlando and I did the shootings.

911 OPERATOR: What's your name?

SUSPECT: My name is, I Pledge of Allegiance to Abu Bakr al-Baghdadi, of the Islamic State.

His actual name was Omar Mateen and on what was the sixth day of Ramadan, in the middle of the presidential campaign, he shot and killed 49 people with a semiautomatic military-style rifle at the Pulse nightclub in Orlando, Florida. This was exactly the kind of act of domestic terrorism the White House was worried about. Mateen, the 29-year-old American-born son of Afghan immigrants, had grown up in Port St. Lucie, Florida, about 100 miles south of Orlando.

Several hours after the attack, ISIS claimed responsibility for the shooting in a statement released over an encrypted telephone app. Shortly afterward, Donald Trump tweeted:

> Appreciate the congrats for being right on radical Islamic terrorism. I don't want congrats, I want toughness & vigilance. We must be smart!

Earlier in the campaign, Trump had claimed that he was "the first guy who really predicted terrorism," saying, "I can feel it, like I can feel a good location in real estate."[38] After the shooting, Trump did not seem to blame ISIS or Baghdadi; he pointed his finger instead at American Muslims. "They have to cooperate with law enforcement and turn in the people who they know are bad . . . But you know what? They didn't turn them in. And you know what? We had death and destruction."[39]

In the online celebration among digital jihadis after the nightclub shooting, many had posted screenshots of Abu Muhammad al-Adnani, ISIS's best-known spokesperson, and the man the intelligence community considered the prime mover behind the group's international attacks.[40]

Less than a month before, in a 31-minute audio file loaded to the web, Adnani had rewritten ISIS's narrative. What had always distinguished ISIS from al-Qaeda was that ISIS aspired to be a state with actual territory. But now, Adnani, in the face of battlefield defeats in Ramadi and the likely loss of Mosul, was signaling a retreat from the idea of the physical Caliphate.

"Were we defeated when we lost cities in Iraq and were in the desert without any city or land? And would we be defeated and you be victorious if you were to take Mosul or Sirte or Raqqa or even all the cities and we were to return to our initial conditions? Certainly not! True defeat," he said, would come only "if you were able to remove the Koran from Muslims' hearts."

Adnani was redefining success from holding and governing territory to having Islam in your heart. Not the territory without, but the territory within. So, he told his supporters, do not come to the Caliphate but attack the enemy where you are. He called on them to strike during Ramadan.

"And we specifically direct this to soldiers and supporters of the Kilafah in Europe and America. O slaves of Allah, O Muwahhiddin! . . . Truly, the smallest act you do in their lands is more beloved to us than the biggest act done here; it is more effective for us and more harmful to them."

The far enemy had become the near enemy. This was the global whistle to lone wolves in Europe and America. The coalition had basically won the physical war against the Caliphate in Iraq and Syria, but Adnani was saying the truest Caliphate lived inside its supporters' hearts. This is what we all worried about. That the war would migrate from Iraq and Syria to Miami and New York and San Francisco—to the homeland.

After almost three years of assembling the anti-ISIS messaging coalition, we decided to hold its final meeting of the Obama administration in Washington. It was one week after the Orlando terrorist attack. I opened the daylong session by talking about how ISIS was repositioning its brand. How they had been mostly eliminated from Iraq and Syria. How the flow of foreign fighters had decreased by 90 percent. How their continued losses on the military battlefield were changing their tactics on the information battlefield. How they were moving from an ideological brand seeking to rule territory to an umbrella brand for grievance, hate, and psychopathology. How instead of promoting the image of a bountiful Caliphate, they were creating a criminal organization for the marginalized. How they were no longer a state but a malignant state of mind.

As always, I talked about how far we'd come: the creation of the messaging group itself; the launch of the Global Engagement Center; the success of the Sawab Center; the prospective messaging centers in Malaysia and other places. I explained how the new Global Engagement Center would fight other forms of disinformation under a new administration.

Our keynote presentation was from General Mike Nagata, who was now at the National Counterterrorism Center. I had gotten to know Mike from my earliest days in the job, and he was one of the smartest people in the world on the ISIS brand. Someone once told me the Defense Department sees the world through the prism of threats, the State Department through the prism of possibilities. General Nagata was one of the rare people who could do both. His talk was called "Going Dark"—and it was about how ISIS messaging was moving underground. In many ways, as with the domestic attacks in San Bernardino and Miami, this migration to the dark web was a result of the success of our information war against them. The first part of Nagata's presentation was how ISIS was migrating off public social media platforms and onto private encrypted ones, like Telegram, Signal, Wickr, Threema, and WhatsApp. (Nagata jokingly referred to Telegram as "Terrorgram.") ISIS's leaders and communicators, he said, all used

VPNs—virtual private networks—to post and communicate. They mostly inhabited the dark web, which was a completely anonymous platform where they could hide their identities. "Their conversation is more and more difficult to see," he said. "We need to adapt to this new information battlefield."

Nagata went on to talk about the actual battlefield, saying that the worse ISIS did on the physical battlefield, the more likely they would stage terrorist attacks outside it. Nagata explained that there were three kinds of attacks: directed, enabled, and inspired. "The hardest thing for them to do is a directed attack," he said, "and the easiest is an inspired attack." In fact, for inspired attacks, like those in Orlando or San Bernardino, they didn't have to do anything at all. "It's the reverse for us," he said. "The hardest thing for us to prevent is an inspired attack and the easiest is a directed attack."

Nagata noted that there had been a few dozen planned attacks since 2014. Most of them had been interrupted. Nevertheless, polls showed that the American public felt insecure. It was not entirely rational, he said, but it was the reality. He did not have to say it, because everyone understood it, but the current political environment featured leaders who fanned people's fears. In Europe, he said, we were seeing leaders who demonized immigration. We were seeing the rise of white nationalism. We were seeing it here, too. He noted that NATO was seeing an increase in Russian disinformation about immigration. Social scientists were pointing to the rise of what they called authoritarian voters—voters who were attracted to candidates who preached the need for an iron fist and a disdain for "the other."[41]

As he finished, Nagata came back to the point that he'd been making since I first connected with him two years before. "This is a war," he said, "but it's also an argument. The question is, How do we win the argument, because the argument will go on long after the war on the ground is over." He said the only way to win the argument was to provide a positive alternative. "We need to offer a better deal," he said, "and right now we're not."

Telling America's Story

The final "workshop" for all State public affairs officers was to be in the last few weeks before the election. In my first few months at State, we'd had a big conference where all the public affairs officers from around the world returned for meetings and discussions. But when I wanted to schedule one for my last year, I was told by the office of management that Congress was not looking kindly on State spending on "conferences" during this election year, and that all of them had been killed. But, if you wanted to call it a "workshop," they said, Congress would be none the wiser.

About 300 public affairs officers were assembled in the Acheson Auditorium, and I opened the "workshop" by saying that all of them were on the front lines of a global information war, and more and more, our opponents were waging a war against truth—against the very idea that there was an objective reality that we could all agree on. I called the problem of combating disinformation one of the signature challenges of the 21st century. Not only around the world, but here in America.

Everyone was pretty quiet, but when it came time for questions and comments, there was one subject that people wanted to talk about: Donald Trump. They weren't shy about it either. The chief public affairs officer from Brazil stood up and spoke for many when he said: "Every day, we get questions about life in America. The demonstration in Charlotte was like a thunderclap. People asked, Are there really Nazis in America? Is there apartheid in America? Why don't you like Muslims in America?" Some applause from the audience. It seemed every single person had a similar story to tell.

Here are a few of the comments:

"People say, 'We don't recognize America anymore.'" (Indonesia)

"Everyone is worried that it will become impossible to study abroad in America if you are a person of color." (Hong Kong)

"People are asking, 'Does democracy work? Will the U.S. now abandon us?'" (Pakistan)

"They used to look at America as a model of democracy and rule of law and anticorruption. Now, they see American apartheid." (South Africa)

"They say, 'You Americans are complete hypocrites.'" (Turkey)

"They ask me all the time, 'You always say Article 5 of NATO is inviolate, but will you say that if Trump is president?'" (Lithuania)

"The people who are scared around the world are the people who live in illiberal democracies. They say, 'We know about strongmen and dictators, you don't.'" (Hungary)

I could only repeat the same platitudes about how, in a democracy, voters choose and we abide by the result. Even if Secretary Clinton won, they said—and most folks assumed that would be the outcome—America has been deeply damaged by Trump's rhetoric. American presidential elections are not local affairs but global ones. People around the world feel they have a vote—and a stake in the outcome.

All the questions I got were fundamentally the same. People around the world asking, "All that stuff you've been telling us for so long—about democracy and human rights and fairness and diversity—it's not really true, is it?" American public diplomacy is ultimately about values. And now people around the world were saying that this story was a fiction. It's not as though people around the world had never said that before. We'd been called hypocrites long before Donald Trump decided to run for president. But we'd never had someone running for president who so explicitly rejected those values both in his ideology and in his behavior. That was something new.

So many people approached me privately to ask, What happens if he wins? How can we do our job? Should I resign?

I told them not to worry.

From Russia with Love

In the year before the election, the Russian government had forced the closing of all 29 American Centers in Russia, including our flagship center in the middle of Moscow, which had its lease rescinded after a 22-year partnership with the Library of Foreign Literature.[42]

American Centers—sometimes called American Spaces or American Corners—were libraries or reading rooms where people could find American books, periodicals, and videos. They were a Cold War legacy, but they had gotten a new life in many countries because they offered Wi-Fi, which was not always easy to come by, and because we didn't monitor what people did online.

After Russia started shutting down the centers, our ambassador, John Tefft, formulated a fallback plan. He wanted to build a new $10 million American Center on the grounds of the current Moscow embassy. The money to build it would have to come through the Public Diplomacy budget, and he had been suggesting for six months that I come to Moscow to look at the site.

Tefft had visited with me a few months earlier. A burly Midwest-erner with a walrus mustache, clunky black glasses, and a shock of white hair, he looked more like he might have been Russia's ambassador to the U.S. Tefft was a fluent Russian-speaker who had previously served as ambassador to Ukraine, Georgia, and Lithuania. He was a propo-nent of old-fashioned cultural diplomacy and wasn't a big fan of our counter-Russian disinformation efforts.

Over the past two years, as relations with Moscow had continued to erode, the NSC and the State Department were none too keen on people going to Russia. So, when I agreed to go, planning for the visit began, and so did resistance to it. In State parlance, there were a lot of anti-bodies to the visit at the White House and at the Russia desk. We were learning more about Russia's role in attacking the American election, and the NSC wasn't keen to stir things up. They most cer-tainly didn't want an American official to go over to Russia and accuse the Russians of tampering with our election. Trump and the Russians were getting ready to call the election "rigged," and no one wanted to give them any more ammunition to do so.

Before my scheduled departure, the NSC arranged for me to have a special intelligence briefing on security. The lead briefer was young, sharply dressed, and no-nonsense. He spoke in staccato sentences.

"Have no expectation of privacy.

"It's a hostile environment, the most hostile there is.

"Harassment and assault of Americans is way up.

"They monitor all communication. Everything is intercepted. Don't send anything that you don't want read. Don't say anything you don't want heard. Don't do anything you don't want seen. Even in your hotel room."

Pause. "Especially in your hotel room.

"They will go into your room while you're at breakfast.

"Sometimes they will leave some clue that they've been there, sometimes not. Sometimes they want you to know you are being surveilled, sometimes they don't. Just assume that you are.

"No detail is too mundane for them to be interested in. From what toothpaste you use to where your shirts are from.

"The FSB [the Federal Security Service, the successor to the KGB] is sophisticated, and they have a long memory. They're patient. A piece of information that seems irrelevant now might prove significant in 10 years.

"Be wary of chance encounters. Better to just assume that nothing is by chance.

"In these encounters, they use stuff they know about you from your Twitter feed or your LinkedIn profile. An attractive woman will say to you something about *Time* magazine or Nelson Mandela. They try to make you think that you know them. You don't.

"They like to use honey traps," he said. "Don't get caught in one."

Exactly one week before the trip, I got a rather forlorn email from Ambassador Tefft. He said that he understood that there were "substantial questions" being raised about some of the events he'd organized. He now feared that it wasn't a trip "fitting" for an Under Secretary and that we should cancel it.

I discovered that the Russia desk at the State Department had been saying no to one particular event that Tefft wanted me to do, a public town hall. They just wanted it to be a sightseeing trip.

I decided to call Tefft, who was clearly frustrated and unhappy. I said all I really wanted to do was show the colors, take a look at the space for the American Center, and have a kind of punctuation point for my time at State dealing with Russian disinformation.

John was immediately relieved and said that planning would continue and that he was excited that I was coming.

Once the trip was back on, it became clear that the Russians weren't terribly excited to have me go either. They set up one official meeting—the bare minimum. It was with the Russian deputy foreign minister, who was responsible for both educational exchanges and the American Centers. The plan was that I would speak to him about the cancellation of FLEX and the closing of all our centers. The trip was two and a half weeks before the election. Jon Finer told me to keep everything as low-key as possible; no Ukraine, no Putin, no Clinton, and no Trump.

If the Russians had tried to find a more inhospitable space for our meeting, I don't know how they could have succeeded. They led me into a narrow trapezoidal room with one grimy window in a faceless building off Red Square. It reminded me of Raskolnikov's yellow room in *Crime and Punishment*.

The meeting was scheduled to be with Deputy Foreign Minister Sergey Ryabkov, who was roughly my equivalent and was designated as the principal person I was to meet with. But there was a plus-one, Dmitry Peskov, the presidential spokesperson, who clearly took the lead. Ryabkov did not open his mouth. I suspect Peskov had come because I'd been editor of *Time*. Peskov was a lean and hungry fellow in a sharp suit who looked like he was dying for a cigarette. No greeting. No welcome. No handshake. He did not look you in the eye. His whole countenance was sour and indifferent.

The first words out of Peskov's mouth were, "Relations between our two countries are at the lowest point since the Cold War." He said this matter-of-factly, as though he were the ticket agent at the Amtrak window telling you train times.

Organizations take their lead from the top, and Peskov seemed to be channeling Putin: chilly, inhospitable, inflexible. He made no effort to be pleasant—or diplomatic.

The two Russians sat there silently after Peskov's opening sentence, and so I just started talking. I recounted our unhappiness with the closing of the American Spaces. Peskov shrugged. I said how disappointed we were with the canceling of FLEX. He shrugged. Finally I protested about the continuing harassment of our diplomats and locally employed staff. Peskov shrugged again—here, if it were possible, he looked even more like he wanted a cigarette.

When I was done, Peskov responded in a bored way that the closing of the American Spaces all had to do with local issues over which Moscow had no control. But when he got to FLEX, he became more animated, saying that Russia did not in any way benefit from it and that it was designed by America to brainwash young Russians into thinking how wonderful the U.S. was and how awful Russia was.

If Peskov's strategy was to shut down any discussion of these issues, it worked. They were so closed off, so hostile, that it felt pointless. The attitude was, This is not a negotiation; there is only one side—ours. It's much easier going into a discussion knowing you were going to say no to everything rather than thinking, Well, maybe I'll agree with 10 percent. I didn't see any point in banging the table.

The meeting didn't end so much as stop. When I finished talking, the Russians just stood up to leave. They were done. They had simply wanted to get through it without any drama or concessions or mistakes. And they succeeded.

Here is the entire Russian press release on the meeting:

> On September 14, Deputy Foreign Minister Sergey
> Ryabkov met with US Under Secretary of State for Public
> Diplomacy and Public Affairs Richard Stengel who is
> currently in Moscow. The officials exchanged opinions on
> issues of Russian-American relations and some international
> topics.[43]

It purposely omitted any mention of Peskov; it was an official haiku of Russian disinformation. So, my first meeting as a government official three years before and now, basically, my last were unsatisfying sit-downs with hostile and taciturn Russian officials.

Most of the rest of the trip was uneventful. I had lunch at Spaso House, the beautiful old embassy, with one of the last remaining independent magazine editors in Moscow, who told me, "Putin is the strongman that Trump plays on TV." I spoke to the embassy public affairs staff, who recounted examples of harassment, of tires being slashed, of homes broken into.[44] The final event of the trip was the town hall, which Tefft felt was the absolute minimum of public diplomacy I needed to do. It remained on the schedule, though Washington was concerned about it.

Jon Finer was not someone who liked to bother you with stuff. But this was the third time Finer had called me before the town hall. He wanted to go over the details. I said it was at the American Center, which I hadn't yet seen. It was with former exchange students and people who were regulars at the Center. He asked whether it was open press. Yes, I said.

Jon said the White House was concerned that I would say something negative about Russia—or about Syria or about Trump or, well, about almost anything on the list of difficult things between the United States and Russia. No one wanted any hiccups just before the election. This was the last visit by a U.S. official to Russia before Election Day. The White House was anxious that it not look like they were helping Hillary or attacking Trump—or Putin, for that matter. They just didn't want to upset anything at this point.

I told Jon that my plan was to make absolutely no news whatsoever. He laughed and said to call him when it was over.

*　*　*

The schedule was for me to go to the American Center about 45 minutes early, to get a tour, and to look at the plans. That was the ostensible reason for my trip, to make a decision about the potential $10 million expansion. My expectations weren't high. I had already seen too many American posts around the world that had become remote garrisons.

But I was pleasantly surprised by what I saw. It was in central Moscow, not outside the city. The envisioned entrance was attractive and not near the main embassy entrance. Visitors wouldn't need to go through the more rigorous security of the embassy proper. And then the plans for the actual center were modern, open, and high-tech. It didn't seem like a fortress at all. I told Tefft that I was a yes.

When I walked into the room where we were holding the town hall, I was relieved. The term "town hall" gives the impression of something large and formal. I'd imagined an auditorium. In fact, it looked like an oversize middle-school classroom. There was a small desk at the entrance where people would fill out name tags with colored Sharpies. The chairs—many of which were those mini-desks you'd actually find in a middle school—were haphazardly arranged. The whole setup couldn't have been more rinky-dink.

Before the town hall, I was to spend a bit of time with former exchange students. They were young and fresh-faced and earnest and could have been modern versions of Soviet-era Young Pioneers, but dressed in jeans and T-shirts. All they wanted to do was talk about what a wonderful time they had in visiting the United States. They were very disappointed about the cancellation of FLEX.

The head of public affairs was going to introduce me at the town hall, and then I was to be interviewed by another member of the PA staff. I had already gone over the softball questions. But the audience was an unknown. I could get a question about Trump or Syria or Putin. Perhaps a journalist in the audience would try to stir up some controversy. But I wasn't too worried. I had the usual bland State and NSC talking points.

When I came out of the makeshift green room, the town hall gathering just looked comically small and unassuming. It was mostly the same exchange students, a few of their friends, and a handful of older people who were regulars at the American Center. Was there a representative from Russian intelligence there? Perhaps. Or a journalist who did not register as a journalist? There was no way to know. The public affairs office introduced me and spent most of the time talking about my years as a journalist and my work with Nelson Mandela.

A young woman stood up and asked, Which is tougher, being editor of *Time* or working in the State Department? I laughed at that. Definitely editor of *Time*.

Next, a young man asked about how to improve relations between America and Russia.

I talked about coming to Russia for the first time in 1980 when I was a grad student, and how much it had changed since then. Moscow seemed so prosperous and modern now. I said there was a natural bond of affection between the Russian people and the American people and that it was mostly governments that got in the way.

Then a young man stood up and asked a question in Russian. Some people began laughing as he spoke. The PAO smiled as well, and said it's a question about the presidential election. How is it affecting public diplomacy, he said, and then he asked me to make a prediction about who will win. People laughed again.

I smiled and said that in terms of public diplomacy, it's been difficult because the election is changing perceptions about America and the democratic process. But if you look back, I said, the Framers of the American Constitution thought democracy was a messy process. They worried about demagogues. They worried about people being fooled. I said there had been some unfortunate political views expressed during the campaign. Prejudice against immigrants and outsiders. Animosity toward the press. They are the values of some Americans, yes, but they are not *American* values. Freedom of speech and of religion, equality before the law—those are the core values of America, even if we don't always live up to them.

And the prediction? the young man said. I smiled and said, the voters will choose. That's the beauty of democracy.

And that was it. I didn't mention Trump's name. I didn't mention Syria. I didn't mention Russian disinformation or hacking or interference in the election. No controversy. No hiccups.

I'd been working on countering Russian disinformation for three years, and here I was in Moscow and there was nothing to counter. A bunch of people had come because they liked America. It just didn't seem like the time or the place to take a swing.

It felt silly to call Finer. I texted him instead:

No news made whatsoever.

Here's what our embassy tweeted after the town hall.

"Social media is just a tool, can be used for good or ill. Your challenge is to use it for good."—@stengel @AMC_Moscow

The Day After

The Quiet Car was never quieter than the morning after the election. It was a gray day. I had taken the Acela hundreds of times over the last three years. That morning, I recognized my fellow travelers, but I did not recognize my country.

I had gone back to New York on Monday night to vote in the election on Tuesday. I took the 8 a.m. train back on Wednesday. My

State inbox was virtually empty; no work emails that morning, unlike the usual deluge. I sent out a note to hold a public diplomacy meeting that afternoon to figure out how we would move forward.

All my worlds, all my concerns of the last three years, had collided. So much of what I had worked for over the last three years seemed to have taken a giant step backward. Trump's victory seemed to have instantly accelerated all the trends we were trying to turn back. The rise of disinformation and nationalism. Trump, after all, had weaponized grievance and vulnerability like both ISIS and Putin. All three exploited—and stoked—the grievances of millions who felt marginalized by modernism.

Trump's election was also an enormous challenge to American public diplomacy and to the American brand. So much of what we believed and promoted as part of the American brand—free speech, freedom of religion, the power of diversity, equality before the law, a level playing field—was challenged by brand Trump. But even deeper values seemed to be under threat, values that I had worked for as a journalist as well—not just free speech, but critical thinking, fact-based debate, the marketplace of ideas.

The idea of America First—even without the term's echoes of pre–World War I isolationism—seemed to be a recipe for America alone, America isolated. Secretary Kerry liked to say that people around the world do not stay up at night worrying about America's engagement; they worry when we're not engaged. In the notes I had sometimes emailed him for speeches, I'd sent some version of this idea several times: that America could not do everything, but there were some things that only America could do. But the truth was, there weren't that many of them. And even if we did not need our allies quite as much as they needed us, we still needed them. The Trump worldview was, no, our allies *and* our adversaries were playing us for suckers.

As I stared out the window, the only thing I felt like doing was to write a note to my two sons. They were 18 and 16. Here's a bit of it.

> You can take from all this the idea that public life is disappointing and unsatisfying. You might say, Why would I want to have any part of it? It's a fair question. And, as Justice Brandeis once said, "the right to be left alone is the most comprehensive of rights and the right most valued by civilized men." You may decide, I want to be left alone to do the things I care about. To be private. That's fine. But don't let this put you off. A different Justice, William O. Douglas, used to say to his clerks, "Find the stream of history and jump in." That stream just got more turbulent and interesting.

The State Department felt like a morgue that morning. When we had that first postelection meeting in the conference room next to my office, there were a lot of red-rimmed eyes. People seemed frozen, numb, unsure what to say.

I had called the meeting to make sure we were helping posts with whatever they needed. It was amazing to me how often people at State seemed to start from scratch after a big event, as though we'd never done this before. Folks, I said, this isn't our first presidential transition. I uttered all the usual platitudes, no less true for being familiar. Democracy means the people rule, and the people have spoken. The peaceful transition of power is the hallmark of American democracy. We still represent America's interests. We have men and women in harm's way all around the world whom we must continue to look after. And, finally, we have only one president at a time. Barack Obama is still president of the United States and will be until January 20.

One longtime foreign service officer said, You know, 60 percent of foreign service officers today have been in their jobs less than 10 years. Most have basically worked for one president, Barack Obama; and two Secretaries of State, Hillary Clinton and John Kerry. They are going to be upset and unnerved. How do we message to them to continue to do their jobs, to feel proud of representing their country? A lot of murmurs around the table.

The foreign service officers were thinking, What will it be like to work under a President Trump? Who will be Secretary of State? They served regardless of who was in the White House or in the Secretary's office on the seventh floor. Politicals like me had no moral quandary. We were all done on January 20. We would all submit our resignation letters that day.

I had been at this information warfare business for the last three years. I desperately wanted to make a difference but was unsure that I had. I mentioned that in my very first conversation with Secretary Kerry, he asked me to help him with figuring out the narrative for the 21st century. He'd mention it every few months at the 8:30, and I would send him a few thoughts. We never came up with a good name, but a few themes seemed clear. Strongmen, authoritarian nationalism, and illiberal democracies were all on the march. Brutal non-state actors like ISIS were on the rise. Big systems were under attack from small systems. The politics of force seemed to be trampling the force of politics. Disinformation was growing while free speech was shrinking. Authoritarian regimes were anti-fact. But the Secretary was by nature an optimist, and he always wanted to add the good news, of which there was a lot: we had cut extreme poverty in half over the last two decades; more people around the world had entered the middle class in the last 50 years than in all of human history; we were living at the least violent time in human history. Yes, all true, all good.

Now suddenly the picture had become darker. Were we now in a world in retreat from progress? A spheres-of-influence world, a world of nationalism and tribalism, a world that disdained facts and knowledge? I know it's hokey, and it's not even true historically, but even with all our many flaws, I believed in America as that city on a hill. Now, that city looked different. We would now have as our president someone who wanted to coat it in gold leaf, put his name on it, and build a wall around it. As one foreign ambassador said to me, "The power to inspire was once America's greatest asset." Now it seemed to be gone.

Looking around that room at the State Department, I knew it was the fundamental conviction of everyone there that among America's finest moments was the period after World War II when we launched the Marshall Plan and led the creation of the postwar global order and the institutions that have helped keep the peace for 75 years after a century of unimaginable suffering. The Secretary of State during much of that time, Dean Acheson, called his memoir *Present at the Creation.* Now, we were all wondering if we were present at the destruction.

PART VII

What to Do About Disinformation

The Problem

The Library of Congress was created in 1800 and has 39 million books.[1] That's a lot of information. Today, the internet generates 100 times that much data every second. Yes, every second. Information is the most important asset of the 21st century. No wonder polls show that people feel bewildered by the proliferation of online news and data. Mixed in that daily tsunami of bits and pixels, there's a lot of information that is false as well as true. About half the Americans who get news from social media say they have unwittingly—or wittingly—shared a false story.

It's a big problem. Disinformation undermines democracy because democracy depends on the free flow of information. That's how people make their decisions. Disinformation undermines the integrity of our choices. "Governments are instituted among Men," the Declaration of Independence states, "deriving their just powers from the consent of the governed." If that consent is acquired through deception, the powers derived from it are not just. That is an attack on the very heart of our democracy.

First, though, let's be clear about what we're talking about. I'm not talking about information or news that is simply wrong or incorrect. I'm talking about information or news that is deliberately false in order to manipulate and mislead people. Incorrect information is an occupational hazard of the media business and it's a problem that people have been trying to fix forever. When I first started at *Time* many years ago, every story had full-time fact-checkers working on it. That was one attempt to avoid mistakes—and even that was far from perfect. Mistakes happen.

Let's define our terms. Part of the problem is that there are no agreed-on definitions of the language we use to describe it. Here's a very quick glossary:

Disinformation: The deliberate creation and distribution of information that is false and deceptive in order to mislead an audience.

Misinformation: Information that is false, though not deliberately; that is created inadvertently or by mistake.

Propaganda: Information that may or may not be true that is designed to engender support for a political view or an ideology.

I'm not partial to the term "fake news" because it has become an epithet applied to any information that you dislike or disagree with. Now, dictators and strongmen around the world describe any story that is critical of them as "fake news." Its very use is usually a form of disinformation itself. The primary culprit behind that is Donald Trump. But the idea of calling news that you don't like "fake" would be familiar to Lenin and Stalin and pretty much every other dictator of the last century. As I said earlier, the Russians were calling Western media fake news long before Trump did. I prefer to use the term "junk news" to describe information that is false, cheap, and misleading and that has been created without regard for its truthfulness. Let's stop using it.

Propaganda is also a tricky term. The word comes from the Catholic Church and the Latin verb *propagare*—its root meaning was the propagation of the faith. Most people see "propaganda" as a pejorative term, but I believe it is—or should be—morally neutral. Like rhetoric, propaganda can be used for good or for ill. Advertising is a form of propaganda. What the United States Information Agency did during the Cold War was a form of propaganda. Advocating for something you believe in can be defined as propaganda. Propaganda is a misdemeanor. Disinformation is a felony.

Just as successful propaganda often uses content that is true, disinformation is often a mixture of truth and falsity. Disinformation doesn't necessarily have to be 100 percent false to be disinformation. In fact, the most effective forms of disinformation are a mixture of information that is both false and true. The Russians are masters of having a kernel of truth in their disinformation. That's in part why it's so effective and hard to fight.

I know it's an awful cliché, but there are no easy answers to the problem of disinformation. I say that based on a lifetime in media and some time in Washington trying to deal with it. As I said in the introduction, the traditional democratic belief that the truth will win out in the marketplace of ideas, a belief enshrined in the Supreme Court's view of the First Amendment, seems a little naive these days. We no longer know what a free and fair marketplace of ideas even looks like.

As I've tried to show throughout this book, democracies aren't very good at fighting disinformation. We are too open. We value free speech and debate. In most ways, that is a strength, but it can be a liability in an information war. Our Constitution and our laws are focused on protecting speech whether it is true or false. That is in part because we've always believed that truth will win out. As a result, we have very few laws or means for punishing or restricting the spread of speech that is false. That now seems like a design flaw. We need to look at hate speech statutes in Europe to see if there is anything worth borrowing. I'm not suggesting amending the First Amendment, but I do think it's worth examining whether speech that engenders prejudice and hatred should have the same protections as other speech.

As a journalist, I'd always been close to a First Amendment absolutist. But in 2015, when I was working on a public diplomacy response to the *Charlie Hebdo* attacks, I began to change my mind. In America, the standard for protected speech has evolved since Holmes's line about "falsely shouting fire in a theater." In *Brandenberg v. Ohio*, the court ruled that speech that led to or directly caused violence was not protected by the First Amendment. When *Charlie Hebdo* published cartoons of Muhammad on its cover, wasn't that speech that was likely to lead to violence? They had been attacked before for doing the same thing. As Garry Trudeau wrote about the *Charlie Hebdo* tragedy, "What free speech absolutists have failed to acknowledge is that because one has the right to offend a group does not mean that one must."[2]

But even outlawing hate speech will not solve the problem of disinformation. So, what can we do to fight disinformation without undermining the values that make us a democracy? As we've seen, government may not be the answer, but it has a role. Stricter government regulation of social media can incentivize the creation of fact-based content and disincentivize the creation of disinformation. Right now, the big social media platforms optimize content that has greater engagement and virality, and such content can sometimes be disinformation or misinformation. I'm suggesting that those incentives can be changed in part through regulation and in part through more informed user choice.

What is most disturbing is that disinformation is being spread in a way and through means that erode trust in public discourse and democratic processes. And that is precisely what the bad actors want to do. The disinformationists don't necessarily want you to believe them— they don't want you to believe anybody. Moreover, as things stand now, there is an alignment of economic interests between the disinformationists and the platforms—both make money when disinformation goes viral. Right now, the creators of disinformation use all the legal tools on social media platforms that are designed to deliver targeted messages to specific audiences. These are the exact same tools—behavioral data analysis, audience segmentation, programmatic ad buying—that make advertising campaigns effective. The Internet Research Agency in St. Petersburg uses the same behavioral data and machine-learning algorithms that Coca-Cola and Nike use.[3]

All the big platforms depend on the harvesting and use of personal information. Your data is the currency of the digital economy. Google, Facebook, Amazon, Microsoft, and Apple—5 of the top 10 largest companies in the world—depend on the collection and use of personal information. Their business model is to sell targeted advertising. They track where you go, what you do, whom you know, and what you want to know about, so they can sell that information to advertisers.

At the heart of this issue is, Who owns your information? These businesses all argue that because they collect, aggregate, and analyze your data, they own it. In the U.S., the law agrees. But in Europe, according to the EU's General Data Protection Regulation, people own their own information. That is the correct model. America needs a digital bill of rights that protects everyone's information as a part of a new social contract. Right now, the law that covers your digital privacy is the U.S. Privacy Act, which was written in 1974, a decade before the internet existed. Today, the possession and ownership of one's personal information has become an inalienable right, akin to the freedoms of speech and worship and assembly protected by our 230-year-old Bill of Rights. The principle is simple: people need to know and be able to control what information is being collected about them, how it is collected, and how it is used.

I'm advocating a mixture of remedies that optimize transparency, accountability, privacy, self-regulation, data protection, and information literacy. That can collectively reduce the creation, dissemination, and consumption of false information. I believe that artificial intelligence and machine learning can be enormously effective in combating falsehood and disinformation. They are necessary but insufficient. All these efforts should be—to use one of the military's favorite terms—mutually reinforcing.[4]

Fixes

Okay, let's get to some potential fixes. I'm putting my proposed fixes and solutions into categories. They are:

- Section 230
- Privacy and Elections

- Algorithms
- Media
- Advertising

Section 230

The goal for legislation should be to create an information environ-ment that is more transparent, is more consumer-focused, and makes the creators and purveyors of disinformation more accountable. Here's the problem: legislation's original sin, the Communications Decency Act of 1996.

The Communications Decency Act (CDA) was one of the first attempts by Congress to regulate content on the internet. But think back for a moment to 1996—it was the era of America Online, Com-puServe, Netscape, Yahoo, and Prodigy. It was pre-Facebook, pre-Google, pre-Twitter—heck, it was pre-MySpace. But these players and new ones were already revolutionizing media and digital commerce. Their economic model was largely based on user-generated content. That's why Section 230 of that act is so important. Section 230 says that online platforms and their users are not considered publishers and have immunity from being sued for the content they post.

> No provider or user of an interactive computer service shall
> be treated as the publisher or speaker of any information
> provided by another information content provider.[5]

That single not-very-clear sentence gives all of today's gigantic platforms blanket immunity from any liability for their content. It shields them from legal liability for the actions of their users. That's enormous. The law basically treats internet service providers as something like the old phone company: as if they were nothing more than pipes through which content flowed. That one sentence in Section 230 allows all the platforms to make billions and billions of dollars on the content you and I give them for free.

The idea that these platforms are not publishers is absurd. Facebook is the largest publisher on the planet—the largest publisher in history. The fact that, for the most part, it is not creating its own content doesn't mean that it's not a publisher. That goes for Twitter, Instagram, Snapchat, and all the rest. They publish nonprofessional user-generated content as well as content produced by professionals to promote other content. No, they do not for the most part commission, edit, and produce content like traditional publishers—though they are all doing more of that. That is what publishing is in the 21st century. They do not merit the broad exemptions from liability that they have.

Ironically, Congress's motivation back in 1996 wasn't so much to shield these new platforms as to protect free speech. Congress didn't want the government to police these platforms and thereby potentially restrict freedom of speech—it wanted the platforms to police themselves. Congress worried that if the platforms were considered publishers, they would be too draconian in policing their content and put a chill on the creation of content by third parties. The courts had suggested that if a platform exercised editorial control by removing offensive language, that made it a publisher and therefore liable for the content on its site. The idea of Section 230 was to give these companies a "safe harbor" to screen harmful content. The rationale was that if they received a general immunity, they would be freer to remove antisocial content that violated their terms of service without violating constitutional free speech provisions. If they were publishers, Congress thought, they might restrict free speech in their zeal to avoid liability and, by the way, it worked: it created an overabundance of free speech. But the unintended consequence was to allow a tidal wave of conspiracy theories and rumors and false and misleading content. It enabled the platforms to make money from content created by their users without making themselves—or their users—liable for it. This certainly protected free speech, but it also protected hate speech and disinformation.

But the problem is that Facebook is not like the old AT&T. Facebook makes money off the content it hosts and distributes. They just call it "sharing." And Facebook makes the same amount off ad revenue from shared content that is false as from shared content that is true. True, the old telephone companies made the same amount of revenue from a call that was a marriage proposal as from one plotting a terrorist attack, but a telephone call was not shared with thousands or millions of people the way a Facebook post can be.

If Section 230 was meant to encourage platforms to limit content that is false or misleading, it's failed. No traditional publisher could survive if it put out the false and untrue content that the platforms do. It would be sued constantly. The law must incentivize the platform companies to be proactive and accoutable in fighting disinformation. Demonstrably false information needs to be removed from the platforms. And that's just the beginning.

But let's be realistic. The companies will fight tooth and nail to keep their immunity. So, revising Section 230 must encourage them to make good-faith efforts to police their content, without making them responsible for every phrase or sentence on their services. It's unrealistic to expect these platforms to vet every tweet or post. One way to do this is to revise the language of the CDA to say that no platform that makes a good faith effort to fulfill its responsibility to delete harmful content and provide information to users about that content can be liable for the damage that it does.[6] It's a start.

Privacy and Elections

More privacy equals less disinformation.

If fewer people have your private information, fewer people can abuse it. If your privacy information is protected, you are less likely to be the target of deceptive advertising and disinformation. An online privacy bill of rights is a good idea. There are a number of bills that are attempting to do this and establish a baseline of privacy protections for users.[7] One thing that should be mandatory in any digital bill of rights: the requirement that platforms obtain consent from users to share or sell their information and notify users about the collection of their data. This is the absolute minimum—but it would be a big step forward.

When it comes to elections, platforms must alert people when a third party uses their private information for online election advertising. Political campaigns have become ever more sophisticated in their ability to use your consumer information to target you with advertising. If they know what movies you like, what shoes you buy, and what books you read, they know what kind of campaign advertising you will be receptive to. At the same time, advertisers must give users the ability to opt out of any content they receive.

These larger changes will undoubtedly take time, but there is one fix that could happen quickly: treat digital and online campaign advertising with the same strictness and rigor as television, radio, and print advertising. Right now, the Federal Election Commission does not do that. Television and radio stations, as well as newspapers, must disclose the source of all political advertising and who is paying for it. That is not true of digital advertising. The Honest Ads Act, which was introduced by Senator Mark Warner, Senator Amy Klobuchar, and the late Senator John McCain, is an attempt to solve the problem of hidden disinformation campaigns by creating a disclosure system for online political advertising.[8] It would require online platforms to obtain and disclose information on who is buying political advertising, as well as who the targeted audience is for those ads. It mandates that platform companies disclose if foreign agents are paying for the ads. And platform companies should also be responsible for identifying bots so that voters know whether they are being targeted by machines or actual human beings. All of this is both necessary and the absolute minimum.

For this regulation to be effective, it must also be done in real time during campaigns. Right now, according to the Federal Election Commission, political campaigns do not have to disclose their ad buys until a year after the fact. That is absurd. People need to know if they are being fed disinformation and falsehoods—and to know in a timely way so that they can factor it in their decision-making. Immediacy is more important during political campaigns than at any other time. Finding out a year later that you were targeted with a false ad by a bot that influenced your vote is worse than useless.

Finally, Congress needs to designate state and local election systems to be national critical infrastructure. That would give the federal government broader powers to intervene in a crisis. The Obama administration tried to do this, but the Republican majority in Congress voted it down. This is an essential change, and should be a bipartisan issue.

Algorithms, Ratings Systems, and Artificial Intelligence

Right now, the algorithms that decide which story goes to the top of Google's search results or your Facebook newsfeed rely in large part on how viral a story is: that is, how often it was linked to or shared by other users. It correlates popularity with value. Or at least what you want to see. The operating assumption is that the more popular a story is, the more important it is, and the more you will care to view it. Sometimes that's true. But if you think a story about a Kardashian quarrel is less important than a story about why nuclear weapons in Pakistan are not secure, then the algorithm isn't working for you. Research shows that stories that are emotional or sensational—which are stories that are more likely to be filled with misinformation—are shared much more widely than less emotional, less sensational stories. In this way, the algorithms are boosting deceptive stories over factual ones. That also incentivizes people to create stories that are emotional and misleading because such stories produce more advertising revenue.

Right now, the algorithms that do this are black boxes that no one can see into. The platform companies should be compelled to be more transparent about their algorithms. If companies had to publicly explain their formulas for relevance and importance, people would be able to make intelligent choices about the search engines they use. Wouldn't you like to know the priorities of the search engine that you use?

Over the past year, there has been a valuable movement toward offering ratings systems for news. Ratings systems allow users to evaluate the trustworthiness of individual stories and the news organizations themselves. Yes, you might like that story about how eating dark chocolate will make you lose weight, but if it comes from a website that is funded by Nestlé, you might have your doubts. A recent study by the Knight Foundation found that when a news rating tool marked a site as reliable, readers' belief in its accuracy went up. A negative rating for a story or brand made users less likely to trust the information.[9]

A number of companies and nonprofits have created such ratings systems. The Trust Project posts "Trust Indicators" for news sites, providing details of an organization's ethics and standards.[10] Slate has a Chrome extension called "This Is Fake," which puts a red banner over content that has been debunked, as well as on sites that are recognized as "serial fabricators."[11] Factmata is a start-up that is attempting to build a community-driven fact-checking system in which people can correct news articles.[12] And I am on the board of advisors of NewsGuard, which labels news sites as trustworthy or not, as determined by extensive research and a rigorous set of criteria.[13]

The greatest potential for detecting and deleting disinformation and "junk news" online is through artificial intelligence and machine learning. This means using computer systems to perform human tasks such as visual perception, speech recognition, decision-making, and reasoning to detect and then delete false and misleading content. There are several different ways machine learning and AI can do this. Content analysis uses keywords to find suspect material. Pattern recognition finds collections or groupings of dubious content. Data-based network analysis can distinguish between online networks that are formed by actual human beings and those that are artificially constructed by bots. Companies can adjust their algorithms to favor human-created networks over artificial ones. The platforms can even offer a predictor, based on sourcing and data and precedent, as to whether a certain piece of content is likely to be false. The good news is that AI is getting better at this every day.

The hard part of using AI and machine learning to disrupt disinformation is that the bad guys can use it too. They are already developing their own systems to understand how their target audiences behave online and how to tailor disinformation for them so that they will share it. The platforms help advertisers and companies find and reach their best audiences, and this works for bad guys as well as good. The platforms have to work to stay one step ahead of the disinformationists by developing more nuanced AI systems to protect their users from disinformation and information they don't want.

The Media

America doesn't have a "fake news" problem—it has a media literacy problem.

Millions of Americans aren't able to tell a made-up story from a factual one. Few Americans examine the provenance of the information they get, and many will trust a story from an unknown source as much as one from the *New York Times*. Few Americans understand how journalism works and are susceptible to those who say journalists are making up stories. And let's face it, your friends are not the best curators of high-quality journalism. At the same time, the disinformationists have gotten better and better at creating stories and websites that appear legitimate. Witness the Russian creation, during the presidential campaign, of sites with names like Denver Guardian and ABCnews.com, which appeared to be genuine news sites.

Schools don't teach media literary. They need to. Students need to be taught how news organizations work, and how to identify the provenance of information. Making journalism a staple of secondary education would go a long way toward solving the "fake news" problem. And it's not just media literacy but civic literacy. In 2004, when I was head of the National Constitution Center in Philadelphia, Sandra Day O'Conner said to me, We're going to pay a terrible price in this country for having stopped teaching civics. We have.

One thing that would help media literacy is for the media itself to become more transparent. News organizations don't do a very good job of explaining how they work. When people see a TV news story or read a newspaper or magazine piece, they have very little idea of what went into it. They don't know how many sources the writer may have talked to, how many pages of notes she took, how many different versions of the story were produced, how it was edited and shaped and fact-checked.

Even though technology has gone through transformational change in the past 20 years, newspaper journalism and TV journalism look a lot like they did in the 1980s. Even online stories are essentially just print stories with better graphics and more photos. News organizations should use all the new digital tools to move into an era of radical transparency, allowing readers and viewers to understand how stories are created, reported, and edited.

What do I mean? Let's take a newspaper story. Online, the story should essentially deconstruct itself. Next to the text, there should be links to the full transcripts of interviews the reporter did. (Of course, if an interview is with an anonymous source on background, that wouldn't be possible.) Those links would also include the URLs of biographies of those in the story. Writers and editors should include links to the primary and secondary sources for the story—all the research—including other news stories, books, video, and scholarly articles. There should be links to other photos or videos that were considered for the story. I would even have a link to the original outline of the story so that the reader could see how it was conceived. The top of each story should feature a digital table of contents that shows each of these aspects of the story. This is a technologically modern and even more open version of what scholars do with footnotes and bibliographies. The basic idea is to show the reader every step of the story and how it turned out the way it did.

Will every reader look through these links? No, of course not. But readers who are trying to find bias or prejudice, or just more information on the subject, will use them. Regular readers will get a better sense of how much work and research went into a story. The story itself then becomes a lesson in media literacy. Publications should have transparency editors and producers whose job it would be to create the digital infrastructure around each story. It's a whole new job category.

Transparency will also help news organizations to constantly live up to their own best practices. Readers will appreciate it.

Now, for one smaller issue related to media literacy.

News organizations must get rid of online clickbait and so-called content recommendation networks and "Sponsored Stories" that Taboola and Outbrain perch at the bottom of the screen and that pretend to be news. You've seen them thousands of times. "This tiny company in your area is destroying a $200 billion industry." "Top gut doctor says to throw out this vegetable immediately." They pretend to be factual content and are designed to fool the least discriminating of users into clicking on them. The companies that produce such content are warehouses of misinformation, rumor, mistakes, and distortion, and they adhere to none of the policies that shape the real news stories on the same page. Their presence at the bottom of the page weakens and undermines the credible journalism above it. I don't care how much revenue they contribute—no amount of money can make up for lost credibility. Please, please get rid of them.

Advertising

When I was editor of *Time* and forever trying to lure print advertisers to the magazine, I'd quote John Wanamaker, founder of the 19th-century department store that bore his name, who famously said, "Half the money I spend on advertising is wasted. The trouble is, I don't know which half." We'd all chuckle. But in the age of digital advertising, advertisers know exactly how much of their advertising is effective—and how much was wasted. Advertisers know exactly how many people look at an ad. They know how many screens you clicked through, how long you stayed on each page, and whether any action was taken, like creating an account or giving your email address. And they certainly know if you actually clicked through to buy their product, which is the holy grail of the online ad business. Using the tools and data provided by most platforms and even news organizations, advertisers can zero in on precisely who might buy their product based on a user's preferences and previous experience.

Advertising is the foundation of the internet economy as well as the digital news business. Last year, for the first time, digital ad revenue exceeded that of television, long the revenue king. Print is now a distant third. Part of the reason for the preeminence of digital is the rise of automated buying. The big platform companies offer advertisers the ability to automatically target the right customers without ever talking to anyone in ad sales. The various tools of behavioral tracking have become so sophisticated and effective that programmatic or automated ad buying has become the industry norm. The days when publishers took ad buyers to fancy lunches are long gone.

Advertisers use ad mediation software provided by the platforms to find the most relevant audiences for their ads. These ad platforms take into account a user's region, device, likes, searches, and purchasing history. Something called dynamic creative optimization, which is a tool that uses artificial intelligence, allows advertisers to optimize their content for the user and find the most receptive audience. Targeted ads are dispatched automatically across thousands of websites and social media feeds. Engagement statistics are logged instantaneously to tell the advertiser and the platform what is working and what is not. The system tailors the ads for the audiences likely to be the most receptive.

Ultimately, the bad guys use all these new tools to find the audiences they want as well. The Russians became experts at using two parts of Facebook's advertising infrastructure: the ads auction and something called Custom Audiences. In the ads auction, potential advertisers submit a bid for a piece of advertising real estate. Facebook not only awards the space to the highest bidder, but also evaluates how clickbaitish the copy is. The more eyeballs the ad will get, the more likely it is to get the ad space, even if the bidder is offering a lower price. Since the Russians did not care about the accuracy of the content they were creating, they were willing to create sensational false stories that became viral. Hence, more ad space.

Facebook creates a custom audience by reading users' cookies and evaluating their behavioral data to put together groups of people with similar interests. Let's say you like the Cleveland Cavaliers, frequent antiquing sites, and shop online at Saks Fifth Avenue: Facebook will put you in a custom audience with other people like you, and advertisers can buy that audience as well as every friend who "looks like you." Yes, the Russians used this too.

But the absolute master of these tactics was the Trump campaign. Plus, they spent exponentially more on these Facebook ads than the Russians did. It's hard to evaluate the influence the Russians had, and people will debate it forever. What is not debatable is that the millions of dollars the Trump campaign spent on their own targeted ads had an exponentially greater influence on voters than anything the Russians did.

Advertising's fancy new tools are worrying (or useful, depending on your point of view), but ultimately the problem with advertising goes much deeper. The original sin of news and information on the web was to make it advertiser-supported. It was, after all, the continuation of a long tradition. But advertising has seriously skewed the news and information business since the days when a boy or girl on a bicycle hurled the paper to your doorstep first thing in the morning. Advertising always subsidized the actual costs of a news organization. The price you paid for your physical paper was only half the cost of producing it and delivering it. So people never had a sense of the true value of news.

In the early days of the internet, news organizations did not charge anything for their content, further skewing users' conception of the cost of information. In those days, people used to say, Information wants to be free—to which I always said, People just want free information. And we gave it to them. Information is not and never has been free.

When the model for digital advertisers became buying audiences rather than brands, advertising became untethered from the quality of the publication that housed it. It prioritized virality and popularity over importance and accuracy. In the old days, when you bought an ad in *Time* or the *New Yorker* or the *Washington Post*, you knew your ad would be next to a story that was smart, well written, and accurate. But today, when you are buying, say, young men between the ages of 18 and 24, your ad can be connected to stories that are inaccurate, salacious, and offensive—because that's what your audience is looking at.

Content charges, subscriptions, and pay walls are all fine, but one unintended consequence is that free junk news goes viral while worthy stories behind pay walls do not. I've been a longtime advocate of micro-charges, but that strategy has never caught on. Now I prefer soft pay walls so some content is free, and is therefore better able to reach scale to rebut mis- and disinformation. When worthy fact-based news is behind pay walls, free junk news racks up even more page views.

Taken together, all of these things I'm proposing would reduce but not eliminate the amount of disinformation in our culture. For all this to work, we need global privacy regulations, a universal definition of disinformation, and legal consequences for purveying it. But even if everything I suggested was done, disinformation would still be with us. Disinformation will always be with us. And that is because the problem is not facts, or the lack of them, or misleading stories filled with conjecture; the problem is us. There are all kinds of fancy cognitive biases and psychological states, but the plain truth is that people are going to believe what they want to believe. It would be wonderful if the human brain came with a lie detector, but it doesn't. That's clearly a design flaw. The saying, "We see the world not as it is, but as we are" has been attributed to the Talmud, Anaïs Nin, and Immanuel Kant. Whatever its provenance, it remains true. But what we can continue to do, and that includes people in government and media and education, is to try to help people see the world as it is, to try to arrive at some shared consensus. The disinformationists want people to think that empirical facts are an elitist conspiracy. That's an extremely dangerous idea. Anything that we do that optimizes transparency, accountability, and information literacy will diminish the power of disinformation. But it won't eliminate it.

POSTSCRIPT

A few weeks before the end of the Obama administration, Congress codified the Global Engagement Center into law in the 2017 National Defense Authorization Act. Its mission was to "lead, synchronize, and coordinate efforts of the Federal Government to recognize, understand, expose, and counter foreign state and non-state propaganda and disinformation efforts aimed at undermining the United States national security interests."[1] The bill allocated funding of $80 million, with $60 million of that to be transferred from the Defense Department at the request of the Secretary of State. Three-quarters of the GEC's budget was designated to counter Russian influence operations. But Secretary of State Rex Tillerson did not request the money for more than a year.[2] Nor did State allocate and spend the $20 million that it was responsible for contributing. When Tillerson finally did make the request, a year and a half into the administration, he asked for half of the $80 million that Congress had authorized.[3] Senators Portman and Murphy, who had sponsored the legislation, said this delay was "indefensible" at a time when "ISIS is spreading terrorist propaganda and Russia is implementing a sophisticated disinformation campaign to undermine the United States and our allies."[4]

Today, the GEC is no longer in the business of creating content to counter disinformation. It has become an entity that uses data science and analytics to measure and better understand disinformation. Over the past two years, a steady stream of people have quit or retired and the GEC has had a hard time hiring replacements, even though it now has the budget to do so. It has not engaged with Russian disinformation. After two years with an acting director, the Trump administration named former navy pilot, intelligence officer, and Fox News reporter Lea Gabrielle to head the GEC.

The U.S.-backed Syrian Defense Forces announced on March 22, 2019, "the total elimination of the so-called Caliphate" from Syria. Trump had prematurely announced ISIS's defeat on several occasions, most prominently in December 2018, when he tweeted that ISIS was defeated and that he was removing all American troops from Syria. The decision was met with hostility by many in the military, and by influential Republican Senators. Both Defense Secretary James Mattis and head of the Global Coalition to Counter ISIS Brett McGurk retired in protest.[5] The National Counterterrorism Center estimates that 14,000 ISIS fighters remain in Syria and Iraq and have blended into the local population. Trump subsequently agreed to keep 400 U.S. troops in Syria.

ISIS's messaging army has also effectively gone underground. Its efforts are no longer to extol the Islamic State, but to recruit potential terrorists who will commit violence in ISIS's name. They use virtual jihadis to direct and inspire terrorist attacks. They are almost completely off public social media platforms and live on encrypted platforms and the dark web.

The Sawab Center continues to grow and has 70 employees. Its Twitter feed has more than 650,000 followers. With the waning of ISIS, the center also counters other forms of extremism and creates social media in support of Islamic harmony.

In March 2017, at the urging of his son-in-law Jared Kushner, President Trump had a formal lunch at the White House with Mohammed bin Salman.[6] Two months later, Trump made his first official foreign trip to Saudi Arabia, where he announced a joint U.S.-Saudi center on fighting extremist messaging.[7] Shortly after this visit, bin Salman became the crown prince, orchestrating the ouster of his cousin Mohammed bin Nayef. As part of his Vision 2030 program, the new crown prince rescinded the ban on women drivers, permitted concerts featuring a female singer, and has allowed women to attend sporting events.[8] In 2018, the CIA concluded that bin Salman had masterminded the grisly killing of *Washington Post* journalist and Saudi citizen Jamal Khashoggi at the Saudi consulate in Istanbul.

Since the 2016 election, a great deal more information emerged about Russian disinformation efforts during the campaign. New studies showed that in addition to creating content for Twitter and Facebook, the Russians were also on Instagram and other platforms like Vine, Gab, and Meetup.[9] Content created by the Internet Research Agency in St. Petersburg reached 126 million people on Facebook and more than 20 million on Instagram.[10] In February 2018, Special Counsel Robert Mueller indicted 13 Russian nationals for conspiring "to defraud the United States" by "interfering with the U.S. political and electoral processes, including the presidential election of 2016."[11] The Mueller indictment against the Internet Research Agency disclosed that employees of the Internet Research Agency organized pro-Trump rallies around the country, including one in West Palm Beach, Florida, where they rented a flatbed truck and hired an actress to portray Hillary Clinton behind bars on the back of the truck. A September 2018 criminal complaint by the Special Counsel's office against one Russian national said the Russian "conspiracy sought to conduct what it called internally 'information warfare against the United States of America.'"[12]

In December 2018, the Senate Intelligence Committee released a white paper on Russian disinformation. It reported that during the presidential campaign, the Internet Research Agency had created more than 10 million tweets—of which 6 million were original—across almost 4,000 accounts. They also produced 1,100 YouTube videos across 17 channels; 116,000 Instagram posts across 133 accounts; and more than 61,000 Facebook posts across 81 pages. They got 77 million engagements on Facebook, 187 million on Instagram, and 73 million on Twitter, where the Russians used paid trolls, newsbots, and repurposed accounts from botnets to target left-leaning and right-leaning users. Most of these accounts were designed to pass as Americans and were registered from U.S. IP addresses.

The white paper had impressive detail on Russian operations targeting African Americans and attempts to suppress voter turnout. It outlined the extensive anti–Hillary Clinton operations as well as support for Julian Assange and WikiLeaks. The IRA also created content that criticized America's role in Syria, supported Russian operations in defense of Syrian president Bashar al-Assad, and encouraged American voters to urge the U.S. to get out of Syria.

The Russians' focus on black audiences was in many ways their most sophisticated targeting. They created a website called Black Matters US and promoted it with ads and content on Facebook, Google+, Instagram, and Twitter. In February 2016, the site had 100,000 subscribers. They created other entities and sites like Blacktivist and Black Guns Matter to both promote Black Matters and increase their total number of African American followers. Black Matters even sold custom T-shirts to raise funds and build its brand. In general, the idea was to sow dissent, spark protests, and amplify conspiracy theories, in order to suppress the black vote. At the same time, they encouraged black voters to vote for Green Party candidate Jill Stein. The number of votes cast for Stein in the three pivotal states of Michigan,

Wisconsin, and Pennsylvania exceeded Trump's margin of victory in each of those states.

The Internet Research Agency spent $100,000 in advertising on Facebook. According to Facebook, the combined ad buy of the Trump and Clinton campaigns on Facebook was $81 million—more than 1,000 times more. Between June 2016 and Election Day in November, the IRA spent about $40,000, compared with the Clinton campaign's total of $28 million and the Trump's campaign's $44 million. The IRA reached many more people through organic means—the posting of divisive content—but of course, so did Trump and Clinton through mainstream media.[13]

So, did the Russian ad campaign sway any voters? As the Senate Intelligence Report says, "The extent to which they changed, rather than merely reinforced minds, is difficult to answer."[14]

When a redacted version of Special Counsel Robert Mueller's report was released in May of 2019, just as this book was going to press, it added relatively little new information on Russian messaging efforts compared to the more comprehensive examination in the February 2018 indictment of the IRA and the July 2018 indictment of the GRU. The Mueller report hinted at but was unable to prove coordination between the Russian disinformationists and the Trump campaign. Coordination, the report says, required "an agreement—tacit or express—between the Trump Campaign and the Russian government," and Mueller did not find one. The report showed, for example, that Donald Trump Jr. and Kellyanne Conway retweeted Russian trolls from the IRA on a number of occasions, but they did so, according to the report, "unwittingly." It also had examples of the Russians and the Trump campaign coordinating on events and even tactics—but no evidence the Trump campaign knew they were dealing with Russians. What Mueller did suggest is that candidate Trump and his campaign welcomed Russian efforts to help him and hurt Hillary Clinton. There is still a tremendous amount that is unknown about what the Russians and the Trump campaign did during the 2016 campaign. More importantly, the Russians have gotten a pass for the moment, and they will continue to engage in information warfare in the 2020 campaign. And they will be even smarter about it.

Which brings us back to the larger issue of information war. If information is power, disinformation is an abuse of power. Ultimately, information war is not a battle of technologies or platforms; it's a battle of ideas. The weapons in this war are new and evolving, but the issues are old and abiding. Do we care about facts and truth? Do we believe that there is such a thing as empirical reality and that we can all agree on it? Do we believe that people and nations are capable of choosing their own destinies? Our adversaries are fighting to prevent people from having agency over their own lives. They are fighting to have autocrats and ideologies make decisions for us. They are fighting to dismantle the infrastructure of truth. They are fighting to undermine the idea that human beings can be moved by fact and reason. They are fighting for relativism, the idea that no idea is worth fighting for. When I was in government, I felt my job was to help people here and around the world determine their own destiny. At the heart of that fight was the idea that people could use information—factual information—to decide what was best for them. That idea is still worth fighting for.

ACKNOWLEDGMENTS

If you don't like this book, you can blame my friend Michael Beschloss. At a lunch we had a few months into the job, I regaled him with stories about the State Department and he was the first person to say to me, You have to write a book! It's all his fault.

Writers need a place to write. When I left the State Department, I didn't have one. My old friend Tom Goodman generously provided the perfect office at Goodman Media and was unstinting in his support and enthusiasm. And I want to thank Evan Spiegel for being able to use the Snap offices and his infinite tolerance of the time I took to finish this book. Andy Lack and Phil Griffin gave me a home at MSNBC and a place to express my alarm at what has been happening to the country.

I've never liked the term "agent," and it does not even begin to do justice to my dear friend Joy Harris, who has been with me every step of the way and has been a champion of this book from first to last. I suspect she's almost as glad as I am that it is finished. How many times did we say we will look back and laugh at this? I owe her an enormous debt.

I've known Morgan Entrekin a long time (I never use a number if it's over twenty!), but until now, I'd never known directly what a superb editor, thinker, and strategist he is. He's every writer's beau ideal of an editor. His enthusiasm is contagious. As you've seen from this book, organizations tend to take on the character of their leader, and everyone at Grove Atlantic was professional, smart, *enthusiastic*, and a pleasure to work with.

I spent a semester at the Shorenstein Center at Harvard's Kennedy School when I finished at State, which helped me to conceive and structure the book. I want to thank Shorenstein's former director Nicco Mele for bringing me up there and helping me to think about the idea of information war. My tireless research assistant at Harvard, Howard Cohen, untied many knots for me, provided invaluable research, and also guidance on what to do about disinformation via his own excellent master's thesis.

When I'm writing I tend to be sealed off and secretive, but I did have some early readers. Chief among them was my once-upon-a-time editor, friend, and boon companion Bill Phillips, who read an early draft and gave sage counsel and support at a critical time. Another old friend and former editor of mine, Alice Mayhew, used her always-acute eye to strengthen the book and also help shape it. My neighbor upstate, Ann Godoff, was a shrewd reader whose ideas were spot-on.

Because I'm not always as careful as I should be about noting sources, Alasdair Phillips-Robins was a godsend. His meticulous fact-checking and deft line editing has made this a much better book.

It seems like a century ago now, but if not for these three people at Time Inc., I would have never made it to the State Department at all. My boss and dear friend John Huey is a true wise man and always looked out for me. His successor, Martha Nelson, continued that wonderful tradition. And my brilliant successor at *Time*, Nancy Gibbs, made the transition a very happy one.

I want to thank my group of longtime pals who have been a source of support (even if they didn't always know it!): Walter Isaacson, Kurt Andersen, Lawrence O'Donnell, Richard Plepler, Michael Lynton, Gary Ginsberg, Robert Gibbs, David Michaelis, Jim Basker, Bob Harrison,

Jim McGuire. Jeff Shell has become a new pal, and couldn't have been better to work with. Mark and Deb D'Arcy offered hospitality and a home away from home upstate.

The folks at the Atlantic Council, and in particular the digital forensics lab, have always been helpful and supportive: my old friend Fred Kempe, Graham Bookie, and Maks Czuperski.

Now, for the State Department. First, and most importantly, I want to thank the men and women of the Foreign Service. I benefited from their dedication and expertise and bravery, which I saw every day. I know I've been tough on the Foreign Service in the book, but that's because they have a vital role to play in conducting our nation's foreign policy and protecting our national security. That's never been more true than right now.

It was an honor to work with John Kerry, who embodies the best of public service and the idea of the public good, something that has been all too rare of late. David Wade was unfailingly helpful, supportive, and wise. Jon Finer was a delight to work with and this book would be twice as good if I knew even half of what he does about foreign policy. My old friend Bill Burns was leaving State as I was arriving, but he graciously took time to coach a rookie.

Even though she's a character in the book, the portrait of Jen Stout drastically underestimates her role and importance in this story. She was my infallible guide to how government worked. Any successes I had were due in large part to her, but the failures were entirely my own. Her guidance has continued through her help on this book and her continuing friendship.

My life at State and in Washington was immeasurably better because of the friendship and support of Evan Ryan and Tony Blinken. My second chief of staff, ambassador Susan Stevenson, represents the best of those who serve and the American public is lucky to have her. My last chief of staff and longtime friend and colleague, Romesh Ratnesar, made it a pleasure to come to the Harry S. Truman building every day. I want to thank Dana Shell Smith for her savvy about State and talent-spotting. And Heather Higginbottom for getting me there in the first place. I lured Nate Rawlings from *Time* to the State Department, and I couldn't have asked for a better aide, colleague, friend, and companion. Josh Lipsky's title was speechwriter, but that doesn't reflect the myriad ways in which he contributed and supported me. Haroon Ullah made himself indispensable on CVE and plenty else besides. I'd be remiss if I didn't mention Gloria Berbena, Macon Phillips, Roxanne Cabral, Larry Schwartz, and Graham Lampa. I had a superb array of special assistants during my time at State, and I am enormously grateful for their hard work, loyalty, and expertise: Bruce Armstrong, Alastair Baskey, Brett Bruen, Phil Beekman, Faris Asad, Amy Christiansen, Todd Miyahira, Sarah Matthews, Matt Miller, Beth Webster, Vicktery Sanchez, Mary Nagel, Mary DeBree, Clayton McCleskey, Manju Sandarangini, and Nick Snyder. Please forgive me if I'm forgetting anyone!

Cathy Pierre and Tyesha Battle were always patient in putting up with me and I think I gave them a few laughs.

As I said, I'd always known I'd serve, which I don't think my wife Mary counted on when we got married. While I get credit for the public service, the sacrifice at home is rarely acknowledged. My family did not move with me to Washington, and I commuted back and forth. It was not easy on them. My wife Mary, as always, held everything together, and was my eternal confidante about life at State. My two sons, Gabriel and Anton, were never far from my mind. I hope it's true that I missed them more than they missed me. Somehow, despite my absence, they have turned out to be two fine young men whom I am enormously proud of. I love them all beyond measure.

NOTES

INTRODUCTION

1. Hunt Allcott and Mathew Gentzkow, "Social Media and Fake News in the 2016 Election," *Journal of Economic Perspectives* 31, no. 2 (2017), 211–236, https://web.stanford.edu/~gentzkow/research/fakenews.pdf; Craig Silverman, "This Analysis Shows How Viral Fake Election News Stories Outperformed Real News on Facebook," *BuzzFeed News*, November 16, 2016, https://www.buzzfeednews.com/article/craigsilverman/viral-fake-election-news-outperformed-real-news-on-facebook.

2. Thomas Jefferson to Uriah Forrest, with Enclosure, December 31, 1787, Founders Online, National Archives, https://founders.archives.gov/documents/Jefferson/01-12-02-0490.

3. Claire Wardle, "Fake News. It's Complicated," *First Draft News*, February 16, 2017, https://medium.com/1st-draft/fake-news-its-complicated-d0f773766c79.

4. *United States v. Schwimmer*. 279 U.S. 644 (May 27, 1929) (Holmes J., dissenting).

5. Learned Hand, "The Spirit of Liberty" speech, New York City, May 21, 1944, Digital History, University of Houston, http://www.digitalhistory.uh.edu/disp_textbook.cfm?smtID=3&psid=1199.

6. "2017 Edelman Trust Barometer," Global Annual Study, http://www.edelman.com/trust2017/.

7. "Under Secretary for Public Diplomacy and Public Affairs," U.S. Department of State, https://www.state.gov/r/.

8. For more on Russia's influence campaigns against the West, see Peter Pomerantsev and Michael Weiss, *The Menace of Unreality: How the Kremlin Weaponizes Information, Culture and Money* (*The Interpreter*, Institute of Modern Russia, 2014), http://www.interpretermag.com/wp-content/uploads/2014/11/The_Menace_of_Unreality_Final.pdf.

9. Adam Taylor, "Before 'Fake News,' There Was Soviet 'Disinformation,'" *Washington Post*, November 26, 2016, https://www.washingtonpost.com/news/worldviews/wp/2016/11/26/before-fake-news-there-was-soviet-disinformation/.

10. Mike Isaac and Daisuke Wakabayashi, "Russian Influence Reached 126 Million Through Facebook Alone," *New York Times*, October 30, 2017, https://www.nytimes.com/2017/10/30/technology/facebook-google-russia.html.

11. Jefferson to Uriah Forrest, with Enclosure, December 31, 1787.

12. *United States v. Rumely*. 345 U.S. 41 (March 9, 1953) (Douglas J., concurring).

PART I: WELCOME TO STATE

THE LOBBY

1. "Harry S. Truman Federal Building, Washington, DC," U.S. General Services Administration, https://www.gsa.gov/historic-buildings/harry-s-truman-federal-building-washington-dc; James Reston, "A New Role for a New State Department," *New York Times*, May 25, 1947.

2. "New State Building April 1947–Present," Buildings of the Department of State, Office of the Historian, https://history.state.gov/departmenthistory/buildings/section28.

COMMS AND THE 9:15

3. Dean Acheson, *Present at the Creation: My Years at the State Department* (New York: W. W. Norton, 1969), 15.

THE FOREIGN SERVICE

4. "8 Steps to Becoming a Foreign Service Officer," U.S. Department of State, https://careers.state.gov/work/foreign-service/officer/test-process/.

5. Daniel Lippman and Nahal Toosi, "Interest in U.S. Diplomatic Corps Tumbles in Early Months of Trump," *Politico*, August 12, 2017, https://www.politico.com/story/2017/08/12/trump-state-department-foreign-service-interest-plummets-241551.

PART II: GETTING THERE

LUCK = OPPORTUNITY + READINESS

1. "Reform and Restructuring of U.S. Foreign Affairs Agencies: Public Diplomacy in the Department of State," U.S. Department of State Bureau of Public Affairs, September 30, 1999, https://1997-2001.state.gov/outreach/publicaffdip/fs_990930_merger.html.

THE CONFIRMATION PROCESS

2. U.S. Congress, Senate, Committee on Foreign Relations, Nominations of the 113th Congress—First Session, 113th Cong., 1st Sess., 2013, 876.

PART III: THE JOB

WRONG FOOT

1. "Russian Expansion to America," Fort Ross Conservancy, https://www.fortross.org/russian-american-company.htm.

RETHINKING RETHINKING

2. Joseph S. Nye, *Soft Power: The Means to Success in World Politics* (New York: PublicAffairs, 2004).

THE BIRTH OF COUNTER-MESSAGING

3. Exec. Order. No. 13584, 76 Fed. Reg. 56945 (September 9, 2011), https://www.federalregister.gov/documents/2011/09/15/2011-23891/developing-an-integrated-strategic-counterterrorism-communications-initiative-and-establishing-a.

BRINGING BACK OUR GIRLS, SLOWLY

4. Oren Dorell, "Terrorists Kidnap More Than 200 Nigerian Girls," *USA Today*, April 21, 2014, https://www.usatoday.com/story/news/world/2014/04/21/parents-234-girls-kidnapped-from-nigeria-school/7958307/.

5. Kevin Uhrmacher and Mary Beth Sheridan, "The Brutal Toll of Boko Haram's Attacks on Civilians," *Washington Post*, April 3, 2016, https://www.washingtonpost.com/graphics/world/nigeria-boko-haram/.

6. Darlene Superville, "First Lady's Address on Kidnapped Nigerian Girls," Associated Press, May 10, 2014, https://www.apnews.com/e7ef77b4259c4b678e94dbe11f88fa96.

WELCOME TO INTERNATIONAL BROADCASTING

7. U.S. Congress, House, Committee on Foreign Affairs, *Terrorist Attack in Benghazi: The Secretary of State's View*, January 23, 2013, 113th Cong., 1st Sess., 2013.

PART IV: INFORMATION WAR

PUTIN'S PULP FICTIONS

1. Vitaly Shevchenko, "'Little Green Men' or 'Russian Invaders'?" BBC, March 11, 2014, https://www.bbc.com/news/world-europe-26532154.

2. Alessandra Prentice, "Ukraine Leader Warns Russia After Armed Men Seize Government HQ in Crimea," *Reuters*, February 27, 2014, https://www.reuters.com/article/us-ukraine-crisis-crimea/ukraine-leader-warns-russia-after-armed-men-seize-government-hq-in-crimea-idUSBREA1P23U20140227.

3. Bill Chappell and Mark Memmott, "Putin Says Those Aren't Russian Forces in Crimea," NPR, March 4, 2014, https://www.npr.org/sections/thetwo-way/2014/03/04/285653335/putin-says-those-arent-russian-forces-in-crimea.

4. "Ukraine Crisis: 'Illegal' Crimean Referendum Condemned," BBC News, March 6, 2014, https://www.bbc.com/news/world-europe-26475508.

5. "Crimea Referendum: Voters 'Back Russia Union,'" BBC News, March 16, 2014, https://www.bbc.com/news/world-europe-26606097.

6. "Ukraine Crisis: Putin Signs Russia-Crimea Treaty," BBC News, March 18, 2014, https://www.bbc.com/news/world-europe-26630062.

7. Karen DeYoung, "U.S. Warns Russia Against Annexing Crimea," *Washington Post*, March 16, 2014, https://www.washingtonpost.com/world/national-security/us-warns-russia-against-annexing-crimea/2014/03/16/2b4a7006-ad45-11e3-9627-c65021d6d572_story.html.

8. Vladimir Putin, "Presenting Officers Appointed to Senior Command Positions" (remarks, Kremlin, Moscow, March 28, 2014), http://en.kremlin.ru/events/president/news/20650.

9. Sam Frizell, "Ukraine Protestors Seize Kiev as President Flees," *Time*, February 22, 2014, http://world.time.com/2014/02/22/ukraines-president-flees-protestors-capture-kiev/.

10. Andrey Slivka, "Rage in Kiev," *New Yorker*, December 11, 2013, https://www.newyorker.com/news/news-desk/rage-in-kiev.

11. Olga Onuch and Gwendolyn Sasse, "What Does Ukraine's #Euromaidan Teach Us About Protest?" *Washington Post*, February 27, 2014, https://www.washingtonpost.com/news/monkey-cage/wp/2014/02/27/what-does-ukraines-euromaidan-teach-us-about-protest/; "Politics of Brutal Pressure," *Economist*, November 22, 2013, https://www.economist.com/eastern-approaches/2013/11/22/politics-of-brutal-pressure.

12. Oksana Grytsenko and Shaun Walker, "Ukrainians Call for Yanukovych to Resign in Protests Sparked by EU U-Turn," *Guardian*, December 2, 2013, https://www.theguardian.com/world/2013/dec/01/ukraine-largest-street-protests-orange-revolution.

13. Evan Osnos, David Remnick, and Joshua Yaffa, "Trump, Putin, and the New Cold War," *New Yorker*, March 6, 2017, https://www.newyorker.com/magazine/2017/03/06/trump-putin-and-the-new-cold-war.

14. David M. Herszenhorn and Ellen Barry, "Putin Contends Clinton Incited Unrest over Vote," *New York Times*, December 8, 2011, https://www.nytimes.com/2011/12/09/world/europe/putin-accuses-clinton-of-instigating-russian-protests.html.

15. "Backing Ukraine's Territorial Integrity, UN Assembly Declares Crimea Referendum Invalid," *UN News*, March 27, 2014, https://news.un.org/en/story/2014/03/464812-backing-ukraines-territorial-integrity-un-assembly-declares-crimea-referendum.

16. "G-7 Leaders Statement," White House, March 2, 2014, https://obamawhitehouse.archives.gov/the-press-office/2014/03/02/g-7-leaders-statement.

17. Jim Acosta, "U.S., Other Powers Kick Russia Out of G8," CNN, March 24, 2014, https://www.cnn.com/2014/03/24/politics/obama-europe-trip/index.html.

18. "Readout of President Obama's Calls with President Hollande and Prime Minister Harper," White House, March 1, 2014, https://obamawhitehouse.archives.gov/the-press-office/2014/03/01/readout-president-obama-s-calls-president-hollande-and-prime-minister-ha.

19. "Readout of the President's Calls with Prime Minister Cameron, President Komorowski, and Chancellor Merkel," White House, March 2, 2014, https://obamawhitehouse.archives.gov/the-press-office/2014/03/02/readout-presidents-calls-prime-minister-cameron-president-komorowski-and.

20. Rebecca Kaplan, "John Kerry Warns of Consequences for Russia After Ukraine Invasion," CBS News, March 2, 2014, https://www.cbsnews

.com/news/john-kerry-warns-of-consequences-for-russia-after-ukraine-invasion/.

"A Message to America"

21. "IS Beheads Captured American James Wright Foley, Threatens to Execute Steven Joel Sotloff," SITE Intelligence Group, August 19, 2014, https://news.siteintelgroup.com/Jihadist-News/is-beheads-captured-american-james-foley-threatens-to-execute-another.html.
22. "IS Supporters React to James Foley Beheading Video," SITE Intelligence Group, August 20, 2014, http://news.siteintelgroup.com/blog/index.php/categories/jihad/entry/238-is-supporters-react-to-james-foley-beheading-video.
23. Chris Good, "Secret Service 'Aware' of Apparent ISIS Flag Photo in Front of the White House," ABC News, August 14, 2014, https://abcnews.go.com/US/secret-service-aware-apparent-isis-flag-photo-front/story?id=24985241.
24. Brian Stelter, "James Foley Beheading Video: Would You Watch It?" CNN, August 21, 2014, https://www.cnn.com/2014/08/20/us/isis-beheading-social-media/index.html.

Punching Back

25. "President Putin's Fiction: 10 False Claims About Ukraine," U.S. State Department, March 5, 2014, https://2009-2017.state.gov/r/pa/prs/ps/2014/03/222988.htm.
26. Peter Baker, "Point by Point, State Department Rebuts Putin on Ukraine," *New York Times*, March 5, 2014, https://www.nytimes.com/2014/03/06/world/europe/point-by-point-state-dept-rebuts-putin-on-ukraine.html.

The Republic of Fear

27. "Journalists Killed in Syria," Committee to Protect Journalists, https://cpj.org/data/killed/mideast/syria/?status=Killed&motiveConfirmed%5B%5D=Confirmed&type%5B%5D=Journalist&cc_fips%5B%5D=SY&start_year=2011&end_year=2014&group_by=location.
28. "Emotional Plea from Mother of Steven Sotloff, American ISIS Captive," NBC News, August 27, 2014, https://www.nbcnews.com/storyline/isis-terror/emotional-plea-mother-steven-sotloff-american-isis-captive-n190186.
29. Dan Lamothe, "Here's the Transcript of the Video Showing Steven Sotloff's Reported Execution," *Washington Post*, September 2, 2014, https://

www.washingtonpost.com/news/checkpoint/wp/2014/09/02/heres-the-transcript-of-the-video-showing-steven-sotloffs-reported-execution/.

30. Steven Erlanger, Julie Hirschfeld Davis, and Stephen Castle, "NATO Plans a Special Force to Reassure Eastern Europe and Deter Russia," *New York Times*, September 5, 2014, https://www.nytimes.com/2014/09/06/world/europe/nato-summit.html.

31. Julie Hirschfeld-Davies, "After Beheading of Steven Sotloff, Obama Pledges to Punish ISIS," *New York Times*, September 3, 2014, https://www.nytimes.com/2014/09/04/world/middleeast/steven-sotloff-isis-execution.html.

32. For more on ISIS's propaganda campaigns, see Greg Miller and Souad Mekhennet, "Inside the Surreal World of the Islamic State's Propaganda Machine," *Washington Post*, November 20, 2015, https://www.washingtonpost.com/world/national-security/inside-the-islamic-states-propaganda-machine/2015/11/20/051e997a-8ce6-11e5-acff-673ae92ddd2b_story.html.

THE DANGERS OF TRANSPARENCY

33. Jacob Silverman, "The State Department's Twitter Jihad," *Politico*, July 22, 2014, https://www.politico.com/magazine/story/2014/07/the-state-departments-twitter-jihad-109234.

SATIRE IS WHAT CLOSES ON SATURDAY NIGHT

34. John Oliver, "John Oliver—ISIS," YouTube video, 4:29, posted by Bob Pablo, September 8, 2014, https://www.youtube.com/watch?v=M_WWPHbcqZc.

35. Helene Cooper, "U.S. Drops Snark in Favor of Emotion to Undercut Extremists," *New York Times*, July 28, 2016, https://www.nytimes.com/2016/07/29/world/middleeast/isis-recruiting.html.

#HASHTAGDIPLOMACY

36. Amanda Wills, "Ukraine Wants Action, but U.S. Sends Hashtags Instead," *Mashable*, March 28, 2014, https://mashable.com/2014/03/28/united-for-ukraine/#VfqN3EeuuPq1.

THE SECRETARY IS ON THE LINE

37. Massimo Calabresi, "Hillary Clinton and the Rise of Smart Power," *Time*, November 7, 2011, http://content.time.com/time/magazine/article/0,9171,2097973,00.html.

38. David M. Herszenhorn and Ellen Barry, "Putin Contends Clinton Incited Unrest over Vote," *New York Times*, December 8, 2011, https://www .nytimes.com/2011/12/09/world/europe/putin-accuses-clinton-of -instigating-russian-protests.html.

PART V: THE BATTLE IS ENGAGED

A COALITION OF THE UNWILLING

1. "Transcript of Obama's Remarks on the Fight Against ISIS," *New York Times*, September 10, 2014, https://www.nytimes.com/2014/09/11/world/ middleeast/obamas-remarks-on-the-fight-against-isis.html.

EVERY BATTLE IS WON OR LOST BEFORE IT'S FOUGHT

2. Heath A. Conley, James Mina, Ruslan Stefanov, and Martin Vladimirov, *The Kremlin Playbook: Understanding Russian Influence in Central and Eastern Europe* (New York: Rowman Littlefield, 2016).
3. Arch Puddington, "Flacks for Autocrats: An American Growth Industry," Freedom House, June 29, 2017, https://freedomhouse.org/blog/flacks -autocrats-american-growth-industry.

LINES OF EFFORT

4. "History," National Counterterrorism Center, https://www.dni.gov/index .php/nctc-who-we-are/history.

YOU HAVE YOUR TRUTH—WE HAVE OURS

5. "US Puts Up $500K to Fight Russian Media in Baltics," *Sputnik*, October 10, 2015, https://sputniknews.com/world/201508101025570995/.
6. Peter Pomerantsev, in discussion with the author, 2015. See also Pomerantsev's excellent work *Nothing Is True and Everything Is Possible: The Surreal Heart of the New Russia* (New York: PublicAffairs, 2014).
7. "America House Opens with a Photo Exhibit and a Welcome to Ukrainians," U.S. Embassy Kyiv, May 20, 2015, https://ua.usembassy.gov/america -house-opens-photo-exhibit-welcome-ukrainians/.

THE GRAY ZONE

8. "George F. Kennan on Organizing Political Warfare," History and Public Policy Program Digital Archive, Wilson Center, April 30, 1948, https:// digitalarchive.wilsoncenter.org/document/114320.

9. Casey Michael, "America's Neo-Nazis Don't Look to Germany for Inspiration. They Look to Russia," *Washington Post*, August 22, 2017, https://www.washingtonpost.com/news/democracy-post/wp/2017/08/22/americas-neo-nazis-dont-look-to-germany-for-inspiration-they-look-to-russia/.

10. "Putin Q&A: Full Transcript," *Time*, 2007, http://content.time.com/time/specials/2007/personoftheyear/article/0,28804,1690753_1690757_1695787-1,00.html.

WE'RE NOT THE AUDIENCE

11. For more on ISIS's history, strategy, and ideology, see Michael Weiss and Hassan Hassan, *ISIS: Inside the Army of Terror* (New York: Regan Arts, 2016); William McCants, *The ISIS Apocalypse: The History, Strategy, and Doomsday Vision of the Islamic State* (New York: St. Martin's Press, 2015); and Jessica Stern and J. M. Berger, *ISIS: The State of Terror* (New York: HarperCollins, 2015).

QUESTION MORE

12. "State Dept Sideshow: Jen Psaki's Most Embarrassing Fails, Most Entertaining Grillings," *RT*, June 1, 2014, https://www.rt.com/usa/162608-jen-psaki-fails-grilling/.

13. Jill Dougherty, "How the Media Became One of Putin's Most Powerful Weapons," *Atlantic*, April 21, 2015, https://www.theatlantic.com/international/archive/2015/04/how-the-media-became-putins-most-powerful-weapon/391062/.

14. Nikolaus von Twickel, "Russia Today Courts Viewers with Controversy," *Moscow Times*, March 23, 2010, https://www.rbth.com/articles/2010/03/23/230310_rt.html.

15. Casey Michael, "Putin's Magnificent Messaging Machine," *Politico*, August 25, 2015, https://www.politico.com/magazine/story/2015/08/25/putin-rt-soviet-propaganda-121734.

16. Rosie Gray, "Russia Today's New Ad Campaign Suggests It Could Have Prevented the Iraq War," *BuzzFeed News*, August 18, 2014, https://www.buzzfeednews.com/article/rosiegray/russia-todays-new-ad-campaign-suggests-it-could-have-prevent.

17. Katie Zavadski, "Putin's Propaganda TV Lies About Its Popularity," *Daily Beast*, September 17, 2015, https://www.thedailybeast.com/putins-propaganda-tv-lies-about-its-popularity.

18. John Kerry, "Remarks on Ukraine," U.S. Department of State, April 24, 2014, https://2009-2017.state.gov/secretary/remarks/2014/04/225166.htm.

19. Richard Stengel, "Russia Today's Disinformation Campaign," *U.S. Department of State Official Blog*, April 29, 2014, http://2007-2017-blogs.state.gov/stories/2014/04/29/russia-today-s-disinformation-campaign2679.html.

20. Margarita Simonyan, "Who's Really 'Presenting Lies as Facts'? How State Dept. Exposes Itself to Propaganda," *RT*, April 30, 2014, https://www.rt.com/op-ed/155960-presenting-lies-facts-propaganda-exposure/.

My Bad

21. Scott Neuman and Bill Chappell, "Obama: Evidence MH17 Hit by Missile from Rebel-Held Area of Ukraine," NPR, July 18, 2014, https://www.npr.org/sections/thetwo-way/2014/07/18/332496334/malaysia-airlines-flight-mh17-plane-crash-what-we-know.

22. Steven Pifer and Hannah Thoburn, "A New Tragedy in Ukraine: The Shootdown of Malaysian Airlines Flight 17," Brookings Institute, July 17, 2014, https://www.brookings.edu/blog/up-front/2014/07/17/a-new-tragedy-in-ukraine-the-shootdown-of-malaysian-airlines-flight-17/.

23. "Russian Media: MH17 Was Shot Down by Ukrainian Army; Their Target Was Putin's Plane," Baltic News Network, July 18, 2014, https://bnn-news.com/russian-media-mh17-shot-ukrainian-army-target-putins-plane-116613.

24 Carl Schrek, "Catch Carlos If You Can," Radio Free Europe/Radio Liberty, March 14, 2018, https://www.rferl.org/a/catch-carlos-if-you-can-mh17-russia-ukraine/29065244.html.

25. Jessica Chasmar, "'My Bad': State Dept. Official Apologizes for #UnitedForGaza Tweet," July 20, 2014, https://www.washingtontimes.com/news/2014/jul/20/my-bad-state-dept-official-apologizes-unitedforgaz/.

26. "Oops! Rookie Diplomat Rick Stengel Sorry for #UnitedforGaza Tweet," *Forward*, July 21, 2014, https://forward.com/news/breaking-news/202484/oops-rookie-diplomat-rick-stengel-sorry-for-unit/.

27. Jacob B., "'What a Jackass': US Under Secretary of State Apologizes After Tweeting 'United for Gaza' Hashtag," Twitchy, July 20, 2014, https://twitchy.com/jacobb-38/2014/07/20/what-a-jackass-us-under-secretary-of-state-apologizes-after-tweeting-united-for-gaza-hashtag/.

28. Warner Todd Huston, "'My Bad': State Dept. Official Deletes Tweet with Hashtag Backing Hamas," Breitbart, July 21, 2014, https://www.breitbart.com/politics/2014/07/21/my-bad-state-sept-official-praises-hamas-on-twitter-then-retracts/.

BLUNDERING ON

29. Babak Dehghanpisheh, "Family of Missing Journalist Austin Tice Pleads for Information," November 12, 2012, https://www.washingtonpost.com/world/middle_east/family-of-missing-journalist-austin-tice-pleads-for-information/2012/11/12/5762398c-2d01-11e2-89d4-040c9330702a_story.html.
30. Jeryl Bier, "State Dept. Wishes 'RIP' to Living Captives of Terrorists," *Weekly Standard*, January 6, 2015, https://www.weeklystandard.com/jeryl-bier/state-dept-wishes-rip-to-living-captives-of-terrorists.

RECALIBRATING ON RUSSIA

31. Note for the Secretary, *Combating Putin's Information War*, December 1, 2014.

WHAT'S IN A NAME?

32. "Cruz on ISIS: Solution Is Military Power, Not Expanded Medicaid in Iraq," Fox News, February 18, 2015, https://insider.foxnews.com/2015/02/18/cruz-isis-solution-military-power-not-expanded-medicaid-iraq.
33. Eric Schmitt, "U.S. Intensifies Effort to Blunt ISIS's Message," *New York Times*, February 16, 2015, https://www.nytimes.com/2015/02/17/world/middleeast/us-intensifies-effort-to-blunt-isis-message.html.
34. Kayla Yandoli, "15 Poop Horror Stories That Will Make You Feel Better About Yourself," *BuzzFeed*, June 20, 2014, https://www.buzzfeed.com/kaylayandoli/hurbly-grblies; Adrienne LaFrance and Robinson Meyer, "The Eternal Return of BuzzFeed," *Atlantic*, April 15, 2015, https://www.theatlantic.com/technology/archive/2015/04/the-eternal-return-of-buzzfeed/390270/.

PETULANCE AS POLICY

35. "About the Program," FLEX, http://discoverflex.org/about-program/.
36. Neil MacFarquhar and Michael R. Gordon, "Russia Cancels Exchange Program After a Student Seeks U.S. Asylum," *New York Times*, October

4, 2014, https://www.nytimes.com/2014/10/05/world/europe/russia-cancels-exchange-program-after-a-student-seeks-us-asylum.html.

37. Masha Gessen, "Who Controls a Gay Russian Teen-Ager's Story?" *New Yorker*, October 13, 2014, https://www.newyorker.com/news/news-desk/gay-russian-teenager-media-coverage.

38. Gessen, "Who Controls a Gay Russian Teen-Ager's Story?"

39. Will Englund, "U.S. Relations with Russia Face Critical Tests in 2014 as Putin, Obama Fail to Fulfill Expectations," *Washington Post*, January 2, 2014, https://www.washingtonpost.com/world/europe/us-relations-with-russia-face-critical-tests-in-2014-as-putin-obama-fail-to-fulfill-expectations/2014/01/02/a46c880c-4562-11e3-95a9-3f15b5618ba8_story.html.

40. Miriam Elder, "Russia Passes Law Banning Gay 'Propaganda,'" *Guardian*, June 11, 2013, https://www.theguardian.com/world/2013/jun/11/russia-law-banning-gay-propaganda.

BUSINESS AS USUAL

41. Hamdi Alkhshali and Catherine E. Schoichet, "ISIS Seizes Control of Key Iraqi City Ramadi as Government Forces Pull Back," CNN, May 17, 2015, https://www.cnn.com/2015/05/17/asia/isis-ramadi/index.html.

42. Note for the Secretary, *Paris*, June 9, 2015.

43. Mark Mazzetti and Michael R. Gordon, "ISIS Is Winning the Social Media War, U.S. Concludes," *New York Times*, June 12, 2015, https://www.nytimes.com/2015/06/13/world/middleeast/isis-is-winning-message-war-us-concludes.html.

44. Elisabeth Bulmiller and Mark Landler, "U.S. Envoy Urges Caution on Forces for Afghanistan," *New York Times*, November 11, 2009, https://www.nytimes.com/2009/11/12/us/politics/12policy.html.

45. Greg Jaffe and Greg Miller, "Secret U.S. Cable Warned of Pakistani Havens," *Washington Post*, February 24, 2012, https://www.washingtonpost.com/world/national-security/secret-us-cable-warned-of-pakistani-havens/2012/02/24/gIQAgMnYYR_story.html.

46. Rashmee Roshan Lall, "ISIL Makes the US Wake Up and Smell the Coffee," *National*, June 17, 2015, https://www.thenational.ae/opinion/isil-makes-the-us-wake-up-and-smell-the-coffee-1.98088.

HOLDING FIRE

47. "Investigation by the Dutch Safety Board," Government of the Netherlands, October 13, 2015, https://www.government.nl/topics/mh17 -incident/investigation-by-the-dutch-safety-board.

48. Office of the Press Secretary, "Statement by NSC Spokesperson Ned Price on the Dutch Safety Board Report on the Downing of Malaysia Airlines Flight 17," White House, October 13, 2015, https://obamawhitehouse .archives.gov/the-press-office/2015/10/13/statement-nsc-spokesperson -ned-price-dutch-safety-board-report-downing.

49. U.S. Department of State, Office of Press Relations, "The Dutch Safety Board's Final Report on the Shootdown of Malaysia Airlines Flight MH17," U.S. Department of State, October 13, 2015, https://obama whitehouse.archives.gov/the-press-office/2015/10/13/statement-nsc -spokesperson-ned-price-dutch-safety-board-report-downing.

FOR WHOM THE BELL TROLLS

50. Aric Toler, "Inside the Kremlin Troll Army Machine: Templates, Guidelines, and Paid Posts," *GlobalVoices*, March 14, 2015, https://globalvoices .org/2015/03/14/russia-kremlin-troll-army-examples/; Adrian Chen, "The Agency," *New York Times*, June 2, 2015, https://www.nytimes .com/2015/06/07/magazine/the-agency.html.

51. Toler, "Inside the Kremlin Troll Army Machine."

52. Translated from a lexicon of internet slang terms produced by the Internet Research Agency and leaked in 2015. See Andrei Soshnikov, "Столица политического троллинга" ("The Capital of Political Trolling"), MR7. ru, March 11, 2015, https://mr7.ru/articles/112478/; and Dean Sterling Jones, "Inside the Russian Troll Factory," *Shooting the Messenger*, February 27, 2018, https://shootingthemessenger.blog/2018/02/27/inside-the -russian-troll-factory/.

53. Jones, "Inside the Russian Troll Factory."

54. Translated from documents available at Soshnikov, "The Capital of Political Trolling."

55. Aric Toler, "Fake 'Ukrainian' News Websites Run by Russian 'Troll Army' Offshoots," *GlobalVoices*, November 19, 2014, https://globalvoices .org/2014/11/19/fake-ukrainian-news-websites-run-by-russian-troll-army -offshoots/.

56. Translated from documents available at Soshnikov, "The Capital of Political Trolling."

Part VI: Disruption

Making _____ Great Again

1. "Here's Donald Trump's Presidential Announcement Speech," *Time*, June 16, 2015, http://time.com/3923128/donald-trump-announcement -speech/.

Shutdown

2. Adam Nagourney, Ian Lovett, and Richard Pérez-Peña, "San Bernardino Shooting Kills at Least 14; Two Suspects Are Dead," *New York Times*, December 2, 2015, https://www.nytimes.com/2015/12/03/us/san -bernardino-shooting.htm; Adam Nossiter and Rick Gladstone, "Paris Attacks Kill More Than 100, Police Say; Border Controls Tightened," *New York Times*, November 13, 2015, https://www.nytimes.com/2015/11/14/ world/europe/paris-shooting-attacks.html.

3. Jenna Johnson and David Weigel, "Donald Trump Calls for 'Total' Ban on Muslims Entering United States," *Washington Post*, December 8, 2015, https://www.washingtonpost.com/politics/2015/12/07/e56266f6-9d2b -11e5-8728-1af6af208198_story.html.

4. Philip Bump, "Donald Trump's Call to Ban Muslim Immigrants Is Based on a Very Shoddy Poll," *Washington Post*, December 7, 2015, https://www. washingtonpost.com/news/the-fix/wp/2015/12/07/donald-trumps-call-to -ban-muslims-from-coming-to-the-u-s-has-a-very-bad-poll-at-its-center/.

5. "Outcry as Donald Trump Calls for US Muslim Ban," BBC News, December 8, 2015, https://www.bbc.com/news/av/world-us-canada-35036567/ outcry-as-donald-trump-calls-for-us-muslim-ban.

6. U.S. Department of Defense, Press Operations, "Department of Defense Press Briefing by Pentagon Press Secretary Peter Cook in the Pentagon Briefing Room," U.S. Department of Defense, December 8, 2015, https:// dod.defense.gov/News/Transcripts/Transcript-View/Article/633414/ department-of-defense-press-briefing-by-pentagon-press-secretary -peter-cook-in/.

7. Gardiner Harris, David E. Sanger, and David M. Herszenhorn, "Obama Increases Number of Syrian Refugees for U.S. Resettlement to 10,000," *New York Times*, September 10, 2015, https://www.nytimes

.com/2015/09/11/world/middleeast/obama-directs-administration-to
-accept-10000-syrian-refugees.html.

"LISA"

8. Lucian Kim, "Russia Having Success in Hybrid War Against Germany," *Reuters*, February 7, 2016, http://blogs.reuters.com/great
-debate/2016/02/07/russia-having-success-in-hybrid-war-against
-germany/; Sam Jones, "Putin Has West in Cross Hairs with Social
Media Offensive," *Financial Times*, June 1, 2016, https://www.ft.com/
content/5de9c57a-2809-11e6-8ba3-cdd781d02d89?mhq5j=e1.

9. Kim, "Russia Having Success in Hybrid War Against Germany."

10. Ken Gude, "Russia's Fifth Column," Center for American Progress,
March 17, 2017, https://www.americanprogress.org/issues/security/
reports/2017/03/15/428074/russias-5th-column/.

11. "Was Russia Behind 2015's Cyber Attack on the German Parliament?"
Deutsche Welle, February 2, 2016, https://www.dw.com/en/was-russia
-behind-2015s-cyber-attack-on-the-german-parliament/a-19017553.

12. "Address by President of the Russian Federation," Kremlin, March 18,
2014, http://en.kremlin.ru/events/president/news/20603.

THEY ALWAYS ACCUSE YOU OF WHAT THEY'RE DOING

13. Peter Pomerantsev, "Unplugging Putin TV," *Foreign Affairs*, February
18, 2015, https://www.foreignaffairs.com/articles/russia-fsu/2015-02-18/
unplugging-putin-tv.

14. "Trump Trumped by Twitter Trolls," *RT*, June 16, 2015, https://www
.rt.com/usa/267631-trump-trumped-twitter-trolls/.

15. Mark Maremont and Rob Barry, "Russian Twitter Support for Trump
Began Right After He Started Campaign," *Wall Street Journal*, November
6, 2017, https://www.wsj.com/articles/russian-twitter-support-for-trump
-began-right-after-he-started-campaign-1509964380.

16. Maremont and Barry, "Russian Twitter Support for Trump Began Right
After He Started Campaign."

THE BREXIT PREDICATE

17. Amanda Taub, "A Lesson from Brexit: On Immigration, Feelings
Trump Facts," *New York Times*, June 26, 2016, https://www.nytimes
.com/2016/06/27/world/europe/brexit-economy-immigration-britain
-european-union-democracy.html.

18. Vivian Salama, "Trump in Paris: The Curious Case of His Friend Jim," AP, July 12, 2017, https://apnews.com/e18f254c4ac84e6bab4ceed56401cc65.

19. "Women Face 'Mass Sex Attacks' by Migrants If No Brexit—Farage," *RT*, June 5, 2016, https://www.rt.com/uk/345473-nigel-farage-sex-attacks/.

20. "'EU Migrant Crisis Proposals Will Open Britain's Doors to Jihadists,' Says Nigel Farage," *RT*, April 29, 2015, https://www.rt.com/uk/254121 -migrant-crisis-farage-eu/; Patrick Foster, "Kremlin-Backed Broadcaster RT Offers Nigel Farage His Own Show," September 7, 2016, https:// www.telegraph.co.uk/news/2016/09/07/kremlin-backed-broadcaster-rt -offers-nigel-farage-his-own-show/.

21. Nigel Farage, "TTIP Is About Giant Corporates Dominating Our Economies," Breitbart, June 11, 2015, https://www.breitbart.com/ europe/2015/06/11/farage-for-breitbart-ttip-is-about-giant-corporates -dominating-our-economies/; Nigel Farage, "UK Migration Cover Up: The Government Must Release The REAL Figures Immediately," Breitbart, December 17, 2015, https://www.breitbart.com/europe/2015/12/17/ farage-for-breitbart-uk-migration-cover-up-the-government-must -release-the-real-figures-immediately/; "EXCLUSIVE—Farage Tells Breitbart: 'Obama Visit Caused "Brexit Bounce," Swayed Vote in Favour of Leave,'" Breitbart, June 24, 2016, https://www.breitbart.com/ europe/2016/06/24/listen-nigel-farage-on-momentous-eu-referendum -win/.

22. Robert Hutton and Thomas Seal, "UKIP's Farage Champions Trump at Rally in Mississippi," Bloomberg News, August 24, 2016, https://www .bloomberg.com/news/articles/2016-08-25/ukip-s-farage-champions -trump-at-rally-in-mississippi; Ben Jacobs and Dan Roberts, "Nigel Farage Fights Donald Trump's Corner in Post-Debate Spin Room," *Guardian*, October 10, 2016, https://www.theguardian.com/us-news/2016/ oct/10/nigel-farage-fights-donald-trumps-corner-in-post-debate-spin -room.

23. Matt Burgess, "Here's the First Evidence Russia Used Twitter to Influence Brexit," *Wired*, November 10, 2017, https://www.wired.co.uk/article/ brexit-russia-influence-twitter-bots-internet-research-agency.

THE PRINCE OF DARKNESS

24. Jeffrey Goldberg, "The Obama Doctrine," *Atlantic*, April 2016, https:// www.theatlantic.com/magazine/archive/2016/04/the-obama-doctrine/ 471525/.

WHO HAS THE PEN?

25. Executive Order 13721 of March 14, 2016, "Developing an Integrated Global Engagement Center to Support Government-wide Counterterrorism Communications Activities Directed Abroad and Revoking Executive Order 13584," *Federal Register* 81, no. 52: 14685–14688, https://www.govinfo.gov/content/pkg/FR-2016-03-17/pdf/2016-06250.pdf.

GOING FOR IT

26. Will Englund, "In Ukraine, Sens. McCain, Murphy Address Protesters, Promise Support," *Washington Post*, December 15, 2013, https://www.washingtonpost.com/world/in-ukraine-us-sens-mccain-murphy-address-protesters/2013/12/15/be72cffe-65b0-11e3-997b-9213b17dac97_story.html.

27. Daniela Altimari, "Murphy Brings McCain to Hartford to Speak About Ukraine War," *Hartford Courant*, March 9, 2015, https://www.courant.com/politics/hc-murphy-mccain-ukraine-20150309-story.html.

28. Countering Information Warfare Act of 2016, S. 2692, 114th Congress (2016).

THE BAR SCENE IN STAR WARS

29. U.S. Congress, House, Committee on Foreign Affairs, *Countering the Virtual Caliphate: The State Department's Performance*, 114th Cong., 2nd sess., 2016, 5.

INTERFERENCE

30. Alexander Dugin, "Dugin's Guideline—In Trump We Trust," YouTube video, 8:08, posted by Katehon Think Tank, March 4, 2016, https://www.youtube.com/watch?v=aOWIoMtIvDQ.

31. Dmitri Alperovitch, "Bears in the Midst: Intrusion into the Democratic National Committee," CrowdStrike, June 15, 2016, https://www.crowdstrike.com/blog/bears-midst-intrusion-democratic-national-committee/.

32. Eric Lipton, David E. Sanger, and Scott Shane, "The Perfect Weapon: How Russian Cyberpower Invaded the U.S.," *New York Times*, December 13, 2016, https://www.nytimes.com/2016/12/13/us/politics/russia-hack-election-dnc.html.

33. Louis Nelson, "Trump Accuses DNC of 'Hacking' Its Own Oppo Research on Him," *Politico*, June 15, 2016, https://www.politico.com/story/2016/06/donald-trump-opposition-224397.

34. David E. Sanger and Eric Schmitt, "Spy Agency Consensus Grows That Russia Hacked D.N.C.," *New York Times*, July 26, 2016, https://www.nytimes.com/2016/07/27/us/politics/spy-agency-consensus-grows-that-russia-hacked-dnc.html.

35. Tom Hamburger and Karen Tumulty, "WikiLeaks Releases Thousands of Documents About Clinton and Internal Deliberations," *Washington Post*, July 22, 2016, https://www.washingtonpost.com/news/post-politics/wp/2016/07/22/on-eve-of-democratic-convention-wikileaks-releases-thousands-of-documents-about-clinton-the-campaign-and-internal-deliberations/.

36. "Donald Trump News Conference," C-SPAN, July 27, 2016, https://www.c-span.org/video/?413263-1/donald-trump-urges-russia-find-hillary-clinton-emails-criticizes-record-tpp.

37. Alexander Mallin, "Trump: Crimea's People Prefer Russia, but If He's Elected Putin Is 'Not Going into Ukraine,'" ABC News, July 31, 2016, https://abcnews.go.com/ThisWeek/trump-crimeas-people-prefer-russia-elected-putin-ukraine/story?id=41029437.

The Far Enemy Is the Near Enemy

38. Ben Schreckinger, "A Family Trumpsgiving in South Carolina," *Politico*, November 24, 2015, https://www.politico.com/story/2015/11/donald-trump-south-carolina-family-216202.

39. Ryan Teague Beckwith, "Read Donald Trump's Speech on the Orlando Shooting," *Time*, June 13, 2016, http://time.com/4367120/orlando-shooting-donald-trump-transcript/.

40. Adam Withnall, "Isis Official Calls for 'Lone Wolf' Attacks in US and Europe During Ramadan," May 22, 2016, https://www.independent.co.uk/news/world/middle-east/isis-official-calls-for-lone-wolf-attacks-in-us-and-europe-during-ramadan-a7042296.html.

41. See, for example, Amanda Taub, "The Rise of American Authoritarianism," *Vox*, March 1, 2016, https://www.vox.com/2016/3/1/11127424/trump-authoritarianism; Jonathan Haidt, "The Key to Trump Is Stenner's Authoritarianism," *Righteous Mind*, January 6, 2017, http://righteousmind.com/the-key-to-trump-is-stenners-authoritarianism/.

From Russia with Love

42. Anna Dolgov, "Russian Authorities Close Down American Center in Moscow," *Moscow Times*, September 17, 2015, https://www.themoscowtimes

.com/2015/09/17/russian-authorities-close-down-american-center-in
-moscow-a49623.

43. "Press Release on Deputy Foreign Minister Sergey Ryabkov's Meeting with US Under Secretary of State for Public Diplomacy and Public Affairs Richard Stengel," Ministry of Foreign Affairs of the Russian Federation, September 14, 2016, http://www.mid.ru/en/maps/us/-/asset_publisher/unVXBbj4Z6e8/content/id/2439579.

44. Similar stories would later become public; for example, Roland Oliphant, "Moscow's Spies Accused of Breaking into American Diplomats' Homes, Killing a Pet and Paying for Smear Stories," *Daily Telegraph*, June 28, 2016, http://www.telegraph.co.uk/news/2016/06/28/moscows-spies-accused -of-breaking-into-american-diplomats-homes/.

PART VII: WHAT TO DO ABOUT DISINFORMATION

THE PROBLEM

1. "General Information," Library of Congress, https://www.loc.gov/about/general-information/.
2. From Garry Trudeau's speech at George Polk Awards ceremony, published in the *Atlantic*.
3. For more on how disinformationists have used the tools of the internet to spread discord, see Dipayan Ghosh and Ben Scott, *Digital Deceit: The Technologies Behind Precision Propaganda on the Internet* (Cambridge, MA: Shorenstein Center, Harvard Kennedy School, 2018), https://www.newamerica.org/public-interest-technology/policy-papers/digitaldeceit/.
4. For more on legislative and technological solutions to the problems of misinformation and disinformation, see Howard Cohen, "Tech Tock . . . Time Is Running Out to Find Solutions to Mis- and Disinformation and Privacy Problems," Harvard Kennedy School, May 2018, https://www.belfercenter.org/sites/default/files/files/publication/PAE%20Cohen%20-%20web.pdf.

SECTION 230

5. Communications Decency Act, 47 U.S.C. § 230 (1996).
6. For a longer discussion of possible amendments to Section 230, see Tim Hwang, "Dealing with Disinformation: Evaluating the Case for CDA 230 Amendment," MIT Media Lab, December 17, 2017, https://ssrn.com/abstract=3089442.

Privacy and Elections

7. Ed Markey, U.S. Senator from Massachusetts, "As Facebook CEO Zuckerberg Testifies to Congress, Senators Markey and Blumenthal Introduce Privacy Bill of Rights," April 10, 2018, https://www.markey.senate.gov/news/press-releases/as-facebook-ceo-zuckerberg-testifies-to-congress-senators-markey-and-blumenthal-introduce-privacy-bill-of-rights.

8. Mark R. Warner, U.S. Senator from Virginia, "The Honest Ads Act," October 19, 2017, https://www.warner.senate.gov/public/index.cfm/the-honest-ads-act?page=1.

Algorithms, Ratings Systems, and Artificial Intelligence

9. "Assessing the Effect of News Source Ratings on News Content," Knight Foundation, June 27, 2018, https://knightfoundation.org/reports/assessing-the-effect-of-news-source-ratings-on-news-content.

10. "Frequently Asked Questions," Trust Project, https://thetrustproject.org/faq/.

11. Will Oremus, "Only You Can Stop the Spread of Fake News," *Slate*, December 13, 2016, https://slate.com/technology/2016/12/introducing-this-is-fake-slates-tool-for-stopping-fake-news-on-facebook.html.

12. "About," Factmata, https://factmata.com/about.html.

13. "How It Works," NewsGuard, https://www.newsguardtech.com/how-it-works/.

Postscript

1. "Global Engagement Center," U.S. Department of State, https://www.state.gov/r/gec/.

2. Nahal Toosi, "Tillerson Spurns $80 Million to Counter ISIS, Russian Propaganda," *Politico*, August 2, 2017, https://www.politico.com/story/2017/08/02/tillerson-isis-russia-propaganda-241218.

3. Nahal Toosi, "State, Defense Agree on $40M Fund to Fight Foreign Propaganda," *Politico*, February 26, 2018, https://www.politico.com/story/2018/02/26/state-defense-russia-propaganda-426626.

4. Joel Gehrke, "Senators to Rex Tillerson: Fight Russian Propaganda," *Washington Examiner*, August 2, 2017, https://www.washingtonexaminer.com/senators-to-rex-tillerson-fight-russian-propaganda.

5. Shannon van Sant, "U.S. Envoy to the Coalition Against ISIS Resigns Over Trump's Syria Policy," NPR, December 22, 2018, https://www

.npr.org/2018/12/22/679535003/u-s-envoy-to-the-coalition-against-isis
-resigns-over-trumps-syria-policy.

6. Julie Hirschfeld Davis, "Trump Meets Saudi Prince as U.S. and Kingdom
Seek Warmer Relations," *New York Times*, March 14, 2017, https://www
.nytimes.com/2017/03/14/world/middleeast/mohammed-bin-salman
-saudi-arabia-trump.html.

7. "Saudi to Open Militant-Monitoring Center During Trump Visit,"
Reuters, May 20, 2017, https://www.reuters.com/article/us-usa-trump
-gulf-centre/saudi-to-open-militant-monitoring-center-during-trump
-visit-idUSKCN18G09P.

8. Spencer Feingold, "Saudi Women Attend Soccer Match for First Time,"
CNN, January 12, 2018, https://www.cnn.com/2018/01/12/middleeast/
saudi-women-attend-first-soccer-match/index.html.

9. Paige Leskin, "Russia's Disinformation Campaign Wasn't Just on Facebook and Twitter. Here Are All the Social Media Platforms Russian Trolls
Weaponized During the 2016 US Elections," *Business Insider*, December
18, 2018, https://www.businessinsider.com/all-social-apps-russian-trolls
-used-spread-disinformation-2018-12.

10. Jonathan Albright, Renee DiResta, Ryan Fox, Ben Johnson, Robert
Matney, Kris Shaffer, Becky Ruppel, and David Sullivan, *The Tactics and
Tropes of the Internet Research Agency* (New Knowledge, 2018), https://
cdn2.hubspot.net/hubfs/4326998/ira-report-rebrand_FinalJ14.pdf.

11. Matt Apuzzo and Sharon LaFraniere, "13 Russians Indicted as Mueller Reveals Effort to Aid Trump Campaign," *New York Times*, February
18, 2018, https://www.nytimes.com/2018/02/16/us/politics/russians
-indicted-mueller-election-interference.html.

12. U.S. Department of Justice, Office of Public Affairs, "Russian National
Charged with Interfering in U.S. Political System," press release, October 19, 2018, https://www.justice.gov/opa/pr/russian-national-charged
-interfering-us-political-system.

13. Kurt Wagner, "Donald Trump and Hillary Clinton Spent $81 Million on
Facebook Ads Before Last Year's Election," *Recode*, November 1, 2017,
https://www.recode.net/2017/11/1/16593066/trump-clinton-facebook
-advertising-money-election-president-russia; Sarah Frier, "Trump's Campaign Said It Was Better at Facebook. Facebook Agrees," *Bloomberg News*,
April 3, 2018, https://www.bloomberg.com/news/articles/2018-04-03/
trump-s-campaign-said-it-was-better-at-facebook-facebook-agrees.

14. Albright et al., *Tactics and Tropes of the Internet Research Agency*, 58.

INDEX